Dialectic of Enlightenment

THEODOR W. ADORNO
& MAX HORKHEIMER

Translated by
John Cumming

V

VERSO

London · New York

First published as *Dialektik der Aufklarung*
© Social Studies Association, Inc., New York, 1944
German reissue © S, Fischer Verlag GmbH 1969

English translation first published by Herder & Herder, New York, 1972
© Herder & Herder, Inc., 1972
First published in Great Britain by Allen Lane 1973

First published by Verso/NLB 1979
© NLB 1979
This edition published by Verso 1997
© Verso 1997

Reprinted 1999, 2008

Verso
UK: 6 Meard Street, London W1F 0EG
USA: 180 Varick Street, New York, NY 10014-4606

Verso is the imprint of New Left Books

ISBN 978-1-85984-154-9

British Library Cataloguing in Publication Data
A catalogue record for this book is available from the British Library

Library of Congress Cataloging-in-Publication Data
A catalog record for this book is available from the Library of Congress

Printed in Sweden by ScandBook AB, Falun 2008

CONTENTS

For Friedrich Pollock

PREFACE TO THE
NEW EDITION

THE first edition of *The Dialectic of Enlightenment* was published by Querido of Amsterdam in 1947. The book made its reputation only by degrees, and has now been out of print for a long time. We have decided to reissue it after more than twenty years, not only in answer to many requests but because we believe that not a few of the ideas it contains are still apposite to the times and have to a large extent determined our later theory. No outsider will find it easy to discern how far we are both responsible for every sentence. We jointly dictated lengthy sections; and the vital principle of the *Dialectic* is the tension between the two intellectual temperaments conjoined in it.

We would not now maintain without qualification every statement in the book: that would be irreconcilable with a theory which holds that the core of truth is historical, rather than an unchanging constant to be set against the movement of history. The work was written when the end of the Nazi terror was within sight; nevertheless, in not a few places the reality of our times is formulated in a way no longer appropriate to contemporary experience. And yet—even at that time—our assessment of the transition to the world of the administered life was not too simplistic.

In a period of political division into immense power-blocks, set objectively upon collison, the sinister trend continues. The conflicts in the Third World and the renewed growth of totalitarianism are just as little mere historical episodes as, according to the *Dialectic*, was Fascism in its time. Today critical thought (which does not abandon its commitment even in the face of progress) demands support for the residues of freedom, and for tendencies toward true humanism, even if these seem powerless in regard to the main course of history.

The development toward total integration recognized in this book is interrupted, but not abrogated. It threatens to advance beyond dictatorships and wars. The prognosis of the related conversion of enlightenment into positivism, the myth of things as they actually are, and finally the identification of intellect and that which is inimical to the spirit, has been overwhelmingly confirmed. Our conception of history does not presume any dispensation from it; nor does it imply a positivistic search for information. It is a critique of philosophy, and therefore refuses to abandon philosophy.

The book was written in America, whence we returned to Germany, convinced that there we could achieve more, in practice as well as in theory, than elsewhere. Together with Friedrich Pollock (to whom this book was originally dedicated on his fiftieth, and now his sixty-fifth, birthday), we have once again built up the Institut für Sozialforschung in an attempt to develop the conception formulated in the *Dialectic*. In the extension of our theory and the accompanying mutual experiences, Gretel Adorno has been a precious helper.

We have been far more sparing with alterations to the text than is usual with new editions of works published some decades before. We did not want to retouch what we had written—not even the obviously inadequate places. To have brought the text up to date would, ultimately, have demanded nothing less than a new book. That today it is more a question of preserving freedom, and of extending and developing it, instead—however indirectly—of accelerating the advance toward an administered world, is something that we have also emphasized in our later writings. Essentially, we have restricted our revision to the correction of printer's errors and the like. Such restraint tends to afford the book the status of documentation; yet we hope that it has more than that to offer.

Frankfurt am Main
April 1969

MAX HORKHEIMER
THEODOR W. ADORNO

INTRODUCTION

WHEN we began this work, the first samples of which we dedicate to Friedrich Pollock, we had hoped to be able to have the finished whole ready for his fiftieth birthday. But the more intensively we pursued our task, the clearer it became that our own powers were disproportionate to it. It turned out, in fact, that we had set ourselves nothing less than the discovery of why mankind, instead of entering into a truly human condition, is sinking into a new kind of barbarism. We underestimated the difficulties of interpretation, because we still trusted too much in the modern consciousness. Even though we had known for many years that the great discoveries of applied science are paid for with an increasing diminution of theoretical awareness, we still thought that in regard to scientific activity our contribution could be restricted to the criticism or extension of specialist axioms. Thematically, at any rate, we were to keep to the traditional disciplines: to sociology, psychology, and epistemology.

However, the fragments united in this volume show that we were forced to abandon this conviction. If the assiduous maintenance and verification of the scientific heritage are an essential part of knowledge (especially where zealous positivists have treated it as useless ballast and consigned it to oblivion), in the present collapse of bourgeois civilization not only the pursuit but the meaning of science has become problematical in that regard. What the brazen Fascists hypocritically laud and pliable humanist experts naïvely put into practice—the indefatigable self-destructiveness of enlightenment—requires philosophy to discard even the last vestiges of innocence in regard to the habits and tendencies of the spirit of the age. When public opinion has reached a state in which thought inevitably becomes a commodity, and language the means of promoting that commodity, then the attempt to trace the course of such depravation has to deny any allegiance to current linguistic and conceptual conventions, lest their world-historical consequences thwart it entirely.

If it were only a question of the obstacles resulting from the self-oblivious instrumentalization of science, then a critique of social problems could at least attach itself to trends opposed to the accepted scientific mode; yet even these are affected by the total process of production. They have changed no less than the ideology to which they referred. They suffer what triumphant thought has always suffered. If it willingly emerges from its critical element to become a mere means at the disposal of an existing order, then despite itself it tends to convert the positive it elected to defend into something negative and destructive. The philosophy which put the fear of death into infamy in the eighteenth century, despite all the book-burnings and piles of corpses, chose to serve that very infamy under Napoleon. Ultimately, Comte's school of apologetic usurped the succession to the inflexible Encyclopedists, and joined hands with everything that the latter had formerly rejected. The metamorphoses of criticism into affirmation do not leave the theoretical content untouched, for its truth evaporates. Now, of course, a mechanized history outstrips such intellectual developments, and the official apologists—who have other concerns—liquidate the history that helped them to their place in the sun, before it can prostitute itself.

When examining its own guilty conscience, thought has to forgo not only the affirmative use of scientific and everyday conceptual language, but just as much that of the opposition. There is no longer any available form of linguistic expression which has not tended toward accommodation to dominant currents of thought; and what a devalued language does not do automatically is proficiently executed by societal mechanisms. There are analogies in all areas for the censors voluntarily maintained by film companies faced otherwise with the threat of increased overheads. The process which a literary text has to undergo, if not in the anticipatory maneuvers of its author, then certainly in the combined efforts of readers, editors, sub-editors and ghost writers in and outside publishing houses, exceeds any censorship in thoroughness. To make its functions wholly superfluous would seem to be the ambition of the educational system, despite all salutary reforms. Believing that without strict limitation to the verification of facts and probability theory, the cognitive spirit would prove all too susceptible to charlatanism and superstition, it makes a parched ground ready and avid for charlatanism and superstition. Just as prohibition has always offered access to the poisonous product, so the obstruction of the theoretical faculty paved the way for political error and madness. And even so far as men have not yet succumbed to political delusion, the mechanisms of censorship—both internal and external—will deprive them of the means of resistance.

The dilemma that faced us in our work proved to be the first phenomenon for investigation: the self-destruction of the Enlightenment. We are wholly convinced—and therein lies our *petitio principii*—that social freedom is inseparable from enlightened thought. Nevertheless, we believe that we have just as clearly recognized that the notion of this very way of thinking, no less than the actual historic forms—the social institutions—with which it is interwoven, already contains the seed of the reversal universally apparent today. If enlightenment does not accommodate reflection on this recidivist element, then it seals its own fate. If consideration of the destructive aspect of progress is left to its enemies, blindly pragmatized thought loses its transcending quality and, its relation to truth. In the enigmatic readiness of the technologically educated masses to fall under the sway of any despotism, in its self-destructive affinity to popular paranoia, and in all uncomprehended absurdity, the weakness of the modern theoretical faculty is apparent.

We believe that these fragments will contribute to the health of that theoretical understanding, insofar as we show that the prime cause of the retreat from enlightenment into mythology is not to be sought so much in the nationalist, pagan and other modern mythologies manufactured precisely in order to contrive such a reversal, but in the Enlightenment itself when paralyzed by fear of the truth. In this respect, both concepts are to be understood not merely as historico-cultural (*geistesgeschichtlich*) but as real. Just as the Enlightenment expresses the actual movement of civil society as a whole in the aspect of its idea as embodied in individuals and institutions, so truth is not merely the rational consciousness but equally the form that consciousness assumes in actual life. The dutiful child of modern civilization is possessed by a fear of departing from the facts which, in the very act of perception, the dominant conventions of science, commerce, and politics—cliché-like—have already molded; his anxiety is none other than the fear of social deviation. The same conventions define the notion of linguistic and conceptual clarity which the art, literature and philosophy of the present have to satisfy. Since that notion declares any negative treatment of the facts or of the dominant forms of thought to be obscurantist formalism or—preferably—alien, and therefore taboo, it condemns the spirit to increasing darkness. It is characteristic of the sickness that even the best-intentioned reformer who uses an impoverished and debased language to recommend renewal, by his adoption of the insidious mode of categorization and the bad philosophy it conceals, strengthens the very power of the established order he is trying to break. False clarity is only another name for myth; and myth has always been obscure and enlightening at one and the same time: always using the devices of familiarity and straightforward dismissal to avoid the labor of conceptualization.

The fallen nature of modern man cannot be separated from social progress. On the one hand the growth of economic productivity furnishes the conditions for a world of greater justice; on the other hand it allows the technical apparatus and the social groups which administer it a disproportionate superiority to the rest of the population. The individual is wholly devalued in relation to the economic powers, which at the same time press the control of society over nature to hitherto unsuspected heights. Even though the individual disappears before the apparatus which he serves, that apparatus provides for him as never before. In an unjust state of life, the impotence and pliability of the masses grow with the quantitative increase in commodities allowed them. The materially respectable and socially deplorable rise in the living standard of the lower classes is reflected in the simulated extension of the spirit. Its true concern is the negation of reification; it cannot survive where it is fixed as a cultural commodity and doled out to satisfy consumer needs. The flood of detailed information and candy-floss entertainment simultaneously instructs and stultifies mankind.

The issue is not that of culture as a value, which is what the critics of civilization, Huxley, Jaspers, Ortega y Gasset and others, have in mind. The point is rather that the Enlightenment *must examine itself*, if men are not to be wholly betrayed. The task to be accomplished is not the conservation of the past, but the redemption of the hopes of the past. Today, however, the past is preserved as the destruction of the past. Whereas a worthwhile education was a privilege until the nineteenth century, and one paid for by the increased suffering of the uneducated, in the twentieth century factory space has been purchased by melting down all cultural values in a gigantic crucible. Perhaps that would not be so high a price as the defenders of culture suppose, if the selling-out of culture did not contribute to the conversion of economic triumphs into their opposite.

Under existing conditions the gifts of fortune themselves become elements of misfortune. Their quantity, in default of a social subject, operated during the internal economic crises of times past as so-called "surplus production"; today, because of the enthronement of power-groups as that social subject, it produces the international threat of Fascism: progress becomes regression. That the hygienic shop-floor and everything that goes with it, the people's car or the sportsdrome, leads to an insensitive liquidation of metaphysics, would be irrelevant; but that in the social whole they themselves become a metaphysics, an ideological curtain behind which the real evil is concentrated, is not irrelevant. This is the starting-point of our deliberations.

The first study, which provides the theoretical basis for the second, is an attempt to focus understanding more clearly upon the nexus of rationality and social actuality, and upon what is inseparable therefrom—that of nature and the mastery of nature. The accompanying critique of enlightenment is intended to prepare the way for a positive notion of enlightenment which will release it from entanglement in blind domination.

Broadly speaking, the critical section of the first study concentrates on two theses: myth is already enlightenment; and enlightenment reverts to mythology. In the two excursuses, these theses are demonstrated in terms of specific phenomena. The first traces the dialectic of myth and enlightenment in the *Odyssey,* as one of the earliest representative testimonies of Western bourgeois civilization. At the midpoint are the notions of sacrifice and renunciation, in which appear the difference as well as the unity of mythic nature and enlightened mastery of nature. The second excursus is concerned with Kant, Sade, and Nietzsche, who mercilessly elicited the implications of the Enlightenment. Here we show how the submission of everything natural to the autocratic subject finally culminates in the mastery of the blindly objective and natural. This tendency evens out all the antinomies of bourgeois thought—even that of moral rigor and absolute amorality.

The essay on the "culture industry" demonstrates the regression of enlightenment to ideology which finds its typical expression in cinema and radio. Here enlightenment consists above all in the calculation of effectiveness and of the techniques of production and distribution; in accordance with its content, ideology expends itself in the idolization of given existence and of the power which controls technology. In the treatment of this contradiction the culture industry is taken more seriously than it would implicitly require. But since its appeal to its own properly commercial nature, its acknowledgment of a qualified truth, has long been a subterfuge that it uses to evade responsibility for lies, our analysis keeps to the products' objectively inherent claim to be aesthetic images which accordingly embody truth, and demonstrates the nullity of social being in the nihilism of that claim. The section on the "culture industry" is even more fragmentary than the others.

The argument and thesis of "Elements of Anti-Semitism" is concerned with the actual reversion of enlightened civilization to barbarism. Not merely the ideal but the practical tendency to self-destruction has always been characteristic of rationalism, and not only in the stage in which it appears undisguised. In this sense we offer the main lines of a philosophical prehistory of anti-Semitism. Its "irrationalism" is deduced from the nature of the dominant *ratio* itself, and the world which corresponds to its image. This chapter is directly related to empirical research carried out at the Institut für Sozialforschung, the foundation established and maintained by Felix Weil, and without which not merely our studies but a good part of the theoretical work of German emigrants that continued despite Hitler would not have been possible. We wrote the first three theses in conjunction with Leo Löwenthal, with whom we have worked on many scientific problems since our first years together in Frankfurt.

The last part of this book contains sketches and drafts which belong in part to the area of thought of the foregoing essays without being precisely locatable there, and in part offer advance summaries of problems to be treated in forthcoming works. Most of them are concerned with a dialectical anthropology.

May 1944   *Los Angeles, California*

The book as published contains no important alterations of the text written during the war. All that has been added subsequently is the last thesis of "Elements of Anti-Semitism."

June 1947   MAX HORKHEIMER
                                             THEODOR W. ADORNO

DIALECTIC OF ENLIGHTENMENT

THE CONCEPT
OF ENLIGHTENMENT

IN the most general sense of progressive thought, the Enlightenment has always aimed at liberating men from fear and establishing their sovereignty. Yet the fully enlightened earth radiates disaster triumphant. The program of the Enlightenment was the disenchantment of the world; the dissolution of myths and the substitution of knowledge for fancy. Bacon, the "father of experimental philosophy,"[1] had defined its motives. He looked down on the masters of tradition, the "great reputed authors" who first "believe that others know that which they know not; and after themselves know that which they know not. But indeed facility to believe, impatience to doubt, temerity to answer, glory to know, doubt to contradict, end to gain, sloth to search, seeking things in words, resting in part of nature; these and the like have been the things which have forbidden the happy match between the mind of man and the nature of things; and in place thereof have married it to vain notions and blind experiments: and what the posterity and issue of so honorable a match may be, it is not hard to consider. Printing, a gross invention; artillery, a thing that lay not far out of the way; the needle, a thing partly known before: what a change have these three things made in the world in these times; the one in state of learning, the other in the state of war, the third in the state of treasure, commodities, and navigation! And those, I say, were but stumbled upon and lighted upon by chance. Therefore, no doubt, the sovereignty of man lieth hid in knowledge; wherein many things are reserved, which kings with

1. Voltaire, *Lettres Philosophiques*, XII, *Œuvres Complètes* (Garnier: Paris, 1879), Vol. XXII, p. 118.

their treasure cannot buy, nor with their force command; their spials and intelligencers can give no news ... 'em, their seamen and discoverers cannot sail where they gr... now we govern nature in opinions, but we are thrall unto her in necessity: but if we would be led by her in invention, we should command her by action."[2]

Despite his lack of mathematics, Bacon's view was appropriate to the scientific attitude that prevailed after him. The concordance between the mind of man and the nature of things that he had in mind is patriarchal: the human mind, which overcomes superstition, is to hold sway over a disenchanted nature. Knowledge, which is power, knows no obstacles: neither in the enslavement of men nor in compliance with the world's rulers. As with all the ends of bourgeois economy in the factory and on the battlefield, origin is no bar to the dictates of the entrepreneurs: kings, no less directly than businessmen, control technology; it is as democratic as the economic system with which it is bound up. Technology is the essence of this knowledge. It does not work by concepts and images, by the fortunate insight, but refers to method, the exploitation of others' work, and capital. The "many things" which, according to Bacon, "are reserved," are themselves no more than instrumental: the radio as a sublimated printing press, the dive bomber as a more effective form of artillery, radio control as a more reliable compass. What men want to learn from nature is how to use it in order wholly to dominate it and other men. That is the only aim. Ruthlessly, in despite of itself, the Enlightenment has extinguished any trace of its own self-consciousness. The only kind of thinking that is sufficiently hard to shatter myths is ultimately self-destructive. In face of the present triumph of the factual mentality, even Bacon's nominalist credo would be suspected of a metaphysical bias and come under the same verdict of vanity that he pronounced on scholastic philosophy. Power and knowledge are synonymous.[3] For Bacon as for Lu-

---

2. Bacon, "In Praise of Human Knowledge" (*Miscellaneous Tracts upon Human Knowledge*), *The Works of Francis Bacon*, ed. Basil Montagu (London, 1825), Vol. I, pp. 254ff.
3. Cf. Bacon, *Novum Organum, Works*, Vol. XIV, p. 31.

ther, "knowledge that tendeth but to satisfaction, is but as a courtesan, which is for pleasure, and not for fruit or generation." Not "satisfaction, which men call truth," but "operation," "to do the business," is the "right mark": for ". . . what is the true end, scope, or office of knowledge, which I have set down to consist not in any plausible, delectable, reverend or admired discourse, or any satisfactory arguments, but in effecting and working, and in discovery of particulars not revealed before, for the better endowment and help of man's life."[4] There is to be no mystery—which means, too, no wish to reveal mystery.

The disenchantment of the world is the extirpation of animism. Xenophanes derides the multitude of deities because they are but replicas of the men who produced them, together with all that is contingent and evil in mankind; and the most recent school of logic denounces—for the impressions they bear—the words of language, holding them to be false coins better replaced by neutral counters. The world becomes chaos, and synthesis salvation. There is said to be no difference between the totemic animal, the dreams of the ghost-seer, and the absolute Idea. On the road to modern science, men renounce any claim to meaning. They substitute formula for concept, rule and probability for cause and motive. Cause was only the last philosophic concept which served as a yardstick for scientific criticism: so to speak because it alone among the old ideas still seemed to offer itself to scientific criticism, the latest secularization of the creative principle. Substance and quality, activity and suffering, being and existence: to define these concepts in a way appropriate to the times was a concern of philosophy after Bacon—but science managed without such categories. They were abandoned as *idola theatri* of the old metaphysics, and assessed as being even then memorials of the elements and powers of the prehistory for which life and death disclosed their nature in myths and became interwoven in them. The categories by which Western philosophy defined its everlasting natural order marked the spots once occupied by Oncus and Persephone, Ariadne and Nereus. The pre-Socratic cosmologies pre-

4. Bacon, "Valerius Terminus: Of the Interpretation of Nature" (*Miscellaneous Tracts upon Human Knowledge*), *Works,* Vol. I, p. 281.

serve the moment of transition. The moist, the indivisible, air, and fire, which they hold to be the primal matter of nature, are already rationalizations of the mythic mode of apprehension. Just as the images of generation from water and earth, which came from the Nile to the Greeks, became here hylozoistic principles, or elements, so all the equivocal multitude of mythical demons were intellectualized in the pure form of ontological essences. Finally, by means of the Platonic ideas, even the patriarchal gods of Olympus were absorbed in the philosophical *logos*. The Enlightenment, however, recognized the old powers in the Platonic and Aristotelian aspects of metaphysics, and opposed as superstition the claim that truth is predicable of universals. It asserted that in the authority of universal concepts, there was still discernible fear of the demonic spirits which men sought to portray in magic rituals, hoping thus to influence nature. From now on, matter would at last be mastered without any illusion of ruling or inherent powers, of hidden qualities. For the Enlightenment, whatever does not conform to the rule of computation and utility is suspect. So long as it can develop undisturbed by any outward repression, there is no holding it. In the process, it treats its own ideas of human rights exactly as it does the older universals. Every spiritual resistance it encounters serves merely to increase its strength.[5] Which means that enlightenment still recognizes itself even in myths. Whatever myths the resistance may appeal to, by virtue of the very fact that they become arguments in the process of opposition, they acknowledge the principle of dissolvent rationality for which they reproach the Enlightenment. Enlightenment is totalitarian.

Enlightenment has always taken the basic principle of myth to be anthropomorphism, the projection onto nature of the subjective.[6] In this view, the supernatural, spirits and demons, are mirror images of men who allow themselves to be frightened by natural phenomena. Consequently the many mythic figures can

5. Cf. Hegel, *Phänomenologie des Geistes* (*The Phenomenology of Spirit*), *Werke*, Vol. II, pp. 410ff.

6. Xenophanes, Montaigne, Hume, Feuerbach, and Salomon Reinach are at one here. See, for Reinach: *Orpheus*, trans. F. Simmons (London & New York, 1909), pp. 9ff.

all be brought to a common denominator, and reduced to the human subject. Oedipus' answer to the Sphinx's riddle: "It is man!" is the Enlightenment stereotype repeatedly offered as information, irrespective of whether it is faced with a piece of objective intelligence, a bare schematization, fear of evil powers, or hope of redemption. In advance, the Enlightenment recognizes as being and occurrence only what can be apprehended in unity: its ideal is the system from which all and everything follows. Its rationalist and empiricist versions do not part company on that point. Even though the individual schools may interpret the axioms differently, the structure of scientific unity has always been the same. Bacon's postulate of *una scientia universalis*,[7] whatever the number of fields of research, is as inimical to the unassignable as Leibniz's *mathesis universalis* is to discontinuity. The multiplicity of forms is reduced to position and arrangement, history to fact, things to matter. According to Bacon, too, degrees of universality provide an unequivocal logical connection between first principles and observational judgments. De Maistre mocks him for haboring *"une idole d'échelle."*[8] Formal logic was the major school of unified science. It provided the Enlightenment thinkers with the schema of the calculability of the world. The mythologizing equation of Ideas with numbers in Plato's last writings expresses the longing of all demythologization: number became the canon of the Enlightenment. The same equations dominate bourgeois justice and commodity exchange. "Is not the rule, *'Si inaequalibus aequalia addas, omnia erunt inaequalia,'* an axiom of justice as well as of the mathematics? And is there not a true coincidence between commutative and distributive justice, and arithmetical and geometrical proportion?"[9] Bourgeois society is ruled by equivalence. It makes the dissimilar comparable by reducing it to abstract quantities. To the Enlightenment, that which does not reduce to numbers, and ultimately to the one, becomes illusion; modern positivism writes it off as literature.

7. Bacon, *De Augmentis Scientiarum, Works*, Vol. VIII, p. 152.
8. *Les Soirées de Saint-Pétersbourg* (5ième entretien), *Œuvres Complètes* (Lyon, 1891), Vol. IV, p. 256.
9. Bacon, *Advancement of Learning, Works*, Vol. II, p. 126.

Unity is the slogan from Parmenides to Russell. The destruction of gods and qualities alike is insisted upon.

Yet the myths which fell victim to the Enlightenment were its own products. In the scientific calculation of occurrence, the computation is annulled which thought had once transferred from occurrence into myths. Myth intended report, naming, the narration of the Beginning; but also presentation, confirmation, explanation: a tendency that grew stronger with the recording and collection of myths. Narrative became didactic at an early stage. Every ritual includes the idea of activity as a determined process which magic can nevertheless influence. This theoretical element in ritual won independence in the earliest national epics. The myths, as the tragedians came upon them, are already characterized by the discipline and power that Bacon celebrated as the "right mark." In place of the local spirits and demons there appeared heaven and its hierarchy; in place of the invocations of the magician and the tribe the distinct gradation of sacrifice and the labor of the unfree mediated through the word of command. The Olympic deities are no longer directly identical with elements, but signify them. In Homer, Zeus represents the sky and the weather, Apollo controls the sun, and Helios and Eos are already shifting to an allegorical function. The gods are distinguished from material elements as their quintessential concepts. From now on, being divides into the *logos* (which with the progress of philosophy contracts to the monad, to a mere point of reference), and into the mass of all things and creatures without. This single distinction between existence proper and reality engulfs all others. Without regard to distinctions, the world becomes subject to man. In this the Jewish creation narrative and the religion of Olympia are at one: ". . . and let them have dominion over the fish of the sea, and over the fowl of the air, and over the cattle, and over all the earth, and over every creeping thing that creepeth upon the earth."[10] "O Zeus, Father Zeus, yours is the dominion of the heavens, and you oversee the works of man, both wicked and just, and even the wantonness of the beasts; and righteousness

10. Genesis I. 26 (AV).

8

is your concern."[11] "For so it is that one atones straightaway, and another later; but should one escape and the threatening decree of the gods not reach him, yet it will certainly be visited at last, if not upon him then upon his children or another generation."[12] Only he who always submits survives in the face of the gods. The awakening of the self is paid for by the acknowledgement of power as the principle of all relations. In view of the unity of this *ratio,* the divorcement between God and man dwindles to the degree of irrelevancy to which unswervable reason has drawn attention since even the earliest critique of Homer. The creative god and the systematic spirit are alike as rulers of nature. Man's likeness to God consists in sovereignty over existence, in the countenance of the lord and master, and in command.

Myth turns into enlightenment, and nature into mere objectivity. Men pay for the increase of their power with alienation from that over which they exercise their power. Enlightenment behaves toward things as a dictator toward men. He knows them in so far as he can manipulate them. The man of science knows things in so far as he can make them. In this way their potentiality is turned to his own ends. In the metamorphosis the nature of things, as a substratum of domination, is revealed as always the same. This identity constitutes the unity of nature. It is a presupposition of the magical invocation as little as the unity of the subject. The shaman's rites were directed to the wind, the rain, the serpent without, or the demon in the sick man, but not to materials or specimens. Magic was not ordered by one, identical spirit: it changed like the cultic masks which were supposed to accord with the various spirits. Magic is utterly untrue, yet in it domination is not yet negated by transforming itself into the pure truth and acting as the very ground of the world that has become subject to it. The magician imitates demons; in order to frighten them or to appease them, he behaves frighteningly or makes gestures of appeasement. Even though his task is impersonation, he never conceives of himself

11. Archilochos, fr. 87; quoted by Deussen, *Allgemeine Geschichte der Philosophie,* Vol. II, Pt. 1 (Leipzig, 1911), p. 18.
12. Solon, fr. 13.25 *et seq.,* quoted by Deussen, p. 20.

as does the civilized man for whom the unpretentious preserves of the happy hunting-grounds become the unified cosmos, the inclusive concept for all possibilities of plunder. The magician never interprets himself as the image of the invisible power; yet this is the very image in which man attains to the identity of self that cannot disappear through identification with another, but takes possession of itself once and for all as an impenetrable mask. It is the identity of the spirit and its correlate, the unity of nature, to which the multiplicity of qualities falls victim. Disqualified nature becomes the chaotic matter of mere classification, and the all-powerful self becomes mere possession—abstract identity. In magic there is specific representation. What happens to the enemy's spear, hair or name, also happens to the individual; the sacrificial animal is massacred instead of the god. Substitution in the course of sacrifice marks a step toward discursive logic. Even though the hind offered up for the daughter, and the lamb for the first-born, still had to have specific qualities, they already represented the species. They already exhibited the non-specificity of the example. But the holiness of the *hic et nunc,* the uniqueness of the chosen one into which the representative enters, radically marks it off, and makes it unfit for exchange. Science prepares the end of this state of affairs. In science there is no specific representation: and if there are no sacrificial animals there is no god. Representation is exchanged for the fungible—universal interchangeability. An atom is smashed not in representation but as a specimen of matter, and the rabbit does not represent but, as a mere example, is virtually ignored by the zeal of the laboratory. Because the distinctions in functional science are so fluid that everything is subsumed in the same matter, the scientific object is petrified, and the fixed ritual of former times appears flexible because it attributed the other to the one. The world of magic retained distinctions whose traces have disappeared even in linguistic form.[13] The multitudinous affinities between existents are suppressed by the single relation between the subject who bestows meaning and the meaningless object, between rational signifi-

13. See, for example: Robert H. Lowie, *An Introduction to Cultural Anthropology* (New York, 1940), pp. 344ff.

cance and the chance vehicle of significance. On the magical plane, dream and image were not mere signs for the thing in question, but were bound up with it by similarity or names. The relation is one not of intention but of relatedness. Like science, magic pursues aims, but seeks to achieve them by mimesis —not by progressively distancing itself from the object. It is not grounded in the "sovereignty of ideas," which the primitive, like the neurotic, is said to ascribe to himself;[14] there can be no "over-evaluation of mental processes as against reality" where there is no radical distinction between thoughts and reality. The "unshakable confidence in the possibility of world domination,"[15] which Freud anachronistically ascribes to magic, corresponds to realistic world domination only in terms of a more skilled science. The replacement of the milieu-bound practices of the medicine man by all-inclusive industrial technology required first of all the autonomy of ideas in regard to objects that was achieved in the reality-adjusted ego.

As a linguistically expressed totality, whose claim to truth suppresses the older mythic belief, the national religion or patriarchal solar myth is itself an Enlightenment with which the philosophic form can compare itself on the same level. And now it has its requital. Mythology itself set off the unending process of enlightenment in which ever and again, with the inevitability of necessity, every specific theoretic view succumbs to the destructive criticism that it is only a belief—until even the very notions of spirit, of truth and, indeed, enlightenment itself, have become animistic magic. The principle of fatal necessity, which brings low the heroes of myth and derives as a logical consequence from the pronouncement of the oracle, does not merely, when refined to the stringency of formal logic, rule in every rationalistic system of Western philosophy, but itself dominates the series of systems which begins with the hierarchy of the gods and, in a permanent twilight of the idols, hands down an identical content: anger against insufficient righteousness. Just as the myths already realize enlightenment, so en-

14. Cf. Freud, *Totem und Tabu* (*Totem and Taboo*), *Gesammelte Werke*, Vol. IX, pp. 106ff.
15. *Totem und Tabu*, p. 110.

lightenment with every step becomes more deeply engulfed in mythology. It receives all its matter from the myths, in order to destroy them; and even as a judge it comes under the mythic curse. It wishes to extricate itself from the process of fate and retribution, while exercising retribution on that process. In the myths everything that happens must atone for having happened. And so it is in enlightenment: the fact becomes null and void, and might as well not have happened. The doctrine of the equivalence of action and reaction asserted the power of repetition over reality, long after men had renounced the illusion that by repetition they could identify themselves with the repeated reality and thus escape its power. But as the magical illusion fades away, the more relentlessly in the name of law repetition imprisons man in the cycle—that cycle whose objectification in the form of natural law he imagines will ensure his action as a free subject. The principle of immanence, the explanation of every event as repetition, that the Enlightenment upholds against mythic imagination, is the principle of myth itself. That arid wisdom that holds there is nothing new under the sun, because all the pieces in the meaningless game have been played, and all the great thoughts have already been thought, and because all possible discoveries can be construed in advance and all men are decided on adaptation as the means to self-preservation—that dry sagacity merely reproduces the fantastic wisdom that it supposedly rejects: the sanction of fate that in retribution relentlessly remakes what has already been. What was different is equalized. That is the verdict which critically determines the limits of possible experience. The identity of everything with everything else is paid for in that nothing may at the same time be identical with itself. Enlightenment dissolves the injustice of the old inequality—unmediated lordship and mastery—but at the same time perpetuates it in universal mediation, in the relation of any one existent to any other. It does what Kierkegaard praises his Protestant ethic for, and what in the Heraclean epic cycle is one of the primal images of mythic power; it excises the incommensurable. Not only are qualities dissolved in thought, but men are brought to actual conformity. The blessing that the market does not enquire after one's birth is paid for by the barterer, in that he models the potentialities that are his by birth on the production of the commodities that can be bought in the market. Men were given their individuality as unique in each case, different to all others, so that it might all the more surely be made the same as any other. But because the unique self never wholly disappeared, even after the liberalistic epoch, the Enlightenment has always sympathized with the social impulse. The unity of the manipulated collective consists in the negation of each individual: for individuality makes a mockery of the kind of society which would turn all individuals to the one collectivity. The horde which so assuredly appears in the organization of the Hitler Youth is not a return to barbarism but the triumph of repressive equality, the disclosure through peers of the parity of the right to injustice. The phony Fascist mythology is shown to be the genuine myth of antiquity, insofar as the genuine one saw retribution, whereas the false one blindly doles it out to the sacrifices. Every attempt to break the natural thralldom, because nature is broken, enters all the more deeply into that natural enslavement. Hence the course of European civilization. Abstraction, the tool of enlightenment, treats its objects as did fate, the notion of which it rejects: it liquidates them. Under the leveling domination of abstraction (which makes everything in nature repeatable), and of industry (for which abstraction ordains repetition), the freedom themselves finally came to form that "herd" which Hegel[16] has declared to be the result of the Enlightenment.

The distance between subject and object, a presupposition of abstraction, is grounded in the distance from the thing itself which the master achieved through the mastered. The lyrics of Homer and the hymns of the Rig-Veda date from the time of territorial dominion and the secure locations in which a dominant warlike race established themselves over the mass of vanquished natives.[17] The first god among the gods arose with this civil society in which the king, as chieftain of the arms-

---

16. *Phänomenologie des Geistes*, p. 424.
17. Cf. W. Kirfel, *Geschichte Indiens*, in: *Propyläenweltgeschichte*, Vol. III, pp. 261ff; and G. Glotz, *Histoire Grecque*, Vol. I, in: *Histoire Ancienne* (Paris, 1938), pp. 137ff.

DIALECTIC OF ENLIGHTENMENT

bearing nobility, holds down the conquered to the earth, whereas physicians, soothsayers, craftsmen and merchants see to social intercourse. With the end of a nomadic existence, the social order is created on a basis of fixed property. Mastery and labor are divided. A proprietor like Odysseus "manages from a distance a numerous, carefully gradated staff of cowherds, shepherds, swineherds and servants. In the evening, when he has seen from his castle that the countryside is illumined by a thousand fires, he can compose himself for sleep with a quiet mind: he knows that his upright servants are keeping watch lest wild animals approach, and to chase thieves from the preserves which they are there to protect."[18] The universality of ideas as developed by discursive logic, domination in the conceptual sphere, is raised up on the basis of actual domination. The dissolution of the magical heritage, of the old diffuse ideas, by conceptual unity, expresses the hierarchical constitution of life determined by those who are free. The individuality that learned order and subordination in the subjection of the world, soon wholly equated truth with the regulative thought without whose fixed distinctions universal truth cannot exist. Together with mimetic magic, it tabooed the knowledge which really concerned the object. Its hatred was extended to the image of the vanquished former age and its imaginary happiness. The chthonic gods of the original inhabitants are banished to the hell to which, according to the sun and light religion of Indra and Zeus, the earth is transformed.

Heaven and hell, however, hang together. Just as the name of Zeus, in non-exclusive cults, was given to a god of the underworld as well as to a god of light;[19] just as the Olympian gods had every kind of commerce with the chthonic deities: so the good and evil powers, salvation and disaster, were not unequivocally distinct. They were linked together like coming up and passing away, life and death, summer and winter. The gloomy and indistinct religious principle that was honored as *mana* in

18. Glotz, p. 140.
19. See Kurt Eckermann, *Jahrbuch der Religionsgeschichte und Mythologie* (Halle, 1845), Vol. I, p. 241; and O. Kern, *Die Religion der Griechen* (Berlin, 1926), Vol. I, pp. 181ff.

14

the earliest known stages of humanity, lives on in the radiant world of Greek religion. Everything unknown and alien is primary and undifferentiated: that which transcends the confines of experience; whatever in things is more than their previously known reality. What the primitive experiences in this regard is not a spiritual as opposed to a material substance, but the intricacy of the Natural in contrast to the individual. The gasp of surprise which accompanies the experience of the unusual becomes its name. It fixes the transcendence of the unknown in relation to the known, and therefore terror as sacredness. The dualization of nature as appearance and sequence, effort and power, which first makes possible both myth and science, originates in human fear, the expression of which becomes explanation. It is not the soul which is transposed to nature, as psychologism would have it; *mana*, the moving spirit, is no projection, but the echo of the real supremacy of nature in the weak souls of primitive men. The separation of the animate and the inanimate, the occupation of certain places by demons and deities, first arises from this pre-animism, which contains the first lines of the separation of subject and object. When the tree is no longer approached merely as tree, but as evidence for an Other, as the location of *mana*, language expresses the contradiction that something is itself and at one and the same time something other than itself, identical and not identical.[20] Through the deity, language is transformed from tautology to language. The concept, which some would see as the sign-unit for whatever is comprised under it, has from the beginning been instead the product of dialectical thinking in which everything is always that which it is, only because it becomes that which it is not. That was the original form of objectifying definition, in which concept and thing are separated. The same form which is already far advanced in the Homeric epic and confounds itself in modern positivist science. But this dialectic remains impotent to the extent that it develops from the cry of terror

20. This is how Hubert and Mauss interpret "sympathy," or *mimesis*: "*L'un est le tout, est dans l'un, la nature triomphe de la nature.*" H. Hubert and M. Mauss, "*Théorie générale de la Magie*," in: *L'Année Sociologique*, 1902–3, p. 100.

15

which is the duplication, the tautology, of terror itself. The gods cannot take fear away from man, for they bear its petrified sound with them as they bear their names. Man imagines himself free from fear when there is no longer anything unknown. That determines the course of demythologization, of enlightenment, which compounds the animate with the inanimate just as myth compounds the inanimate with the animate. Enlightenment is mythic fear turned radical. The pure immanence of positivism, its ultimate product, is no more than a so to speak universal taboo. Nothing at all may remain outside, because the mere idea of outsideness is the very source of fear. The revenge of the primitive for death, when visited upon one of his kin, was sometimes appeased by reception of the murderer into his own family;[21] this, too, signified the infusion of alien blood into one's own, the generation of immanence. The mythic dualism does not extend beyond the environs of existence. The world permeated by *mana* and even the world of Indian and Greek myth know no exits, and are eternally the same. Every birth is paid for with death, every fortune with misfortune. Men and gods may try in their short space to assess fate in other terms than the blind course of destiny, but in the end existence triumphs over them. Even their justice, which is wrested from fatality, bears the marks of fatality: it corresponds to the look which men—primitives, Greeks and barbarians alike—cast from a society of pressure and misery on the circumambient world. Hence, for mythic and enlightened justice, guilt and atonement, happiness and unhappiness were sides of an equation. Justice is subsumed in law. The shaman wards off danger by means of its image. Equivalence is his instrument; and equivalence regulates punishment and reward in civilization. The mythic representations can also be traced back in their entirety to natural conditions. Just as the Gemini—the constellation of Castor and Pollux—and all other symbols of duality refer to the inevitable cycle of nature, which itself has its ancient sign in the symbol of the egg from which they came, so the balance held by Zeus, which symbolizes the justice of the

21. Cf. Westermarck, *Ursprung der Moralbegriffe* (Leipzig, 1913), Vol. I, p. 402.

entire patriarchal world, refers back to mere nature. The step from chaos to civilization, in which natural conditions exert their power no longer directly but through the medium of the human consciousness, has not changed the principle of equivalence. Indeed, men paid for this very step by worshipping what they were once in thrall to only in the same way as all other creatures. Before, the fetishes were subject to the law of equivalence. Now equivalence itself has become a fetish. The blindfold over Justitia's eyes does not only mean that there should be no assault upon justice, but that justice does not originate in freedom.

The doctrine of the priests was symbolic in the sense that in it sign and image were one. Just as hieroglyphs bear witness, so the word too originally had a pictorial function, which was transferred to myths. Like magical rites, myths signify self-repetitive nature, which is the core of the symbolic: a state of being or a process that is presented as eternal, because it incessantly becomes actual once more by being realized in symbolic form. Inexhaustibility, unending renewal and the permanence of the signified are not mere attributes of all symbols, but their essential content. The representations of creation in which the world comes forth from the primal mother, the cow, or the egg, are symbolic—unlike the Jewish Genesis. The elders' mockery of the all-too-human gods left the core untouched. The gods were not wholly individual. They still had something of *mana* in them, for they embodied nature as universal power. With their pre-animistic characteristics they are prominent in the Enlightenment. Beneath the coy veil of the Olympian *chronique scandaleuse,* there was already apparent the doctrine of the mixture, pressure, and impact of the elements, which presently established itself as science and turned the myths into fantastic images. With the clean separation of science and poetry, the division of labor it had already helped to effect was extended to language. For science the word is a sign: as sound, image, and word proper it is distributed among the different arts, and is not permitted to reconstitute itself by their addition, by synesthesia, or in the composition of the *Gesamtkunstwerk.* As a system of signs, language is required to resign itself to calculation in order to know nature, and must discard the claim to be like her. As image, it is required to resign itself to mirror-imagery in order to be nature entire, and must discard the claim to know her. With the progress of enlightenment, only authentic works of art were able to avoid the mere imitation of that which already is. The practicable antithesis of art and science, which tears them apart as separate areas of culture in order to make them both manageable as areas of culture ultimately allows them, by dint of their own tendencies, to blend with one another even as exact contraries. In its neo-positivist version, science becomes aestheticism, a system of detached signs devoid of any intention that would transcend the system: it becomes the game which mathematicians have for long proudly asserted is their concern. But the art of integral representability, even in its techniques, subscribed to positive science, and in fact adapts to the world yet again, becoming ideological duplication, partisan reproduction. The separation of sign and image is irremediable. Should unconscious self-satisfaction cause it once again to become hypostatized, then each of the two isolated principles tends toward the destruction of truth.

In the relationship of intuition (i.e. direct perception) and concept, philosophy already discerned the gulf which opened with that separation, and again tries in vain to close it: philosophy, indeed, is defined by this very attempt. For the most part it has stood on the side from which it derives its name. Plato banned poetry with the same gesture that positivism used against the theory of ideas (*Ideenlehre*). With his much-renowned art, Homer carried out no public or private reforms, and neither won a war nor made any discovery. We know of no multitude of followers who might have honored or adored him. Art must first prove its utility.[22] For art, as for the Jews, imitation is proscribed. Reason and religion deprecate and condemn the principle of magic enchantment. Even in resigned self-distancing from real existence, as art, it remains dishonest; its practitioners become travelers, latterday nomads who find no

22. Cf. Plato, *Republic*, Book X.

abiding home under the established what-has-come-to-be. Nature must no longer be influenced by approximation, but mastered by labor. The work of art still has something in common with enchantment: it posits its own, self-enclosed area, which is withdrawn from the context of profane existence, and in which special laws apply. Just as in the ceremony the magician first of all marked out the limits of the area where the sacred powers were to come into play, so every work of art describes its own circumference which closes it off from actuality. This very renunciation of influence, which distinguishes art from magical sympathy, retains the magic heritage all the more surely. It places the pure image in contrast to animate existence, the elements of which it absorbs. It is in the nature of the work of art, or aesthetic semblance, to be what the new, terrifying occurrence became in the primitive's magic: the appearance of the whole in the particular. In the work of art that duplication still occurs by which the thing appeared as spiritual, as the expression of *mana*. This constitutes its aura. As an expression of totality art lays claim to the dignity of the absolute. This sometimes causes philosophy to allow it precedence to conceptual knowledge. According to Schelling, art comes into play where knowledge forsakes mankind. For him it is "the prototype of science, and only where there is art may science enter in."[23] In his theory, the separation of image and sign is "wholly canceled by every single artistic representation."[24] The bourgeois world was but rarely open to such confidence in art. Where it restricted knowledge, it usually did so not for the sake of art, but in order to make room for faith. Through faith the militant religiousness of the new age hoped to reconcile Torquemada, Luther, Mohammed, spirit and real life. But faith is a privative concept: it is destroyed as faith if it does not continually display its contradistinction to, or conformity with, knowledge. Since it is always set upon the restriction of knowledge, it is itself restricted. The attempt of Protestant faith to find, as in prehistory, the transcendental principle of truth (without which

23. *Erster Entwurf eines Systems der Naturphilosophie*, S. 5, *Werke*, Abt. 1, Vol. II p. 623.
24. *Ibid.*, p. 626.

belief cannot exist) directly in the word itself, and to reinvest this with symbolic power, has been paid for with obedience to the word, and not to the sacred. As long as faith remains unhesitatingly tied—as friend or foe—to knowledge, it perpetuates the separation in the very course of the struggle to overcome it: its fanaticism is the occasion of its untruth, the objective admission that he who only has faith, for that very reason no longer has it. Bad conscience is its second nature. In the secret consciousness of the deficiency—necessarily inherent in faith—of its immanent contradiction in making reconciliation a vocation, lies the reason why the integrity of all believers has always been a sensitive and dangerous thing. The atrocities of fire and sword, counter-Reformation and Reformation, have occurred not as exaggerations but as realizations of the principle of faith itself. Faith constantly reveals itself to be of the same cut as the world-history which it would dictate to—in modern times, indeed, it becomes its favorite instrument, its particular stratagem. It is not merely the Enlightenment of the eighteenth century that, as Hegel confirmed, is relentless but—as no one knew better than he—the advance of thought itself. The lowest and the highest insight alike manifest that distance from truth which makes apologists liars. The paradoxical nature of faith ultimately degenerates into a swindle, and becomes the myth of the twentieth century; and its irrationality turns it into an instrument of rational administration by the wholly enlightened as they steer society toward barbarism.

When language enters history its masters are priests and sorcerers. Whoever harms the symbols is, in the name of the supernatural powers, subject to their earthly counterparts, whose representatives are those chosen organs of society. What happened previously is hid in darkness. The dread which gives birth to *mana*, wherever it is met within ethnology, is always sanctioned, at least by the tribal elders. Unidentified, volatile *mana* was rendered consistent by men and forcibly materialized. Soon the magicians peopled every spot with emanations and made a multiplicity of sacred rites concordant with the variety of sacred places. They expanded their professional knowledge and their influence with the expansion of the spirit world and its characteristics. The nature of the sacred being transferred itself to the magicians, who were privy to it. In the first stages of nomadic life the members of the tribe still took an individual part in the process of influencing the course of nature. Men hunted game, while women did the work which could be produced without strict command. It is impossible to determine to what extent habit contributed to so simple an arrangement. In it, the world is already divided into the territory of power and the profane area; as the emanation of *mana*, the course of nature is elevated to become the norm, and submission to it is required. But even though, despite all submission, the savage nomad still participated in the magic which determined the lines of that submission, and clothed himself as his quarry in order to stalk it, in later times intercourse with spirits and submission were assigned to different classes: the power is on the one side, and obedience on the other. For the vanquished (whether by alien tribes or by their own cliques), the recurrent, eternally similar natural processes become the rhythm of labor according to the beat of cudgel and whip which resounds in every barbaric drum and every monotonous ritual. The symbols undertake a fetishistic function. In the process, the recurrence of nature which they signify is always the permanence of the social pressure which they represent. The dread objectified as a fixed image becomes the sign of the established domination of the privileged. Such is the fate of universal concepts, even when they have discarded everything pictorial. Even the deductive form of science reflects hierarchy and coercion. Just as the first categories represented the organized tribe and its power over the individual, so the whole logical order, dependency, connection, progression, and union of concepts is grounded in the corresponding conditions of social reality—that is, of the division of labor.[25] But of course this social character of categories of thought is not, as Durkheim asserts, an expression of social solidarity, but evidence of the inscrutable unity of society and domination. Domination lends increased consistency and force to the social whole in which it establishes itself. The

25. See E. Durkheim, *"De Quelques Formes Primitives de Classification,"* in: *L'Année Sociologique,* Vol. IV, 1903, pp. 66ff.

division of labor to which domination tends serves the dominated whole for the end of self-preservation. But then the whole
as whole, the manifestation of its immanent reason, necessarily
leads to the execution of the particular. To the individual,
domination appears to be the universal: reason in actuality.
Through the division of labor imposed on them, the power of
all the members of society—for whom as such there is no other
course—amounts over and over again to the realization of the
whole, whose rationality is reproduced in this way. What is
done to all by the few, always occurs as the subjection of individuals by the many: social repression always exhibits the
masks of repression by a collective. It is this unity of the collectivity and domination, and not direct social universality,
solidarity, which is expressed in thought forms. By virtue of the
claim to universal validity, the philosophic concepts with which
Plato and Aristotle represented the world, elevated the conditions they were used to substantiate to the level of true reality.
These concepts originated, as Vico puts it,[26] in the marketplace
of Athens; they reflected with equal clarity the laws of physics,
the equality of full citizens and the inferiority of women, children and slaves. Language itself gave what was asserted, the
conditions of domination, the universality that they had assumed as the means of intercourse of a bourgeois society. The
metaphysical emphasis, and sanction by means of ideas and
norms, were no more than a hypostatization of the rigidity and
exclusiveness which concepts were generally compelled to assume wherever language united the community of rulers with
the giving of orders. As a mere means of reinforcing the social
power of language, ideas became all the more superfluous as
this power grew, and the language of science prepared the way
for their ultimate desuetude. The suggestion of something still
akin to the terror of the fetish did not inhere in conscious justification; instead the unity of collectivity and domination is
revealed in the universality necessarily assumed by the bad
content of language, both metaphysical and scientific. Metaphysical apology betrayed the injustice of the *status quo* least

26. Giambattista Vico, *Scienza Nuova* (*Principles of a New Science
of the Common Nature of Nations*).

of all in the incongruence of concept and actuality. In the impartiality of scientific language, that which is powerless has wholly lost any means of expression, and only the given finds its neutral sign. This kind of neutrality is more metaphysical than metaphysics. Ultimately, the Enlightenment consumed not just the symbols but their successors, universal concepts, and spared no remnant of metaphysics apart from the abstract fear of the collective from which it arose. The situation of concepts in the face of the Enlightenment is like that of men of private means in regard to industrial trusts: none can feel safe. Even if logical positivism still allowed leeway to probability, ethnological positivism puts it in its place: "Our vague ideas of chance and quintessence are pale shadows of this much richer notion"[27]— that is, of magical substance.

As a nominalist movement, the Enlightenment calls a halt before the *nomen,* the exclusive, precise concept, the proper name. Whether—as some assert[28]—proper names were originally species names as well, can no longer be ascertained, yet the former have not shared the fate of the latter. The substantial ego refuted by Hume and Mach is not synonymous with the name. In Jewish religion, in which the idea of the patriarchate culminates in the destruction of myth, the bond between name and being is still recognized in the ban on pronouncing the name of God. The disenchanted world of Judaism conciliates magic by negating it in the idea of God. Jewish religion allows no word that would alleviate the despair of all that is mortal. It associates hope only with the prohibition against calling on what is false as God, against invoking the finite as the infinite, lies as truth. The guarantee of salvation lies in the rejection of any belief that would replace it: it is knowledge obtained in the denunciation of illusion. Admittedly, the negation is not abstract. The contesting of every positive without distinction, the stereotype formula of vanity, as used by Buddhism, sets itself above the prohibition against naming the Absolute with names: just as far above as its contrary, pantheism; or its caricature,

27. Hubert and Mauss, *op. cit.,* p. 118.
28. See Tönnies, *"Philosophische Terminologie,"* in: *Psychologisch-Soziologische Ansicht* (Leipzig, 1908), p. 31.

bourgeois skepticism. Explanations of the world as all or nothing are mythologies, and guaranteed roads to redemption are sublimated magic practices. The self-satisfaction of knowing in advance and the transfiguration of negativity into redemption are untrue forms of resistance against deception. The justness of the image is preserved in the faithful pursuit of its prohibition. This pursuit, "determinate negativity"[29] does not receive from the sovereignty of the abstract concept any immunity against corrupting intuition, as does skepticism, to which both true and false are equally vain. Determinate negation rejects the defective ideas of the absolute, the idols, differently than does rigorism, which confronts them with the Idea that they cannot match up to. Dialectic, on the contrary, interprets every image as writing. It shows how the admission of its falsity is to be read in the lines of its features—a confession that deprives it of its power and appropriates it for truth. With the notion of determinate negativity, Hegel revealed an element that distinguishes the Enlightenment from the positivist degeneracy to which he attributes it. By ultimately making the conscious result of the whole process of negation—totality in system and in history—into an absolute, he of course contravened the prohibition and himself lapsed into mythology.

This did not happen merely to his philosophy as the apotheosis of progressive thought, but to the Enlightenment itself, as the sobriety which it thought distinguished it from Hegel and from metaphysics. For enlightenment is as totalitarian as any system. Its untruth does not consist in what its romantic enemies have always reproached it for: analytical method, return to elements, dissolution through reflective thought; but instead in the fact that for enlightenment the process is always decided from the start. When in mathematical procedure the unknown becomes the unknown quantity of an equation, this marks it as the well-known even before any value is inserted. Nature, before and after the quantum theory, is that which is to be comprehended mathematically; even what cannot be made to agree, indissolubility and irrationality, is converted by means

29. *Phänomenologie des Geistes*, p. 65.

of mathematical theorems. In the anticipatory indentification of the wholly conceived and mathematized world with truth, enlightenment intends to secure itself against the return of the mythic. It confounds thought and mathematics. In this way the latter is, so to speak, released and made into an absolute instance. "An infinite world, in this case a world of idealities, is conceived as one whose objects do not accede singly, imperfectly, and as if by chance to our cognition, but are attained by a rational, systematically unified method—in a process of infinite progression—so that each object is ultimately apparent according to its full inherent being . . . In the Galilean mathematization of the world, however, *this selfness* is idealized under the guidance of the new mathematics: in modern terms, it becomes itself a mathematical multiplicity."[30] Thinking objectifies itself to become an automatic, self-activating process; an impersonation of the machine that it produces itself so that ultimately the machine can replace it. Enlightenment[31] has put aside the classic requirement of thinking about thought—Fichte is its extreme manifestation—because it wants to avoid the precept of dictating practice that Fichte himself wished to obey. Mathematical procedure became, so to speak, the ritual of thinking. In spite of the axiomatic self-restriction, it establishes itself as necessary and objective: it turns thought into a thing, an instrument—which is its own term for it. But this kind of mimesis, in which universal thought is equalized, so turns the actual into the unique, that even atheism itself is subjected to the ban on metaphysics. For positivism, which represents the court of judgment of enlightened reason, to digress into intelligible worlds is no longer merely forbidden, but meaningless prattle. It does not need—fortunately—to be atheistic, because objectified thinking cannot even raise the problem. The positivist censor lets the established cult escape as willingly as art— as a cognition-free special area of social activity; but he will

30. Edmund Husserl, *"Die Krisis der europäischen Wissenschaften und die transzendentale Phänomenologie,"* in: *Philosophia* (Belgrade, 1936), pp. 95ff.

31. Cf. Schopenhauer, *Parerga und Paralipomena*, Vol. II, S. 356; *Werke*, ed. Deussen, Vol. V, p. 671.

never permit that denial of it which itself claims to be knowledge. For the scientific mind, the separation of thought from
business for the purpose of adjusting actuality, departure from
the privileged area of real existence, is as insane and self-
destructive as the primitive magician would consider stepping
out of the magic circle he has prepared for his invocation; in
both cases the offense against the taboo will actually result in
the malefactor's ruin. The mastery of nature draws the circle
into which the criticism of pure reason banished thought. Kant
joined the theory of its unceasingly laborious advance into infinity with an insistence on its deficiency and everlasting limitation. His judgment is an oracle. There is no form of being in
the world that science could not penetrate, but what can be
penetrated by science is not being. According to Kant, philosophic
judgment aims at the new; and yet it recognizes nothing new,
since it always merely recalls what reason has always deposited
in the object. But there is a reckoning for this form of thinking
that considers itself secure in the various departments of science
—secure from the dreams of a ghost-seer: world domination
over nature turns against the thinking subject himself; nothing
is left of him but that eternally same *I think* that must accom-
pany all my ideas. Subject and object are both rendered ineffectual. The abstract self, which justifies record-making and systematization, has nothing set over against it but the abstract
material which possesses no other quality than to be a substrate
of such possession. The equation of spirit and world arises
eventually, but only with a mutual restriction of both sides. The
reduction of thought to a mathematical apparatus conceals the
sanction of the world as its own yardstick. What appears to be
the triumph of subjective rationality, the subjection of all
reality to logical formalism, is paid for by the obedient subjection of reason to what is directly given. What is abandoned
is the whole claim and approach of knowledge: to comprehend
the given as such; not merely to determine the abstract spatio-
temporal relations of the facts which allow them just to be
grasped, but on the contrary to conceive them as the super-
ficies, as mediated conceptual moments which come to fulfill-

ment only in the development of their social, historical, and human significance. The task of cognition does not consist in mere apprehension, classification, and calculation, but in the determinate negation of each im-mediacy. Mathematical formalism, however, whose medium is number, the most abstract form of the immediate, instead holds thinking firmly to mere immediacy. Factuality wins the day; cognition is restricted to its repetition; and thought becomes mere tautology. The more the machinery of thought subjects existence to itself, the more blind its resignation in reproducing existence. Hence enlightenment returns to mythology, which it never really knew how to elude. For in its figures mythology had the essence of the *status quo:* cycle, fate, and domination of the world reflected as the truth and deprived of hope. In both the pregnancy of the mythical image and the clarity of the scientific formula, the everlastingness of the factual is confirmed and mere existence pure and simple expressed as the meaning which it forbids. The world as a gigantic analytic judgment, the only one left over from all the dreams of science, is of the same mold as the cosmic myth which associated the cycle of spring and autumn with the kidnapping of Persephone. The uniqueness of the mythic process, which tends to legitimize factuality, is deception. Originally the carrying off of the goddess was directly synonymous with the dying of nature. It repeated itself every autumn, and even the repetition was not the result of the buried one but the same every time. With the rigidification of the consciousness of time, the process was fixed in the past as a unique one, and in each new cycle of the seasons an attempt was made ritually to appease fear of death by recourse to what was long past. But the separation is ineffective. Through the establishment of a unique past, the cycle takes on the character of inevitability, and dread radiates from the age-old occurrence to make every event its mere repetition. The absorption of factuality, whether into legendary prehistory or into mathematical formalism, the symbolical relation of the contemporary to the mythic process in the rite or to the abstract category in science, makes the new appear as the predetermined, which is accordingly the old. Not existence but knowledge is without hope, for in the pictorical or mathematical symbol it appropriates and perpetuates existence as a schema.

In the enlightened world, mythology has entered into the profane. In its blank purity, the reality which has been cleansed of demons and their conceptual descendants assumes the numinous character which the ancient world attributed to demons. Under the title of brute facts, the social injustice from which they proceed is now as assuredly sacred a preserve as the medicine man was sacrosanct by reason of the protection of his gods. It is not merely that domination is paid for by the alienation of men from the objects dominated: with the objectification of spirit, the very relations of men—even those of the individual to himself—were bewitched. The individual is reduced to the nodal point of the conventional responses and modes of operation expected of him. Animism spiritualized the object, whereas industrialism objectifies the spirits of men. Automatically, the economic apparatus, even before total planning, equips commodities with the values which decide human behavior. Since, with the end of free exchange, commodities lost all their economic qualities except for fetishism, the latter has extended its arthritic influence over all aspects of social life. Through the countless agencies of mass production and its culture the conventionalized modes of behavior are impressed on the individual as the only natural, respectable, and rational ones. He defines himself only as a thing, as a static element, as success or failure. His yardstick is self-preservation, successful or unsuccessful approximation to the objectivity of his function and the models established for it. Everything else, idea and crime, suffers the force of the collective, which monitors it from the classroom to the trade union. But even the threatening collective belongs only to the deceptive surface, beneath which are concealed the powers which manipulate it as the instrument of power. Its brutality, which keeps the individual up to scratch, represents the true quality of men as little as value represents the things which he consumes. The demonically distorted form which things and men have assumed in the light of unprejudiced cognition, indicates domination, the principle which effected the specification of *mana* in spirits and gods and occurred in the jugglery of magicians and medicine men. The fatality by means of which prehistory sanctioned the incomprehensibility of death is transferred to wholly comprehensible real existence. The noontide panic fear in which men suddenly became aware of nature as totality has found its like in the panic which nowadays is ready to break out at every moment: men expect that the world, which is without any issue, will be set on fire by a totality which they themselves are and over which they have no control.

The mythic terror feared by the Enlightenment accords with myth. Enlightenment discerns it not merely in unclarified concepts and words, as demonstrated by semantic language-criticism, but in any human assertion that has no place in the ultimate context of self-preservation. Spinoza's *"Conatus sese conservandi primum et unicum virtutis est fundamentum"*[32] contains the true maxim of all Western civilization, in which the religious and philosophical differences of the middle class are reconciled. The self (which, according to the methodical extirpation of all natural residues because they are mythological, must no longer be either body or blood, or soul, or even the natural I), once sublimated into the transcendental or logical subject, would form the reference point of reason, of the determinative instance of action. Whoever resigns himself to life without any rational reference to self-preservation would, according to the Enlightenment—and Protestantism—regress to prehistory. Impulse as such is as mythic as superstition; to serve the god not postulated by the self is as idiotic as drunkenness. Progress has prepared the same fate for both adoration and descent into a state of directly natural being, and has anathematized both the self-abandonment of thought and that of pleasure. The social work of every individual in bourgeois society is mediated through the principle of self; for one, labor will bring an increased return on capital; for others, the energy for extra labor. But the more the process of self-preservation is effected by the bourgeois division of labor, the more it requires the self-alienation of the individuals who must model their body and

32. *Ethica,* Pars. IV. Propos, XXII. Coroll.

soul according to the technical apparatus. This again is taken into account by enlightened thought: in the end the transcendental subject of cognition is apparently abandoned as the last reminiscence of subjectivity and replaced by the much smoother work of automatic control mechanisms. Subjectivity has given way to the logic of the allegedly indifferent rules of the game, in order to dictate all the more unrestrainedly. Positivism, which finally did not spare thought itself, the chimera in a cerebral form, has removed the very last insulating instance between individual behavior and the social norm. The technical process, into which the subject has objectified itself after being removed from the consciousness, is free of the ambiguity of mythic thought as of all meaning altogether, because reason itself has become the mere instrument of the all-inclusive economic apparatus. It serves as a general tool, useful for the manufacture of all other tools, firmly directed toward its end, as fateful as the precisely calculated movement of material production, whose result for mankind is beyond all calculation. At last its old ambition, to be a pure organ of ends, has been realized. The exclusiveness of logical laws originates in this unique functional significance, and ultimately in the compulsive nature of self-preservation. And self-preservation repeatedly culminates in the choice between survival and destruction, apparent again in the principle that of two contradictory propositions only one can be true and only one false. The formalism of this principle, and of the entire logic in which form it is established, derives from the opacity and complexity of interests in a society in which the maintenance of forms and the preservation of individuals coincide only by chance. The derivation of thought from logic ratifies in the lecture room the reification of man in the factory and the office. In this way the taboo encroaches upon the anathematizing power, and enlightenment upon the spirit which it itself comprises. Then, however, nature as true self-preservation is released by the very process which promised to extirpate it, in the individual as in the collective destiny of crisis and armed conflict. If the only norm that remains for theory is the ideal of unified science, practice must be subjected to the irrepressible process of world history. The self that is wholly comprehended

30

by civilization resolves itself in an element of the inhumanity which from the beginning has aspired to evade civilization. The primordial fear of losing one's own name is realized. For civilization, pure natural existence, animal and vegetative, was the absolute danger. One after the other, mimetic, mythic and metaphysical modes of behavior were taken as superseded eras, any reversion to which was to be feared as implying a reversion of the self to that mere state of nature from which it had estranged itself with so huge an effort, and which therefore struck such terror into the self. In every century, any living reminiscence of olden times, not only of nomadic antiquity but all the more of the pre-patriarchal stages, was most rigorously punished and extirpated from human consciousness. The spirit of enlightenment replaced the fire and the rack by the stigma it attached to all irrationality, because it led to corruption. Hedonism was moderate, finding the extreme no less odious than did Aristotle. The bourgeois ideal of naturalness intends not amorphous nature, but the virtuous mean. Promiscuity and asceticism, excess and hunger, are directly identical, despite the antagonism, as powers of disintegration. By subjecting the whole of life to the demands of its maintenance, the dictatorial minority guarantees, together with its own security, the persistence of the whole. From Homer to modern times, the dominant spirit wishes to steer between the Scylla of a return to mere reproduction and the Charybdis of unfettered fulfillment; it has always mistrusted any star other than that of the lesser evil. The new German pagans and warmongers want to set pleasure free once more. But under the pressure of labor, through the centuries, pleasure has learned self-hatred, and therefore in the state of totalitarian emancipation remains mean and disabled by self-contempt. It remains in the grip of the self-preservation to which it once trained reason—deposed in the meantime. At the turning points of Western civilization, from the transition to Olympian religion up to the Renaissance, Reformation, and bourgeois atheism, whenever new nations and classes more firmly repressed myth, the fear of uncomprehended, threatening nature, the consequence of its very materialization and objectification, was reduced to animistic superstition, and the subjugation of nature

31

was made the absolute purpose of life within and without. If in the end self-preservation has been automated, so reason has been abandoned by those who, as administrators of production, entered upon its inheritance and now fear it in the persons of the disinherited. The essence of enlightenment is the alternative whose ineradicability is that of domination. Men have always had to choose between their subjection to nature or the subjection of nature to the Self. With the extension of the bourgeois commodity economy, the dark horizon of myth is illumined by the sun of calculating reason, beneath whose cold rays the seed of the new barbarism grows to fruition. Under the pressure of domination human labor has always led away from myth—but under domination always returns to the jurisdiction of myth.

The entanglement of myth, domination, and labor is preserved in one of the Homeric narratives. Book XII of the Odyssey tells of the encounter with the Sirens. Their allurement is that of losing oneself in the past. But the hero to whom the temptation is offered has reached maturity through suffering. Throughout the many mortal perils he has had to endure, the unity of his own life, the identity of the individual, has been confirmed for him. The regions of time part for him as do water, earth, and air. For him, the flood of that-which-was has retreated from the rock of the present, and the future lies cloudy on the horizon. What Odysseus left behind him entered into the nether world; for the self is still so close to prehistoric myth, from whose womb it tore itself, that its very own experienced past becomes mythic prehistory. And it seeks to encounter that myth through the fixed order of time. The threefold schema is intended to free the present moment from the power of the past by referring that power behind the absolute barrier of the unrepeatable and placing it at the disposal of the present as practicable knowledge. The compulsion to rescue what is gone as what is living instead of using it as the material of progress was appeased only in art, to which history itself appertains as a presentation of past life. So long as art declines to pass as cognition and is thus separated from practice, social practice tolerates it as it tolerates pleasure. But the Sirens' song has not yet been rendered powerless by reduction to the condition of art. They know "everything that ever happened on this so fruitful earth,"[33] including the events in which Odysseus himself took part, "all those things that Argos' sons and the Trojans suffered by the will of the gods on the plains of Troy."[34] While they directly evoke the recent past, with the irresistible promise of pleasure as which their song is heard, they threaten the patriarchal order which renders to each man his life only in return for his full measure of time. Whoever falls for their trickery must perish, whereas only perpetual presence of mind forces an existence from nature. Even though the Sirens know all that has happened, they demand the future as the price of that knowledge, and the promise of the happy return is the deception with which the past ensnares the one who longs for it. Odysseus is warned by Circe, that divinity of reversion to the animal, whom he resisted and who therefore gives him strength to resist other powers of disintegration. But the allurement of the Sirens remains superior; no one who hears their song can escape. Men had to do fearful things to themselves before the self, the identical, purposive, and virile nature of man, was formed, and something of that recurs in every childhood. The strain of holding the I together adheres to the I in all stages; and the temptation to lose it has always been there with the blind determination to maintain it. The narcotic intoxication which permits the atonement of deathlike sleep for the euphoria in which the self is suspended, is one of the oldest social arrangements which mediate between self-preservation and self-destruction—an attempt of the self to survive itself. The dread of losing the self and of abrogating together with the self the barrier between oneself and other life, the fear of death and destruction, is intimately associated with a promise of happiness which threatened civilization in every moment. Its road was that of obedience and labor, over which fulfillment shines forth perpetually—but only as illusive appearance, as devitalized beauty. The mind of Odys-

33. *Odyssey* 12.191. (Since the authors' translation differs at certain concise points from the best-known English versions, this and other passages quoted here are near-literal prose renderings of the German. —Tr.).

34. *Odyssey* 12.189–90.

seus, inimical both to his own death and to his own happiness, is aware of this. He knows only two possible ways to escape. One of them he prescribes for his men. He plugs their ears with wax, and they must row with all their strength. Whoever would survive must not hear the temptation of that which is unrepeatable, and he is able to survive only by being unable to hear it. Society has always made provision for that. The laborers must be fresh and concentrate as they look ahead, and must ignore whatever lies to one side. They must doggedly sublimate in additional effort the drive that impels to diversion. And so they become practical.—The other possibility Odysseus, the seigneur who allows the others to labor for themselves, reserves to himself. He listens, but while bound impotently to the mast; the greater the temptation the more he has his bonds tightened—just as later the burghers would deny themselves happiness all the more doggedly as it drew closer to them with the growth of their own power. What Odysseus hears is without consequence for him; he is able only to nod his head as a sign to be set free from his bonds; but it is too late; his men, who do not listen, know only the song's danger but nothing of its beauty, and leave him at the mast in order to save him and themselves. They reproduce the oppressor's life together with their own, and the oppressor is no longer able to escape his social role. The bonds with which he has irremediably tied himself to practice, also keep the Sirens away from practice: their temptation is neutralized and becomes a mere object of contemplation—becomes art. The prisoner is present at a concert, an inactive eavesdropper like later concertgoers, and his spirited call for liberation fades like applause. Thus the enjoyment of art and manual labor break apart as the world of prehistory is left behind. The epic already contains the appropriate theory. The cultural material is in exact correlation to work done according to command; and both are grounded in the inescapable compulsion to social domination of nature.

Measures such as those taken on Odysseus' ship in regard to the Sirens form presentient allegory of the dialectic of enlightenment. Just as the capacity of representation is the measure of domination, and domination is the most powerful thing that can be represented in most performances, so the capacity of representation is the vehicle of progress and regression at one and the same time. Under the given conditions, exemption from work—not only among the unemployed but even at the other end of the social scale—also means disablement. The rulers experience existence, with which they need no longer concern themselves, only as a substratum, and hence wholly ossify into the condition of the commanding self. Primitive man experienced the natural thing merely as the evasive object of desire. "But the master, who has interposed the servant between it and himself, in this way relates himself only to the dependence of the thing and enjoys it pure; however, he leaves the aspect of [its] independence to the servant, who works upon it."[35] Odysseus is represented in labor. Just as he cannot yield to the temptation to self-abandonment, so, as proprietor, he finally renounces even participation in labor, and ultimately even its management, whereas his men—despite their closeness to things—cannot enjoy their labor because it is performed under pressure, in desperation, with senses stopped by force. The servant remains enslaved in body and soul; the master regresses. No authority has yet been able to escape paying this price, and the apparent cyclical nature of the advance of history is partly explained by this debilitation, the equivalent of power. Mankind, whose versatility and knowledge become differentiated with the division of labor, is at the same time forced back to anthropologically more primitive stages, for with the technical easing of life the persistence of domination brings about a fixation of the instincts by means of heavier repression. Imagination atrophies. The disaster is not merely that individuals might remain behind society or its material production. Where the evolution of the machine has already turned into that of the machinery of domination (so that technical and social tendencies, always interwoven, converge in the total schematization of men), untruth is not represented merely by the outdistanced. As against that, adaptation to the power of progress involves the progress of power, and each time anew brings about those degenerations which show not unsuccessful but successful progress to be its

35. *Phänomenologie des Geistes*, p. 146.

contrary. The curse of irresistible progress is irresistible regression.

This regression is not restricted to the experience of the sensuous world bound up with the circumambient animate, but at the same time affects the self-dominant intellect, which separates from sensuous experience in order to subjugate it. The unification of intellectual functions by means of which domination over the senses is achieved, the resignation of thought to the rise of unanimity, means the impoverishment of thought and of experience: the separation of both areas leaves both impaired. The restriction of thought to organization and administration, practiced by rulers from the cunning Odysseus to the naïve managing directors of today, necessarily implies the restriction which comes upon the great as soon as it is no longer merely a question of manipulating the small. Hence the spirit becomes the very apparatus of domination and self-domination which bourgeois thought has always mistakenly supposed it to be. The stopped ears which the pliable proletarians have retained ever since the time of myth have no advantage over the immobility of the master. The over-maturity of society lives by the immaturity of the dominated. The more complicated and precise the social, economic, and scientific apparatus with whose service the production system has long harmonized the body, the more impoverished the experiences which it can offer. The elimination of qualities, their conversion into functions, is translated from science by means of rationalized modes of labor to the experiential world of nations, and tends to approximate it once more to that of the amphibians. The regression of the masses today is their inability to hear the unheard-of with their own ears, to touch the unapprehended with their own hands—the new form of delusion which deposes every conquered mythic form. Through the mediation of the total society which embraces all relations and emotions, men are once again made to be that against which the evolutionary law of society, the principle of self, had turned: mere species beings, exactly like one another through isolation in the forcibly united collectivity. The oarsmen, who cannot speak to one another, are each of them yoked in the same rhythm as the modern worker in the factory, movie theater, and collective. The actual working conditions in society compel conformism—not the conscious influences which also made the suppressed men dumb and separated them from truth. The impotence of the worker is not merely a stratagem of the rulers, but the logical consequence of the industrial society into which the ancient Fate—in the very course of the effort to escape it—has finally changed.

But this logical necessity is not conclusive. It remains tied to domination, as both its reflection and its tool. Therefore its truth is no less questionable than its evidence is irrefutable. Of course thought has always sufficed concretely to characterize its own equivocation. It is the servant that the master cannot check as he wishes. Domination, ever since men settled down, and later in the commodity society, has become objectified as law and organization and must therefore restrict itself. The instrument achieves independence: the mediating instance of the spirit, independently of the will of the master, modifies the directness of economic injustice. The instruments of domination, which would encompass all—language, weapons, and finally machines—must allow themselves to be encompassed by all. Hence in domination the aspect of rationality prevails as one that is also different from it. The "objectivity" of the means, which makes it universally available, already implies the criticism of that domination as whose means thought arose. On the way from mythology to logistics, thought has lost the element of self-reflection, and today machinery disables men even as it nurtures them. But in the form of machines the alienated *ratio* moves toward a society which reconciles thought in its fixed form as a material and intellectual apparatus with free, live, thought, and refers to society itself as the real subject of thought. The specific origin of thought and its universal perspective have always been inseparable. Today, with the transformation of the world into industry, the perspective of universality, the social realization of thought, extends so far that in its behalf the rulers themselves disavow thought as mere ideology. The bad conscience of cliques which ultimately embody economic necessity is betrayed in that its revelations, from the intuitions of the Leader to the dynamic *Weltanschauung*, no longer recognize (in marked contrast to earlier bourgeois apologetics) their own misdeeds as necessary consequences of statutory contexts. The mythological lies of mission and destiny which they use as substitutes never declare the whole truth: gone are the objective laws of the market which ruled in the actions of the entrepreneurs and tended toward catastrophe. Instead the conscious decision of the managing directors executes as results (which are more obligatory than the blindest price-mechanisms) the old law of value and hence the destiny of capitalism. The rulers themselves do not believe in any objective necessity, even though they sometimes describe their concoctions thus. They declare themselves to be the engineers of world history. Only the ruled accept as unquestionable necessity the course of development that with every decreed rise in the standard of living makes them so much more powerless. When the standard of living of those who are still employed to service the machines can be assured with a minimal part of the working time available to the rulers of society, the superfluous reminder, the vast mass of the population, is drilled as yet another battalion—additional material to serve the present and future great plans of the system. The masses are fed and quartered as the army of the unemployed. In their eyes, their reduction to mere objects of the administered life, which preforms every sector of modern existence including language and perception, represents objective necessity, against which they believe there is nothing they can do. Misery as the antithesis of power and powerlessness grows immeasurably, together with the capacity to remove all misery permanently. Each individual is unable to penetrate the forest of cliques and institutions which, from the highest levels of command to the last professional rackets, ensure the boundless persistence of status. For the union boss, let alone the director, the proletarian (should he ever come face to face with him) is nothing but a supernumerary example of the mass, while the boss in his turn has to tremble at the thought of his own liquidation.

The absurdity of a state of affairs in which the enforced power of the system over men grows with every step that takes it out of the power of nature, denounces the rationality of the rational society as obsolete. Its necessity is illusive, no less than the freedom of the entrepreneurs who ultimately reveal their compulsive nature in their inevitable wars and contracts. This illusion, in which a wholly enlightened mankind has lost itself, cannot be dissolved by a philosophy which, as the organ of domination, has to choose between command and obedience. Without being able to escape the confusion which still ensnares it in prehistory, it is nevertheless able to recognize the logic of either-or, of consequence and antimony, with which it radically emancipated itself from nature, as this very nature, unredeemed and self-alienated. Thinking, in whose mechanism of compulsion nature is reflected and persists, inescapably reflects its very own self as its own forgotten nature—as a mechanism of compulsion. Ideation is only an instrument. In thought, men distance themselves from nature in order thus imaginatively to present it to themselves—but only in order to determine how it is to be dominated. Like the thing, the material tool, which is held on to in different situations as the same thing, and hence divides the world as the chaotic, manysided, and disparate from the known, one, and identical, the concept is the ideal tool, fit to do service for everything, wherever it can be applied. And so thought becomes illusionary whenever it seeks to deny the divisive function, distancing and objectification. All mystic unification remains deception, the impotently inward trace of the absolved revolution. But while enlightenment maintains its justness against any hypostatization of utopia and unfailingly proclaims domination to be disunion, the dichotomy between subject and object that it will not allow to be obscured becomes the index of the untruth of that dichotomy and of truth. The proscription of superstition has always signified not only the progress of domination but its compromise. Enlightenment is more than enlightenment—the distinct representation of nature in its alienation. In the self-cognition of the spirit as nature in disunion with itself, as in prehistory, nature calls itself to account; no longer directly, as *mana*—that is, with the alias that signifies omnipotence—but as blind and lame. The decline, the forfeiture, of nature consists in the subjugation of nature without which spirit does not exist. Through the decision in which spirit acknowledges itself to be domination and retreats into nature, it abandons the claim to domination which makes it a vassal of nature. Even though in the flight from necessity, in progress and civilization, mankind cannot hold the course without abandoning knowledge itself, at least it no longer mistakes the ramparts that it erects against necessity (the institutions and practices of subjection that have always redounded on society from the subjugation of nature) for guarantees of the freedom to come. Every progress made by civilization has renewed together with domination that prospect of its removal. Whereas, however, real history is woven out of a real suffering that is not lessened in proportion to the growth of means for its abrogation, the realization of the prospect is referred to the notion, the concept. For it does not merely, as science, distance men from nature, but, as the self-consideration of thought that in the form of science remains tied to blind economic tendency, allows the distance perpetuating injustice to be measured. By virtue of this remembrance of nature in the subject, in whose fulfillment the unacknowledged truth of all culture lies hidden, enlightenment is universally opposed to domination; and the call to check enlightenment resounded even in the time of Vanini[36] less out of fear of exact science than out of that hatred of undisciplined ideas which emerges from the jurisdiction of nature even as it acknowledges itself to be nature's very dread of its own self. The priests always avenged *mana* on the prophet of enlightenment, who propitiated *mana* by a terror-stricken attitude to what went by the name of terror, and the augurs of the Enlightenment were one with the priests in their hybris. In its bourgeois form, the Enlightenment had lost itself in its positivistic aspect long before Turgot and d'Alembert. It was never immune to the exchange of freedom for the pursuit of self-preservation. The suspension of the concept, whether in the name of progress or of culture—which had already long before tacitly leagued themselves against the truth—opened the way for falsehood. And this in a world that verified only evidential propositions, and preserved thought—degraded to the achieve-

36. Lucilio Vanini, a quasi-pantheistic Italian philosopher (1584–1619) sentenced and burned for blasphemy by the Inquisition. —Tr.

ment of great thinkers—as a kind of stock of superannuated clichés, no longer to be distinguished from truth neutralized as a cultural commodity.

But to recognize domination, even in thought itself, as unreconciled nature, would mean a slackening of the necessity whose perpetuity socialism itself prematurely confirmed as a concession to reactionary common sense. By elevating necessity to the status of the basis for all time to come, and by idealistically degrading the spirit for ever to the very apex, socialism held on all too surely to the legacy of bourgeois philosophy. Hence the relation of necessity to the realm of freedom would remain merely quantitative and mechanical, and nature, posited as wholly alien—just as in the earliest mythology—would become totalitarian and absorb freedom together with socialism. With the abandonment of thought, which in its reified form of mathematics, machine, and organization avenges itself on the men who have forgotten it, enlightenment has relinquished its own realization. By taking everything unique and individual under its tutelage, it left the uncomprehended whole the freedom, as domination, to strike back at human existence and consciousness by way of things. But true revolutionary practice depends on the intransigence of theory in the face of the insensibility with which society allows thought to ossify. It is not the material prerequisites of fulfillment—liberated technology as such—which jeopardize fulfillment. That is asserted by those sociologists who are again searching for an antidote, and—should it be a collectivist measure—to master the antidote.[37] Guilt is a context of social delusion. The mythic scientific respect of the peoples of the earth for the *status quo* that they themselves unceasingly produce, itself finally becomes positive fact: the oppressor's fortress in regard to which even revolutionary imagination despises itself as utopism and decays to the condition of pliable trust in the objective tendency of history.

37. "The supreme question which confronts our generation today—the question to which all other problems are merely corollaries—is whether technology can be brought under control . . . Nobody can be sure of the formula by which this end can be achieved . . . We must draw on all the resources to which access can be had . . ." (*The Rockefeller Foundation. A Review for 1943* [New York, 1944], pp. 33ff.).

As the organ of this kind of adaptation, as a mere construction of means, the Enlightenment is as destructive as its romantic enemies accuse it of being. It comes into its own only when it surrenders the last remaining concordance with the latter and dares to transcend the false absolute, the principle of blind domination. The spirit of this kind of unrelenting theory would turn even the mind of relentless progress to its end. Its herald Bacon dreamed of the many things "which kings with their treasure cannot buy, nor with their force command," of which "their spials and intelligencers can give no news." As he wished, they fell to the burghers, the enlightened heirs of those kings. While bourgeois economy multiplied power through the mediation of the market, it also multiplied its objects and powers to such an extent that for their administration not just the kings, not even the middle classes are no longer necessary, but all men. They learn from the power of things to dispense at last with power. Enlightenment is realized and reaches its term when the nearest practical ends reveal themselves as the most distant goal now attained, and the lands of which "their spials and intelligencers can give no news," that is, those of the nature despised by dominant science, are recognized as the lands of origin. Today, when Bacon's utopian vision that we should "command nature by action"—that is, in practice—has been realized on a tellurian scale, the nature of the thralldom that he ascribed to unsubjected nature is clear. It was domination itself. And knowledge, in which Bacon was certain the "sovereignty of man lieth hid," can now become the dissolution of domination. But in the face of such a possibility, and in the service of the present age, enlightenment becomes wholesale deception of the masses.

ODYSSEUS OR MYTH AND ENLIGHTENMENT

As we have seen, the Sirens episode in the Odyssey combines myth and rational labor. In fact, the poem as a whole bears witness to the dialectic of enlightenment. The epic narrative, especially in the most ancient of its various layers, clearly exhibits its close relation to myth: its component adventures have their origin in popular tradition. The Homeric spirit takes over and "organizes" the myths, but contradicts them in the process. Philosophical criticism shows that the usual identification of epic and myth (refuted, in any case, by modern classical philologists) is wholly illusive. *Epos* and *mythos* are two distinct concepts, and indicate two stages in an historical process which can still be discerned where the disparate elements of the Odyssey have been editorially reconciled. If it does not already presuppose a universality of language, the Homeric narrative effects one; by using an exoteric form of representation, it dissolves the hierarchical order of society in the very process of glorifying it. To celebrate the anger of Achilles and the wanderings of Odysseus is already a wistful stylization of what can no longer be celebrated; and the hero of the adventures shows himself to be a prototype of the bourgeois individual, a notion originating in the consistent self-affirmation which has its ancient pattern in the figure of the protagonist compelled to wander. The epic is the historico-philosophic counterpart to the novel, and eventually displays features approximating those characteristic of the novel. The venerable cosmos of the meaningful Homeric world is shown to be the achievement of regulative reason, which destroys myth by virtue of the same rational order in which it reflects it.

The late German Romantic interpreters of classical antiquity, following on Nietzsche's early writings, stressed the bourgeois Enlightenment element in Homer. Nietzsche was one of the few after Hegel who recognized the dialectic of enlightenment. And it was Nietzsche who expressed its antipathy to domination: "The Enlightenment" should be "taken into the people, so that the priests all become priests with a bad conscience—and the same must be done with regard to the State. That is the task of the Enlightenment: to make princes and statesmen unmistakably aware that everything they do is sheer falsehood . . ."[1] On the other hand, Enlightenment had always been a tool for the "great manipulators of government (Confucius in China, the *Imperium Romanum,* Napoleon, the Papacy when it had turned to power and not only to the world) . . . The way in which the masses are fooled in this respect, for instance in all democracies, is very useful: the reduction and malleability of men are worked for as 'progress'!"[2]

The revelation of these two aspects of the Enlightenment as an historic principle made it possible to trace the notion of enlightenment as progressive thought, back to the beginning of traditional history. Nevertheless, Nietzsche's relation to the Enlightenment, and therefore to Homer, was still discordant. Though he discerned both the universal movement of sovereign Spirit (whose executor he felt himself to be) and a "nihilistic" anti-life force is the enlightenment, his pre-Fascist followers retained only the second aspect and perverted it into an ideology. This ideology becomes blind praise of a blind life subject to the same nexus of action by which everything living is suppressed. This is clear in the attitude of the cultural fascists to Homer. They scent out a democratic spirit, characterize the work as redolent of seafarers and traders, and condemn the Ionian epic as all-too-rational expository narrative and a mere communi-

1. Nietzsche, *Nachlass,* Vol. XIV, p. 206.
2. Nietzsche, *Nachlass,* Vol. XV, p. 235.

cation of conventions. This unfavorable judgment from those who feel at one with all obviously direct domination and proscribe all mediation, "liberalism" at any stage of development, has a certain degree of truth in it. In fact the lines from reason, liberalism, and the bourgeois spirit go incomparably farther back than historians who date the notion of the burgher only from the end of medieval feudalism would allow. By continuing to discern the burgher where the older bourgeois humanism fancied it might postulate the sacred dawn that would be its own legitimation, the neo-Romantic reaction identifies world history with enlightenment. The fashionable ideology which is deeply concerned to liquidate enlightenment, unwittingly reveres it, and is compelled to recognize enlightened thought even in the most distant past. The most ancient trace of that thinking threatens the bad conscience of the present-day archaicists; for it offers the possibility of a new release of the whole process they have undertaken to suppress—yet unconsciously advance.

But insight into the anti-mythological, enlightened character of Homer, his extreme difference to chthonic mythology, is inaccurate because limited. For instance, Rudolf Borchardt—the most significant and hence the most impotent of the esoteric representatives of German heavy industry—closes his analysis far too soon. He does not see that the primal powers that are extolled in the poem already represent a phase of enlightenment. By denouncing the epic as narrative fiction without qualifying his categorization, Borchardt fails to perceive what epic and myth actually have in common: domination and exploitation. What he finds mean and vulgar and therefore condemns in the epic—mediation and circulation—is only the development of naked power—the far from noble quality that he lauds in myth. In the alleged genuineness of what is really the archaic principle of blood and sacrifice, there is already something of the bad conscience and deceit of domination proper to that national renewal which today has recourse to the primitive past for the purpose of self-advertisement. Aboriginal myth already contains the aspect of deception which triumphs in the fraudulence of Fascism yet imputes the same practice of lies to the Enlightenment. But there is no work which offers more eloquent testimony of the mutual implication of enlightenment and myth than that of Homer, the basic text of European civilization. In Homer, epic and myth, form and content, do not so much emerge from and contrast with, as expound and elucidate, one another. The aesthetic dualism attests the historico-philosophical tendency: "Apollonian Homer merely continues that general human artistic process to which we owe individuation."[3]

The myths have been transformed in the various layers of the Homeric narrative. But the account given of them there, the unity wrested from the diffuse sagas, is also a description of the retreat of the individual from the mythic powers. In a more profound sense, this is already true of the Iliad. The anger of the mythical son of a goddess against the rational warrior-king and organizer, the undisciplined inactivity of that hero, and finally the encompassing of the dead though victorious by a necessity that is national and Hellenistic, and no longer tribal, mediated through mythic loyalty to the slain comrade, confirms the interaction of prehistory and history proper. It applies to the Odyssey in an even more drastic sense, inasmuch as the Odyssey is closer to the form of the picaresque novel. The opposition of enlightenment to myth is expressed in the opposition of the surviving individual ego to multifarious fate. The eventful voyage from Troy to Ithaca is the way taken through the myths by the self—ever physically weak as against the power of nature, and attaining self-realization only in self-consciousness. The prehistoric world is secularized as the space whose measure the self must take; and the old demons inhabit the distant bounds and islands of the civilized Mediterranean, forced back into the forms of rock and cavern whence they once emerged in the dread remoteness of antiquity. But the epic adventures allow each location a proper name and permit space to be surveyed in a rational manner. Though trembling and shipwrecked, the hero anticipates the work of the compass. Though he is powerless, no part of the sea remains unknown to him, and so his powerlessness also indicates that the mighty powers will be put down. But the evident untruth in myths, the deception of

3. Nietzsche, *Nachlass*, Vol. IX, p. 289.

the claim that the waters and the earth are actually inhabited by demons, the magical deceit of inherited popular religion, becomes in the eyes of the mature traveler something that is merely "misleading," in contradistinction to the unequivocal purposiveness of his own self-preservation, and his return to his homeland and fixed estate. The adventures of Odysseus are all dangerous temptations removing the self from its logical course. He gives way to each allurement as a new experience, trying it out as would a novice still impervious to good advice—sometimes, indeed, out of foolish curiosity, or as a actor ceaselessly rehearsing his parts. "But where there is danger, there salvation grows too":[4] the knowledge which comprises his identity and which enables him to survive, draws its content from experience of the multitudinous, from digression and salvation; and the knowing survivor is also the man who takes the greatest risks when death threatens, thus becoming strong and unyielding when life continues. That is the secret of the process between epic and myth; the self does not constitute the fixed antithesis to adventure, but in its rigidity molds itself only by way of that antithesis: being an entity only in the diversity of that which denies all unity.[5] Like the heroes of all true novels later

4. Hölderlin, "Patmos," Collected Works, Insel Verlag edition (Leipzig, n.d.), p. 230: *"Wo aber Gefahr ist, wächst/Das Rettende auch."*
5. There is direct evidence of this process at the beginning of Book 20. Odysseus notices how the women go to the suitors at night: "And he was angry at heart, like a courageous bitch trying to protect her helpless puppies, barking and showing fight to someone she does not know. So Odysseus' fury rose within him at the thought of these shameless misdeeds. He struck his breast and rebuked his heart thus: 'Be patient, my heart! You suffered far worse things than this that day when the monstrous Cyclops savagely consumed my brave friends. But you suffered it alone until cunning led you out of the cave where you thought death threatened!' Thus he addressed his heart, quelling its stirring in his bosom. Soon his heart obeyed him and staunchly endured. But he himself still rolled to and fro" (20.13–14). The individual as subject is still unreconciled to himself, still unsure. His affective forces (his mettle and his heart) still react independently to him. *"Kradie* or *etor* (the two words are synonymous, 17.22) rebels, and Odysseus strikes his breast, i.e. rebukes his heart and addresses it. His heart beats, therefore his body is reacting against his will. Hence his address is not a mere formal device (as when the hand or foot is addressed in Eurip-

on, Odysseus loses himself in order to find himself; the estrangement from nature that he brings about is realized in the process of the abandonment to nature he contends with in each adventure; and, ironically, when he, inexorable, returns home, the inexorable force he commands itself triumphs as the judge and avenger of the legacy of the powers from which he escaped. At the Homeric level, the identity of the self is so much a function of the unidentical, of dissociated, unarticulated myths, that it must derive itself from those myths. The inner organization of individuality in the form of time is still so weak that the external unity and sequence of adventures remains a spatial change of scenery, of the spots sacred to the local deities by whose virtue the storm drives and tosses. Whenever in later history the self has experienced such debilitation, or the particular representation presupposes such debility in the reader, the narrative account of life has slipped into a sequence of adventures. Laboriously, revocable, in the image of voyaging, historical time is detached from space, the irrevocable pattern of all mythic time.

Artifice is the means by which the adventuring self loses it-

---

ides, to urge them to move), but the heart acts independently" (Wilamowitz-Moellendorff, *Die Heimkehr des Odysseus,* Berlin, 1927, p. 189.) The affect is compared with the animal that man has mastery over: the simile of the bitch belongs to the same stage of experience as the metamorphosis of the companions into swine. The subject, still divided and compelled to use force against the nature within as against that without, "punishes" the heart by forcing it to be patient and, looking ahead, by denying it the immediate present. Striking one's breast became later a gesture of triumph: the victor shows thus that his victory is always won against his own nature. The achievement is attributed to the ratio of self-preservation. ". . . at first the narrator still thinks of his unruly heart as it continues to beat; the *metis* is superior, for it is another inner force and saved Odysseus. Later philosophers would have contrasted it as *nus* or *logistikon* with the imprudent parts of the soul" (Wilamowitz, *op. cit.,* p. 190). The "self"—*autos*—is not spoken of until verse 24, once the repression of instinct by reason has succeeded. If the choice and sequence of words are to be taken as conclusive, the identical "I" of Homer could be seen as primarily the result of a mastery of nature carried out within the individual. This new self trembles within its thing-self—a body—once the heart has been rebuked. In any case, the opposition of aspects of the soul (analyzed in detail by Wilamowitz), which often address one another, seems to confirm the unsure, ephemeral reconciliation of the subject, whose substantiality is no more than the coordination of those aspects.

self in order to preserve itself. The seafarer Odysseus cheats the natural deities, as does the civilized traveler who offers them colored glass beads in exchange for ivory. Only occasionally, of course, does he actually feature as a barterer, when gifts are exchanged. The Homeric gift is halfway between barter and offering. Like a sacrifice, it is intended to pay for forfeited blood (either the stranger's or that of the pirates' captive), and to seal a covenant of peace. But at the same time, the exchange of gifts stands for the principle of equivalence: actually or symbolically the host receives the equivalent value of his effort; the traveler obtains provision for the way—the basic means of returning home. Even if the host receives no direct recompense for his service, he can count on the same for himself or his kin As an offering to the elemental deities, the gift is also a rudimentary insurance against them. The extensive yet dangerous voyaging of early Greece is the pragmatic prerequisite for that. Poseidon himself, Odysseus' elemental enemy, thinks in terms of equivalence when he incessantly complains that Odysseus in the various stages of his voyage receives more in gifts than his full share of the spoils of Troy—had Poseidon allowed him to carry it freely. In Homer, however, this kind of rationalization can be traced back to the sacrifices. Hecatombs of specific magnitude are requited with the favor of the gods. If barter is the secular form of sacrifice, the latter already appears as the magical pattern of rational exchange, a device of men by which the gods may be mastered: the gods are overthrown by the very system by which they are honored.[6]

6. The relationship of sacrifice and exchange was explained in a wholly magical context by Klages (as against Nietzsche's materialistic interpretation): "The necessity of sacrifice pure and simple concerns everyone, because everyone, as we have seen, receives his share—the original *suum cuique*—of life and of all the goods of life, only by continually giving and giving in return. This is not, however, an exchange of goods in the usual sense (which admittedly also owes its primordial origin to the notion of sacrifice), but an exchange of fluids or essences by surrendering one's own soul to the supporting and nurturing life of the world" (Ludwig Klages, *Der Geist als Widersacher der Seele*, Leipzig, 1932, Vol. III, Pt. 2, p. 1409). The dual character of sacrifice, however, the magic self-surrender of the individual to the collective . . . and self-preservation by the technique of this magic, implies an objective

The deception in sacrifice is the prototype of Odyssean cunning; many of Odysseus' stratagems are, so to speak, inset in a context of sacrifice to natural deities.[7] His Olympian allies take advantage of Poseidon's visit to the Ethiopians (the backwoodsmen who still honor him and offer him generous sacrifices) in order to conduct their protégé safely. Deceit is already involved in the very sacrifice that Poseidon accepts with relish: the restriction of the amorphous sea-god to a specific locality, the sacred domain, also restricts his power; and in order to glut himself on Ethiopian bulls, he must forgo the wreaking of his anger on Odysseus. All human sacrifices, when systematically executed, deceive the god to whom they are made: they subject him to the primacy of human ends, and dissolve his power; and the deception of the god carries over smoothly into that practised by the disbelieving priests on the believers. Deceit has its origin in the cult. Odysseus acts as sacrifice and priest at one and the same time. By calculating his own sacrifice, he effectively negates the power to whom the sacrifice is made. In this way he redeems the life he had forfeited. But deceit and artifice are not simply opposed to archaic sacrifice. By means of Odysseus, only the aspect of deception in sacrifice—probably the quintessential reason for the fictitious character of myth—is elevated to self-consciousness. The discovery that symbolic communication with the deity through sacrifice is not actual

contradiction which tends to the development of the rational element in sacrifice. Under the continuing jurisdiction of magic, rationality—as the behavior of the sacrificer—becomes *cunning*. Klages himself, the enthusiastic apologist for myth and sacrifice, has noticed this, and feels compelled to distinguish genuine communication with nature from lies, without finding it possible to derive from magic thinking itself a counterprinciple to the illusion of magical domination of nature, because that illusion in fact constitutes the nature of myth: "It is no longer merely pagan belief but pagan superstition when, say, the god-king on ascending to the throne has to swear that he will henceforth make the sun shine and the field bear its harvest" (Klages, *op. cit.*, p. 1408).

7. This is not refuted by the fact that actual human sacrifices do not occur in Homer. The civilizing tendency of the epic is apparent in the selection of events: "With one exception . . . both Iliad and Odyssey are completely expurgated of the abomination of Human Sacrifice" (Gilbert Murray, *The Rise of the Greek Epic*, Oxford, 1911, p. 150).

must be an age-old human experience. The sacrificial representation that a fashionable irrationalism has so exalted, cannot be separated from the deification of the human sacrifice—the deceit of a priestly rationalization of death by means of an apotheosis of the predestined victim. Something of this trickery, which elevates the frail individual to the status of a vehicle of divine substance, has always been apparent in the ego—which owes its existence to the sacrifice of the present moment to the future. As much as the immortality of the victim, its substantiality is but a semblance and an illusion. It was not without reason that many revered Odysseus as a god.

So long as individuals are sacrificed, and so long as sacrifice implies the antithesis of collective and individual, deceit will be a constant of sacrifice. If belief in sacrificial representation implies recollection of something that was not a primal component of the individual but originated instead in the history of domination, it also becomes untruth in regard to the individual as he has developed. The individual—the self—is man no longer credited with the magical power of representation. The establishment of the self cuts through that fluctuating relation with nature that the sacrifice of the self claims to establish. Every sacrifice is a restoration belied by the actual historical situation in which it occurs. The venerable belief in sacrifice, however, is probably already an impressed pattern according to which the subjected repeat upon themselves the injustice that was done them, enacting it again in order to endure it. It does not restore through representation the direct and only temporarily dislocated communication that present-day mythologists ascribe to it; instead, the institution of sacrifice itself is the occasion of an historic catastrophe, an act of force that befalls men and nature alike. Cunning is only the subjective development of the objective untruth of the sacrifice that redeems it. Perhaps this untruth was always untruth. At one stage[8] of pre-

8. Hardly the oldest stage: "The custom of human sacrifice . . . is more widespread among barbaric and half-civilized peoples than among genuine savages, and in the lowest levels of culture it is scarcely known at all. Among some peoples it has been observed to have increased with the course of time" [in the Society Islands, in Polynesia, in India, and

history sacrifices may have possessed a kind of murderous rationality which even then was hardly separable from the greed of privilege. The predominant theory of sacrifice at the present time traces it to the idea of the collective body, the tribe, into which the blood of its slaughtered member would flow back as energy. Whereas totemism was already ideology in its own time, it nevertheless marks an actual state of affairs in which the dominant form of reason required sacrifice. It is a state of archaic deficiency, in which it is hardly possible to make any distinction between human sacrifice and cannibalism. At times the collective, once its numbers have reached a certain level, can survive only by eating human flesh. Perhaps for certain ethnic or social groups gratification was in some way bound up with cannibalism—a direction of the pleasure instinct now testified to only by distaste for human flesh. Such customs of later times as the *ver sacrum,* by which in times of hunger an entire age group of youths is ritually required to emigrate, bear unmistakable traces of such barbaric and transfigured rationality. The mythic folk religions must have been shown to be illusory long before they acquired a civilized form. When the systematized hunt began to provide the tribe with enough animals to make the consumption of one's fellow tribesmen superfluous, the enlightened hunters and trappers must have been confused by the medicine men's command to surrender themselves as food.[9] The magic collective interpretation of sacrifice, which wholly denies its rationality, is its rationalization: but the neat enlightened assumption that, like ideology today, it could once have been the truth, is too naïve.[10] The latest ideologies are

among the Aztecs]. "With regard to the Africans, Winwood Reade says that the more powerful the nation is, the more significant the practice of sacrifice" (Eduard Westermarck, *Ursprung und Entwicklung der Moralbegriffe,* Leipzig, 1913, Vol. I, p. 363).

9. Among cannibal peoples such as those of West Africa "neither youths nor women . . . are allowed to eat the delicacy" (Westermarck, *op. cit.,* Leipzig, 1909, Vol. II, p. 459).

10. Wilamowitz sees the *nus* as sharply opposed to the *logos* (*Glaube der Hellenen,* Berlin, 1931, Vol. I, pp. 41ff.). For him, myth is a "story as one relates it to oneself," child's legend, untruth, or (inseparable from the foregoing) the highest though unverifiable truth, as in Plato. Whereas

only versions of the most ancient, and revert beyond those previously known only to the same extent that the development of class society belies the previously sanctioned ideologies. The irrationality of sacrifice as so often adduced only reflects the fact that the practice of sacrifice lasted longer than its specific rational necessity—itself already untrue. It is this gap between rationality and irrationality that needs cunning to cover it over. All demythologization is colored by the inevitable experience of the uselessness and superfluousness of sacrifices.

Though its irrationality makes the principle of sacrifice transient, it persists by virtue of its rationality, which has been trans-

---

Wilamowitz is aware of the illusive nature of myths, he equates them with literature. In other words: he looks for them first of all in significative language which they have already caused to become objectively contradictory—a contradiction which, as literature, it then tries to overcome: "Myth is initially spoken discourse; the word never applies to its content" (op. cit.). By hypostatizing this late notion of myth and already presupposing reason to be its clear antithesis, he arrives (implicitly rejecting the view of Bachofen, which he ridicules as fashionable, without even mentioning its defender's name) at a decisive separation of mythology and religion (op. cit., p. 5), in which myth appears not as the older but as the younger stage: "I try to trace the course by which . . . faith developed, underwent various transformations, and eventually became myth" (op. cit., p. 1). The stubborn departmentalism of the Hellenistic scholar prevents him from gaining insight into the dialectic of myth, religion, and enlightenment: "I do not understand the languages from which the currently modish words 'taboo' and 'totem,' 'mana' and 'orenda' are derived, but consider it permissible to keep to the Greeks, and appropriate to consider things Greek in terms proper to the Greeks" (op. cit., p. 10). How it is possible in this way directly to opine that "the germ of Platonic divinity was already present in the most ancient removes of Hellenism," and accord with the viewpoint (put forward by Kirchoff and taken over by Wilamowitz) that sees the oldest core of the Odyssean book precisely in the mythic treatment of nostos, is not clear; in Wilamowitz the central notion of myth itself is without any adequate philosophical articulation. Nevertheless, there is undoubted insight in his resistance to the irrationalism that would glorify myth, and in his insistence on the untruth of myths. His aversion to primitive thought and prehistory emphasizes the more clearly the tension that had always existed between the deceptive word and truth. What Wilamowitz reproaches the later myths for—arbitrary fabrication—must already have been present in the most ancient examples by virtue of the pseudos of sacrifice. This pseudos is related to the very Platonic divinity that Wilamowitz traces back to archaic Hellenism.

formed, but has not disappeared. The self rescues itself from dissolution into blind nature, whose claim is constantly proclaimed in sacrifice. But it is still imprisoned in the natural context as an organism that tries to assert itself against the organic. The dismissal of sacrifice by the rationality of self-preservation is exchange no less than sacrifice itself was. The identically persistent self which arises in the abrogation of sacrifice immediately becomes an unyielding, rigidified sacrificial ritual that man celebrates upon himself by opposing his consciousness to the natural context. This can be seen in the famous Norse myth according to which Odin hung for his own sake as a sacrifice on the tree, and in Klages' thesis that every sacrifice is made by the god to the god, as is still apparent in Christology, in myth in a monotheistic guise.[11] But the level of mythology at which the self appears as a sacrifice to itself is an expression not so much of the original conception of popular religion, but of the inclusion of myth in civilization. In class history, the enmity of the self to sacrifice implied a sacrifice of the self, inasmuch as it was paid for by a denial of nature in man for the sake of domination over non-human nature and over other men. This very denial, the nucleus of all civilizing rationality, is the germ cell of a proliferating mythic irrationality: with the denial of nature in man not merely the *telos* of the outward control of nature but the *telos* of man's own life is distorted and befogged. As soon as man discards his awareness that he himself is nature, all the aims for which he keeps himself alive—social progress, the intensification of all his material and spiritual powers, even consciousness itself—are nullified, and the enthronement of the means as an end, which under late capitalism is tantamount to open insanity, is already perceptible in the prehistory of subjectivity. Man's domination over himself, which grounds his selfhood, is almost always the destruction of the subject in whose service it is undertaken; for the substance which is dominated, suppressed, and dissolved by virtue of self-preservation is none other than that very life as functions of which the achievements of self-preser-

11. The conception of Christianity as a pagan sacrificial religion is essentially derived from Werner Hegemann's *Geretteter Christus* (Potsdam, 1928).

vation find their sole definition and determination: it is, in fact, what is to be preserved. The irrationalism of totalitarian capitalism, whose way of satisfying needs has an objectified form determinated by domination which makes the satisfaction of needs impossible and tends toward the extermination of mankind, has its prototype in the hero who escapes from sacrifice by sacrificing himself. The history of civilization is the history of the introversion of sacrifice. In other words: the history of renunciation. Everyone who practises renunciation gives away more of his life than is given back to him: and more than the life that he vindicates. This is evident in the context of the false society in which everyone is superfluous and is deceived. But society demands that the man who tries to escape from universal, unequal, and unjust exchange, and not renounce but immediately seize the undiminished whole, must thereby lose everything—even the miserable leavings that self-preservation allows him. This immense though superfluous sacrifice is required—against sacrifice itself. Odysseus, too, is the self who always restrains himself[12] and forgets his life, who saves his life

12. For instance, when he fails to kill Polyphemus immediately (9. 302), and when he ignores Antinous' ill-treatment of him in order not to betray his identity (17.460ff.). Compare also the episode with the winds (10.50ff.) and Teiresias' prophecy in the first visit to the Underworld (11.105ff.), which makes the return home independent of the restraint of the spirit. Of course Odysseus' restraint is not definitive but an adjournment of action: he carries out the acts of revenge later, and all the more thoroughly: his patience is perseverance. To some extent his behavior still openly features as spontaneous intention something that is later concealed in total, imperative denial, in order thus to assume irresistible force in the subjection of everything natural. With its transference into the subject, with its emancipation from a mythically given content, this subjection becomes "objective"; objectively self-sufficient in comparison with all particular human aims, it becomes the universal rational law. Already in Odysseus' patience, and unmistakably after the slaughter of the suitors, revenge becomes legal procedure: the ultimate fulfillment of the mythic compulsion becomes the objective instrument of domination. Justice is restrained revenge. But since this legal "patience" is formed on the basis of something outside itself (nostalgia for the homeland), it acquires human characteristics—even traces of confidence—that point beyond the specific revenge that has been refrained from. In fully-developed bourgeois society, both are rescinded: together with thought of revenge, longing becomes taboo—which is, of course, the very enthronement of revenge, mediated as the revenge of the self on itself.

and yet recalls it only as wandering. He also is a sacrifice for the abrogation of sacrifice. His dominative renunciation, as a struggle with myth, represents a society that no longer needs renunciation and domination, which gains mastery over itself not in order to coerce itself and others, but in expiation.

The transformation of sacrifice into subjectivity occurs under the sign of the artifice that was already a feature of sacrifice. In the untruth of artifice, the deceit posited in sacrifice becomes an element of the character, a mutilation of the "buffeted" hero himself, whose countenance was marked by the harsh measures to which he subjected himself in order to survive. This is an expression of the relation between mind and physical strength. The vehicle of mind, the commander (as who the cunning Odysseus is almost always presented) despite all accounts of his heroic deeds, is always physically weaker than the primitive powers with which he must contend for his life. The occasions when the sheer physical strength of the adventurer is celebrated, the fight with Irus the Beggar-King backed by the suitors, and the stringing of the great bow, are athletic exercises. Here self-preservation and physical strength are dissociated: Odysseus' athletic achievements are those of the gentleman who, free from practical cares, can as a self-possessed master devote himself to training. Strength removed from the struggle for survival serves survival: when wrestling with the beggar, who is flabby, undisciplined, and devoid of stamina, or with idlers, Odysseus symbolically treats the deficient as organized society had actually treated them long before, and proves himself to be a nobleman. However, when he encounters primeval powers that are neither domesticated nor etiolated, he doesn't find it so easy. He can never engage in direct conflict with the exotically surviving mythic forces, but has to recognize the status of the sacrificial ceremonies in which he is constantly involved—he dare not contravene them. Instead he formally makes them a prerequisite of his own rational decision, which is always undertaken so to speak within the prehistorical judgment underlying the sacrificial situation. The fact that the old sacrifice itself had in the meantime become irrational, is to the intelligence of the weaker party the mere, acceptable idiocy of ritual. The letter of its law is strictly observed. But the now meaningless sentence contradicts itself in that its very ordinance always provides for its own dissolution. The very spirit that dominates nature repeatedly vindicates the superiority of nature in competition. All bourgeois enlightenment is one in the requirement of sobriety and common sense—a proficient estimate of the ratio of forces. The wish must not be father to the thought. For this reason, however, all power in class society is tied to a nagging consciousness of its own impotence against physical nature and its social descendants—the many. Only consciously contrived adaptation to nature brings nature under the control of the physically weaker. The *ratio* which supplants mimesis is not simply its counterpart. It is itself mimesis: mimesis unto death. The subjective spirit which cancels the animation of nature can master a despiritualized nature only by imitating its rigidity and despiritualizing itself in turn. Imitation enters into the service of domination inasmuch as even man is anthropomorphized for man. The pattern of Odyssean cunning is the mastery of nature through such adaptation. Renunciation, the principle of bourgeois disillusionment, the outward schema for the intensification of sacrifice, is already present *in nuce* in that estimation of the ratio of forces which anticipates survival as so to speak dependent on the concession of one's own defeat, and—virtually—on death. The nimble-witted survives only at the price of his own dream, which he wins only by demystifying himself as well as the powers without. He can never have everything; he has always to wait, to be patient, to do without; he may not taste the lotus or eat the cattle of the Sun-god Hyperion, and when he steers between the rocks he must count on the loss of the men whom Scylla plucks from the boat. He just pulls through; struggle is his survival; and all the fame that he and the others win in the process serves merely to confirm that the title of hero is only gained at the price of the abasement and mortification of the instinct for complete, universal, and undivided happiness.

The formula for the cunning of Odysseus is that the redeemed and instrumental spirit, by resigning itself to yield to nature, renders to nature what is nature's, and yet betrays it in the very process. The mythic monsters whose sphere of power he enters always represent ossified covenants, claims from pre-history. Thus in the stage of development represented by the patriarchal age, the older folk religion appears in the form of its scattered relics: beneath the Olympian heavens they have become images of abstract fate, of immaterial necessity. The fact that it was impossible to choose any route other than that between Scylla and Charybdis may be understood rationalistically as a mythic representation of the superior power of the currents over the small, antique ships. But in the mythic, objectifying transition, the natural relation of strength and impotence has already assumed the character of a legal connection. Scylla and Charybdis have a right to what comes between them, just as Circe does to bewitch those unprepared with the gods' antidote, or Polyphemus to eat the bodies of his guests. Each of the mythic figures is programed always to do the same thing. Each is a figure of repetition: and would come to an end should the repetition fail to occur. All bear traces of something which in the punishment myths of the underworld—those of Tantalus, Sisyphus and the Danaans—is founded upon Olympian justice. They are figures of compulsion: the horrors they suffer are the curse upon them. Mythic inevitability is defined by the equivalence between the curse, the crime which expiates it, and the guilt arising from that, which in its turn reproduces the curse.

All justice in history to date bears the mark of this pattern. In myth each moment of the cycle discharges the previous one, and thereby helps to install the context of guilt as law. Odysseus opposes this situation. The self represents rational universality against the inevitability of fate. Because, however, he meets with the universal and inevitable in a mutual embrace, his rationality necessarily assumes a restrictive form—that of an exception. He must escape the legal conditions which enclose and threaten him, and which are, so to speak, laid down in every mythic figure. He satisfies the sentence of the law so that it loses power over him, by conceding it this very power. It is impossible to hear the Sirens and not succumb to them; therefore he does not try to defy their power. Defiance and infatuation are one and the same thing, and whoever defies them is thereby lost to the myth against which he sets himself. Cunning, however, is defiance in a rational form. Odysseus does not try to take another route that would enable him to escape sailing past the Sirens. And he does not try, say, to presume on the superiority of his knowledge and to listen freely to the temptresses, imagining that his freedom will be protection enough. He abases himself; the ship takes its predestined, fatal course; and he realizes that, however consciously alienated from nature he may be, he remains subject to it if he heeds its voice. He keeps to the contract of his thralldom and struggles in his bonds at the mast, trying to cast himself into the destroyers' arms. But he has found an escape clause in the contract, which enables him to fulfill it while eluding it. The primeval contract does not provide for the possibility of the seafarer listening bound or unbound to the bewitching voices. Bonds belong to a stage when the prisoner is not put to death on the spot. Odysseus recognizes the archaic superior power of the song even when, as a technically enlightened man, he has himself bound. He listens to the song of pleasure and thwarts it as he seeks to thwart death. The bound listener wants to hear the Sirens as any other man would, but he has hit upon the arrangement by which he as subject need not be subjected to them. Despite all the power of his desire, which reflects the power of the demi-goddesses themselves, he cannot pass over to them, for his rowers with wax-stopped ears are deaf not only to the demi-goddesses but to the desperate cries of their commander. The Sirens have their own quality, but in primitive bourgeois history it is neutralized to become merely the wistful longing of the passer-by. The epic says nothing of what happened to the Sirens once the ship had disappeared. In tragedy, however, it would have been their last hour, as it was for the Sphinx when Oedipus solved the riddle, fulfilling its command and thus disenchanting it. For the right of the mythic figures, being that of the stronger, depends only on the impossibility of fulfilling their statutes. If they are satisfied, then the myths right down to their most distant relation will suffer for it. Since Odysseus' successful-unsuccessful encounter with the Sirens all songs have been affected, and

59

Western music as a whole suffers from the contradiction of song in civilization—song which nevertheless proclaims the emotional power of all art music.

With the abrogation of this contract through its literal observance, a change is effected in the historical situation of language, which begins its transition to description. The mythic destiny, *fatum,* was one with the spoken word. The sphere of ideas to which the decrees of fate irrevocably executed by the figures of myth belong, is still innocent of the distinction between word and object. The word must have direct power over fact; expression and intention penetrate one another. Cunning consists in exploiting the distinction. The word is emphasized, in order to change the actuality. In this way, consciousness of intention arises: in his distress, Odysseus becomes aware of the dualism, for he learns that the same word can mean different things. Because both the hero and Nobody are possible connotations of the name Udeis, the former is able to break the anathema of the name. The immutable words remain formulas for the merciless context of nature. In magic its rigidity had already to face that of fate, which it reflected at the same time. There the antithesis between the word and that to which it was assimilated was already present. In the Homeric stage it becomes decisive. In words, Odysseus discovers what is called "formalism" in fully-developed bourgeois society: their perennial obligation is paid for by the fact that they distance themselves from every fulfilling content, and at a distance refer to every possible content—to Nobody as to Odysseus. From the formalism of mythic names and ordinances, which would rule men and history as does nature, there emerges nominalism—the prototype of bourgeois thinking. The artifice of self-preservation depends on the process which decrees the relation between word and thing. Odysseus' two contradictory actions in his encounter with Polyphemus, his answering to the name, and his disowning it, are nevertheless one. He acknowledges himself to himself by denying himself under the name Nobody; he saves his life by losing himself. This linguistic adaptation to death contains the schema of modern mathematics.

Deception as a mode of exchange in which everything proceeds as it should, where the contract is fulfilled and yet the other party is deceived, refers back to an economic type which, if it does not occur in mythic prehistory, does so at least in early antiquity: the age-old practice of "casual exchange" between private households. "Surpluses are casually exchanged, but the principal source of supply is self-production."[13] The behavior of Odysseus the wanderer is reminiscent of that of the casual barterer. In the pathetic image of the beggar, feudal man retains the features of the oriental merchant,[14] who returns with unheard-of riches because for the first time, and contrary to tradition, he has stepped outside the milieu of a domestic economy, and "embarked for other lands." Economically speaking, the adventurous element of his enterprises is none other than the irrational aspect of his *ratio* compared with the hitherto dominant traditional form of economy. This irrational *ratio* has found its echo in cunning as the assimilation of bourgeois reason to the unreason that meets it as an even stronger force. The wily solitary is already *homo œconomicus*, for whom all reasonable things are alike: hence the Odyssey is already a *Robinsonade*. Both Odysseus and Crusoe, the two shipwrecked mariners, make their weakness (that of the individual who parts from the collectivity) their social strength. Delivered up to the mercy of the waves, helplessly isolated, their very isolation forces them recklessly to pursue an atomistic interest. They embody the principle of capitalist economy, even before they have recourse to a servant; but what they preserve materially from the past for the furthering of their new enterprise is evidence for the contention that the entrepreneur has always gone about his competitive business with more initial capital than his mere physicial capacity. Their impotence in regard to nature already acts as an ideology to advance their social hegemony. Odysseus' defenselessness against the breakers is of the same stamp as the traveler's justification of his enrichment at the expense

13. Max Weber, *Wirtschaftsgeschichte* (Munich & Leipzig, 1924), p. 3.
14. Victor Bérard has strongly emphasized (to be sure, not without a degree of apocryphal construction) the Semitic element in the Odyssey. See the chapter on the Phoenicians and the Odyssey in his *Résurrection d'Homère* (Paris, 1930), pp. 111ff.

of the aboriginal savage. This was to be confirmed later on by bourgeois economics in the form of the concept of risk: the possibility of failure becomes the postulate of a moral excuse for profit. From the standpoint of the developed exchange society and its individuals, the adventures of Odysseus are an exact representation of the risks which mark out the road to success. Odysseus lives by the original constitutive principle of civil society: one had the choice between deceit or failure. Deception was the mark of the *ratio* which betrayed its particularity. Hence universal socialization, as outlined in the narratives of the world traveler Odysseus and the solo manufacturer Crusoe, from the start included the absolute solitude which emerged so clearly at the end of the bourgeois era. Radical socialization means radical alienation. Odysseus and Crusoe are both concerned with totality: the former measures whereas the latter produces it. Both realize totality only in complete alienation from all other men, who meet the two protagonists only in an alienated form—as enemies or as points of support, but always as tools, as things.

Admittedly one of the first adventures of the *nostos* proper reaches much further back. The story of the Lotus-eaters goes back well beyond the barbaric age of demonic caricatures and magic deities. Whoever browses on the lotus succumbs, in the same way as anyone who heeds the Sirens' song or is touched by Circe's wand. But the victim does not die: "Yet the Lotus-eaters did not harm the men of our company."[15] The only threats are oblivion and the surrender of will. The curse condemns them to no more than to the primitive state without work and struggle in the "fertile land":[16] "All who ate the lotus, sweeter than honey, thought no more of reporting to us, or of returning. Instead they wished to stay there in the company of the Lotus-eater, picking the lotus and forgetting their homeland."[17] This kind of idyll, which recalls the happiness of narcotic drug addicts reduced to the lowest level in obdurate social orders, who use their drugs to help them endure the unendur-

15. *Odyssey* 9.92ff.
16. *Odyssey* 23.311.
17. *Odyssey* 9.94ff.

able, is impermissible for the adherents of the rationale of self-preservation. It is actually the mere illusion of happiness, a dull vegetation, as meager as an animal's bare existence, and at best only the absence of the awareness of misfortune. But happiness holds truth, and is of its nature a result, revealing itself with the abrogation of misery. Therefore the sufferer who cannot bear to stay with the Lotus-eaters is justified. He opposes their illusion with that which is like yet unlike: the realization of utopia through historical labor; whereas mere lingering in the shade of the image of bliss removes all vigor from the dream. But rationality—Odysseus—acts upon the justice of the case, thereby entering by force the realm of injustice. Odysseus' own action is immediate, and serves domination. This happiness "at the world's bounds"[18] is as impermissible for the rationale of self-preservation as the more dangerous form proved to be in later stages. The indolent are removed by force and transported to the galleys: "But I forced them, weeping, back to the ships, dragged them into the capacious vessels and bound them beneath the benches."[19] The lotus is an Eastern food, and even today—finely shredded—plays a part in Chinese and Indian cooking. Perhaps the tempting power ascribed to it is none other than that of regression to the phase of collecting the fruits of the earth[20] and of the sea—a stage more ancient than agriculture, cattle-rearing and even hunting, older, in fact, than all production. It is hardly accidental that the epic attaches the idea of the idle life to the eating of flowers, even though no such conception adheres to it nowadays. Eating flowers, which still occurs at the dessert stage in the near East, and is known to European children only in terms of cooking with rosewater and candied violets, is promise of a state in which the reproduction of life is independent of conscious self-preservation,

18. Jacob Burckhardt, *Griechische Kulturgeschichte* (Stuttgart, n.d.), Vol. III, p. 95.

19. *Odyssey* 9.98ff.

20. In Indian mythology, Lotus is the goddess of the earth (see Heinrich Zimmer, *Maja*, Stuttgart and Berlin, 1936, pp. 105ff.). If there is a connection with mythic tradition and the old Homeric *nostos*, then the encounter with the Lotus-eaters might be characterized as a stage in the confrontation with the chthonic powers.

and the bliss of the fully contented is detached from the advantages of rationally planned nutrition. The fleeting reminiscence of that most distant and most ancient pleasure attached to the sense of taste is still limited by the almost immediate need actually to consume the food. It points back to prehistory. Whatever the anguish men suffered then, they may not conceive any happiness now that does not draw its virtue from the image of that primal time: "And so we sailed on with heavy hearts."[21]

The next figure to whom the wily-witted Odysseus is driven (to be driven and to be wily are equivalent in Homer), the Cyclops Polyphemus, bears his cartwheel-sized eye as a trace of the same prehistoric world: the single eye recalls the nose and the mouth, more primitive than the symmetry of eyes and ears,[22] which, with the security guaranteed by two unified perceptions, is the virtual prerequisite of identification, depth, and objectivity. Nevertheless, in comparison with the Lotus-eaters, Polyphemus represents a later stage in world development—the barbaric age proper, one of hunters and herdsmen. For Homer, barbarism can be defined as the absence of any systematic agriculture, and the lack of any systematic organization of labor and society governing the disposal of time. He calls the Cyclopes "uncivilized malefactors,"[23] because they (and here there is something akin to an implicit acknowledgement of guilt on the part of civilization itself) "trust in the power of immortal gods, and never lift a hand to sow or till the land; their crops grow without any planning or plowing: wheat, barley, and rich vines whose noble grapes offer wine when fed by Cronion's rain."[24] The fruits of their earth need no legal systematization, and the civilized accusation of anarchy is almost a denunciation of plenitude: "They have neither laws nor assemblies, but dwell in caverns in the mountain rocks, there in their vaulted grottoes; and each man rules his women and children as he wishes, for no one cares what another thinks."[25] This is an already patri-

21. *Odyssey* 9.105.
22. According to Wilamowitz the Cyclopes are "actually animals" (*Glaube der Hellenen*, Vol. I, p. 14).
23. *Odyssey* 9.106.
24. *Odyssey* 9.107ff.
25. *Odyssey* 9.112ff.

archal tribal society, grounded on the subjection of the physically weaker, but as yet unorganized by the yardstick of fixed property and its hierarchy; it is the noncollective aspect of the cave-dwellers, which is the real reason for the lack of objective law and hence provokes the Homeric accusation of savagery— a deficiency of mutual respect. It is interesting in this regard that at a later juncture the narrator's pragmatic exactitude contradicts his civilized judgment: hearing the screams of the blinded Cyclops, his fellow tribesmen come up to help him despite the fact that they are supposed to care not a jot for one another, and only Odysseus' cunning in having given "Nobody" as his name prevents them from aiding Polyphemus.[26] Stupidity and lawlessness are diagnosed as one: when Homer calls the Cyclops a "lawless-minded monster,"[27] this does not mean merely that in his mind he does not respect the laws of civilization, but also that his mind itself, his thinking, is lawless, unsystematic, and rhapsodical, for he cannot solve the bourgeois mental problem of the way in which his uninvited guests can escape from the cave (by clinging to the rams' bellies instead of riding on their backs) and does not see through the sophistic *double-entendre* of Odysseus' false name. Polyphemus, though he trusts in the power of immortality, is, of course, an eater of men, and for this latter reason forgoes his reverence for the gods: "You must be a fool, stranger, or have come from a long way off . . . ." In later times the distinction between fool and stranger was not so nice, and ignorance of local usage was deemed sheer stupidity, however foreign to the locality the stranger might be. —"And here you are telling me to fear the gods and their vengeance! Zeus Cronion and his thunder and the blessed gods mean nothing to the Cyclopes, for we excel them."[28] " 'We excel them,' " reports Odysseus, mockingly; but in fact what was meant was: We are older. The power of the solar system is recognized, but in something like the way in which a feudal type acknowledges that of bourgeois plenty, secretly feeling he is more noble without realizing that the injustice that was done

26. Cf. *Odyssey* 9.403ff.
27. *Odyssey* 9.428.
28. *Odyssey* 9.273ff.

him is of the same stamp as the injustice that he himself represents. The proximate sea-god Poseidon, the father of Polyphemus and Odysseus' enemy, is older than the universal, far-removed sky-god, Zeus, and the feud between elemental folk religion and logocentric legalistic religion is, so to speak, played out on the individual's back. Yet the lawless Polyphemus is not simply the scoundrel which the taboos of civilization make of him, presenting him in the legendary world of enlightened childhood as a Goliath-like ogre. In the poor region in which his survival has assumed a certain order and custom, he is not without redeeming qualities. When he puts the young of his ewes and goats to their udders, the practical action includes concern for the creatures themselves; and, when he is blind, his famous speech to the leading ram whom he calls his friend and asks why this time he is the last of the flock to leave the cave, and whether he is saddened by his master's distress, is moving to a degree equalled only at the highest point of the Odyssey, when the returning wanderer is recognized by the old dog Argos; this affecting quality persists despite the dreadful crudity of the threat with which the passage ends. The giant's behavior has not yet become objectified in the form of "character." He answers the suppliant Odysseus not with a mere outburst of uncontrolled hatred, but only with a refusal of the law that has not yet quite encompassed him. He does not wish to spare Odysseus and his companions "if my own heart does not compel me,"[29] and whether he is really trying to deceive his hearers (as Odysseus reports) is a matter for conjecture. In the euphoria of wine he boastfully offers Odysseus gifts,[30] and only the idea of Odysseus as Nobody bring the evil thought into his mind to eat the chief last of all—perhaps precisely because Odysseus has called himself Nobody and therefore—in terms of the Cyclops' rather elementary sense of humor—counts as non-existent.[31] The physical brutality of the physical superman is always trustworthy. Therefore the fulfillment of the mythic

29. *Odyssey* 9.278.
30. Cf. *Odyssey* 9.355ff.
31. "Ultimately, his so frequently manifest stupidity might be seen as a kind of still-born humor" (Klages, *op. cit.*, p. 1469).

ordinance, always injustice for the judged, also becomes injustice for the natural power which prescribes the law. Polyphemus and the other monsters whom Odysseus tricks, are already models for the evolving line of stupid devils of the Christian era right up to Shylock and Mephistopheles. The stupidity of the giant, an element of his barbaric crudity so long as all goes well for him, represents something better as soon as it is subverted by the one who ought to know better. Odysseus ingratiates himself with Polyphemus and wins his confidence, thereby depriving him of the right to human flesh by the artifice that breaks the ordinance by fulfilling it: "Take, Cyclops, and drink. Wine goes well with human flesh. Find out the excellence of the vintage brought here by the ship that carried us," recommends the bearer of culture.[32]

The adaptation of the *ratio* to its contrary, a state of consciousness that has not as yet developed any fixed identity (as in the case of the gigantic booby) is fully realized, however, in the artifice of the name. It is a trickery found throughout folklore. In the Greek it is a play on words: in the one word the name (Odysseus) and the intention (nobody) are separate. "Odysseus" and "Udeis" still sound the same to modern ears, and it is not difficult to imagine that in one of the dialects in which the story of the return to Ithaca was handed down, the name of the island king sounded exactly the same as the word for nobody. The calculation that, once blinded, Polyphemus would answer his tribesmen's question as to the source of his anguish with the word "Nobody!"—thus concealing the deed and helping the guilty man to escape punishment—is only a thin rationalistic covering. In reality, the subject Odysseus denies his own identity, which makes him a subject, and keeps himself alive by imitating the amorphous. He calls himself Nobody because Polyphemus is not a self, and the confusion of name and thing prevents the deceived savage from evading the trap: his call for retribution stays, as such, magically bound to the name of the one on whom he would be avenged, and this name condemns the call to impotence. Since Odysseus inserts

32. *Odyssey* 9.347ff.

the intention in the name, he withdraws it from the realm of magic. But his self-assertion—as in all epics, as in civilization as a whole—is self-denial. Thereby the self enters that coercive circle of the very natural context from which it tries to escape by imitation. He who calls himself Nobody for hi own sake and manipulates approximation to the state of nature as a means of mastering nature, falls victim to *hubris*. Yet the wily Odysseus cannot help it. On the run, still within the jurisdiction of the giant's flailing hands, he does not merely ridicule him, but reveals his real name and his origin; as if the primitive world still had such power over him (who had always escaped in the past) that, once having been known as nobody, lest he again become nobody, he must restore his own identity with the magic word already dissociated from rational identity. His friends try to warn him against the foolishness of thus declaring his cunning—but to no avail; by the skin of his teeth, he escapes the boulders flung by Polyphemus, whereas his enunciation of his own name probably calls down on him the hatred of Poseidon—who is hardly presented as omniscient. The cunning of the clever man who assumes the form of stupidity turns to stupidity as soon as he surrenders that form. That is the dialectic of eloquence. From antiquity to fascism, Homer has been accused of prating both through his heroes' mouths and in the narrative interpolations. Prophetically, however, Ionian Homer showed his superiority to the Spartans of past and present by picturing the fate which the cunning man—the middleman— calls down upon himself by his words. Speech, though it deludes physical force, is incapable of restraint. Its flow is a parody accompanying the stream of consciousness, thought itself, whose unswerving autonomy acquires an aspect of foolishness—manic foolishness—once it enters reality in the form of discourse, as if thinking corresponded with reality, when in fact the former is superior to the latter merely by virtue of distance. But this distance is also anguish. Therefore it is intelligent tongues (contrary to the proverb) that are always ready to talk by the dozen. The clever man is objectively conditioned by the fear that if he does not unfailingly affirm the nonexistent superiority of the word over force, that superiority will once again be taken from him by force. For the word knows that it is weaker than the nature that it has deceived. Too much talking allows force and injustice to prevail as the actual principle, and therefore prompts those who are to be feared always to commit the very action that is feared. The mythic compulsiveness of the word in prehistory is perpetuated in the disaster which the enlightened word draws down upon itself. Udeis, who compulsively acknowledges himself to be Odysseus, already bears the characteristics of the Jew who, fearing death, still presumes on the superiority which originates in the fear of death; revenge on the middleman occurs not only at the end of bourgeois society, but —as the negative utopia to which every form of coercive power always tends—at its beginning.

In contradistinction to the tales of escape from myth as the savagery of the eater of men, the magical story of Circe refers back again to the magic stage proper. Magic disintegrates the individual, who once again succumbs to it and is thus made to revert to an older biological species. But the force by which this dissolution is brought about is once again oblivion. It uses the fixed order of time to attack the fixed will of the subject, who orientates himself by that order. Circe tempts Odysseus' men to give themselves up to instinct: therefore the animal form of the tempted men has always been connected with a reversion to basic impulse, and Circe has been made the prototype of the courtesan—a development prompted of course by Hermes' lines, which assume that she will take the erotic initiative: "Then, in fright, she will ask you to sleep with her. Do not hesitate before the goddess' bed."[33] Circe's call-sign is ambiguity: she appears first as corrupter and then as helper. Ambiguity is already a mark of her lineage, for she is the daughter of Helios and the granddaughter of Oceanos.[34] The elements of fire and water are undivided in her, and it is this nondifferentiation as opposed to the primacy of a definite aspect of nature (whether matriarchal or patriarchal) which constitutes the nature of promiscuity: the essential quality of the courtesan, reflected

33. *Odyssey* 10.296–97.
34. *Cf. Odyssey* 10.138ff. See also F. C. Bauer, *Symbolik und Mythologie* (Stuttgart, 1824), Vol. I, p. 47.

still in the prostitute's look—*"le regard singulier d'une femme galante."*[35] The courtesan assures happiness and destroys the autonomy of the one she makes happy—this is her equivocation. But she does not necessarily destroy *him:* she affirms an older form of life.[36] Like the Lotus-eaters, Circe does not injure her guests, and even those whom she has made wild animals are peaceful: "Round about there were mountain wolves and long-maned lions which she herself rendered harmless with potent drugs. They did not attack the men but stood on their hind legs, as if fawning upon them, wagging their tails like dogs who surround their master when he leaves the table, because he always brings tasty morsels with him. And so these fierce-clawed wolves and lions fawned upon my men."[37] The enchanted men behave like the wild animals who hear Orpheus playing. The mythic commandment to which they succumb liberates at the same time the repressed nature in them. What is recalled in their reversion to myth is itself myth. The repression of instinct that makes them individuals—selves—and separates them from the animals, was the introversion of repression in the hopelessly closed cycle of nature, to which—as an older theory has it—the name Circe alludes. The forceful magic, on the other hand, which recalls them to an idealized prehistory, not only makes them animals, but—like the idyllic interlude of the Lotus-eaters—brings about, however delusive it may be, the illusion of redemption. But because they have already been men, the civilized epic cannot represent what has happened to them as anything other than unseemly degradation, and in the Homeric account there is hardly any trace of pleasure. It is all the more emphatically discounted, the more civilized the sacrifices are in themselves.[38] Odysseus' companions do not, like earlier guests, becomes sacred creatures of the wilderness, but

35. Cf. Baudelaire, "Le vin du solitaire," *Les Fleurs du Mal.*
36. See J. A. K. Thomson, *Studies in the Odyssey* (Oxford, 1914), p. 153.
37. *Odyssey* 10.212ff.
38. Murray talks of the "sexual expurgations" which he thinks the Homeric poems must have undergone in the course of redactions (Cf. *op. cit.,* pp. 141ff.).

unclean domestic animals—swine. Perhaps a reminiscence of the chthonic cult of Demeter, to whom the pig was sacred, plays a part in the story of Circe.[39] But perhaps it is also the notion of the quasi-human anatomy of the pig and its nakedness which explains the theme: as if the Ionians had the same taboo about commerce with the like that the Jews retain. Perhaps the prohibition of cannibalism is also implicated: as in Juvenal, the taste of human flesh is always described as like that of pork. At any rate, later on all civilizations preferred to call swine those whose instinct was for another pleasure, pigs being animals sanctioned by society for its own ends. Magic and counter-magic in the metamorphosis of the sailors are connected with cabbage and wine; intoxication and waking are bound up with smelling as the increasingly repressed and suppressed sense, it being closest not only to sex but to memory of prehistory.[40] But in the image of the pig the pleasure of smell is already reduced to the unfree snuffling[41] of one who has his nose to the ground and renounces his upright carriage. It is as if the courtesan-enchantress recalled in the course of the ritual to which she subjects the men, that ritual to which patriarchal society repeatedly subjects her. Like her, women under the pressure of civilization are above all inclined to adopt the civilized judgment on woman and to diffame the sex. In the confrontation of enlightenment and myth, the traces of which are preserved in the epic, the powerful temptress is already weak, obsolete and defenseless, and needs the obedient animals as her escorts.[42] As a representative of nature, woman in bourgeois

39. "In general, swine are Demeter's sacrificial animals" (Wilamowitz-Moellendorff, *Der Glaube der Hellenen,* Vol. II, p. 53).

40. Cf. Freud, *Das Unbehagen in der Kultur (Civilization and its Discontents),* in: *Gesammelte Werke,* Vol. XIV (Frankfurt a.M., 1968, 4th ed.), p. 459, footnote.

41. One of Wilamowitz's notes surprisingly indicates the connection between the concept of snuffling and that of the *noos,* autonomous reason: "Schwyzer has quite convincingly related *noos* to snorting and snuffling" (Wilamowitz-Moellendorff, *Die Heimkehr des Odysseus,* p. 191). Of course Wilamowitz does not claim that the etymological connection helps in elucidating the meaning.

42. Cf. *Odyssey* 10.434.

society has become the enigmatic image of irresistibility[43] and powerlessness. In this way she reflects for domination the pure lie that posits the subjection instead of the redemption of nature.

Marriage is the middle way by which society comes to terms with itself. The woman remains the one without power, for power comes to her only by male mediation. Something of this is apparent in the defeat of the courtesan-goddess of the Odyssey, whereas the civilized marriage with Penelope, while older in literary terms, represents a later stage of the objectivity of the patriarchal order. In Odysseus' behavior in Aeaea, the equivocation in the relation of man and woman—desire and command —already assumes the character of a contractually protected exchange. Renunciation is the prerequisite. Odysseus resists the magic of Circe, and thereby partakes of what her magic only deceptively promises to those who do not resist her. Odysseus sleeps with her. But first he makes her swear the great oath of the sacred ones, the Olympian covenant. The oath is intended to protect the man from mutilation, from revenge for the prohibition of promiscuity and for male domination, which—as a permanent deprivation of instinct—is nevertheless a symbolic self-mutilation on the part of the man. The one who resisted her, the lord, the individual whom Circe reproaches (because of his non-transformability) for having "an unassailably firm heart in your breast,"[44] is the one to whose will she subjects herself: "Put your sword away. Let us go to our bed so that joined there in sleep and love we may learn to trust one another."[45] On the pleasure that she ensures, she sets a price: that pleasure has been disdained. The last of the courtesans shows herself to be the first female character. In the transition from saga to story, she makes a decisive contribution to bourgeois frigidity. Her behavior is an enactment of the prohibition of love that later on became all the effective the more love as

43. The consciousness of irresistibility found expression later on in the cult of Aphrodite Peithon, "whose magic is irresistible" (Wilamo-witz-Moellendorff, *Der Glaube der Hellenen*, Vol. II, p. 152).
44. *Odyssey* 10.329.
45. *Odyssey* 10.333ff.

ideology had to perform its work of deception about the hatred of competitors. In the world of commercial exchange, he who gives over the measure is in the wrong; whereas the lover is always he who loves beyond measure. Whereas the sacrifice that he brings is glorified, jealous care is taken to ensure that the lover is not spared a sacrifice. Love itself is the very place where the lover is made to do wrong and punished for his wrongdoing. The incapacity for domination over himself and others to which his love bears witness is reason enough to deny him fulfillment. Society only reproduces and extends solitariness. Even in the most tender instances of emotion the mechanism prevails—even in love itself; in order to approach another at all such bleakness is required as to affect even fulfilment itself. —Circe's power, which subjects men to her and makes them obedient, becomes her obedience to the man who through renunciation refused to submit to her. The influence over nature that the poet ascribes to the goddess Circe dwindles to become priestly prophecy—and even clever foresight as far as the nautical problems ahead are concerned. This lives on in the caricature of female shrewdness. The prophecies of the disempowered enchantress about the Sirens, and Scylla and Charybdis, are ultimately of advantage only to male survival.

How dear a price was paid for the establishment of systematized conditions of sexual reproduction can be dimly seen only in the obscure lines describing the behavior of Odysseus' friends, whom Circe changes back by order of her contractual master. First of all, we read: "They soon became men again—and younger than they had been, and much more handsome in appearance and noble in bearing."[46] But these men who are thus confirmed and strengthened in their manhood are not happy: "Sweet-sour melancholy seized them all and the walls echoed their weeping."[47] Perhaps the oldest wedding hymn sounded like this—the accompaniment to a feast celebrating the rudimentary marriage that lasts only a year. The actual marriage with Penelope has more in common with the former than at first seems the case. Prostitute and wife are the complements of

46. *Odyssey* 10.395ff.
47. *Odyssey* 10.398ff.

73

female self-alienation in the patriarchal world: the wife denotes pleasure in the fixed order of life and property, whereas the prostitute takes what the wife's right of possession leaves free, and—as the wife's secret collaborator—subjects it again to the order of possession: she sells pleasure. Circe and Calypso, the courtesans, like mythic powers of destiny[48] or bourgeois house-wives, are introduced as diligent weavers, whereas Penelope like a courtesan sizes up the homecomer suspiciously, estimating the chances that he might really be just an old beggar, or perhaps a god on his travels. The famous recognition scene with Odysseus is of course truly patrician: "She sat there for a long time without saying a word, astonished beyond measure. At one moment, as she scrutinized his face, he seemed just like her husband; at another, his worn clothes made him unrecognizable."[49] There is no spontaneous reaction, for she does not want to make a mistake, and can hardly permit one under the pressure of the order that so bears down on her. The young Telemachus, who has not yet entirely adapted to his future role, is annoyed by this, but feels he is man enough to rebuke his mother. The charge of stubbornness and hardheartedness that he brings against her is exactly the same as that already made by Circe against Odysseus. If the courtesan makes the patriarchal world-order her own, the monogamous wife is not herself happy with it and does not rest until she has made herself equal with the male character. Thus the marriage partners come to terms. The test Penelope puts the homecomer to concerns the immovable position of the marriage bed; her husband had based it on an olive tree round which he had built the room itself—the olive tree being the symbol of sex and property. Penelope's moving artifice is to speak as if the bed could be moved from its position; furious, her husband answers her with a detailed account of his longlasting piece of woodwork. He is the proto-typical bourgeois—the with-it hobbyist. His do-it-yourself effort is an imitation of the actual labor of a craftsman, from which, in the framework of differentiated conditions of property own-

48. Cf. Bauer, *op. cit.*, and p. 49.
49. *Odyssey* 23.93ff.

ership, he has long been necessarily excluded. He enjoys this for the freedom to do what is really superfluous as far as he is concerned confirms his power of disposal over those who have to do precisely that kind of work in order to live. The cautious Penelope now recognizes Odysseus and fawns upon him with praise of his exceptional effort. But she adds to the praise (which contains a certain element of mockery) a sudden attribution of the reason for all their suffering to the gods' envy of the happiness that only marriage allows, the "promise of permanence":[50] "The immortals sent misery down upon us, thinking it too much that we should enjoy our youth together and then gently reach old age.[51] Marriage does not signify merely the order that requites in life but also solidarity in facing death. Expiation develops in it round about subjection, as in history to date the humane has flourished only and precisely in the savagery that is veiled by humanity. Even if the contract between the partners only calls down that age-old enmity, nevertheless, peacefully growing old together, they can vanish at the same moment like Philemon and Baucis: just as the smoke of the sacrificial altar turns into the wholesome smoke of the fireside. Marriage belongs to the primal rock of myth in the basis of civilization. But its mythic hardness and fixity stand out from myth as the small island kingdom from the infinite sea.

The uttermost stop of the journey proper is no such place of refuge. It is Hades. The souls which the adventurer sees on his first visit to the realm of the dead are primarily the matriarchal images[52] banished by the religion of light: after Odysseus' own mother (to whom he forces himself to behave with patriarcha and expedient rigor),[53] come the ancient heroines. But the

50. Goethe, *Wilhelm Meisters Lehrjahre* (*Wilhelm Meister's Apprenticeship*), *Jubiläum edition* (Stuttgart and Berlin, n.d.), Vol. I, ch. 16, p. 70.
51. *Odyssey* 23.210ff.
52. See Thomson, *op. cit.*, p. 28.
53. "I saw her and my eyes filled with tears, and my heart was moved. Yet I prevented her as well from approaching the blood before I had asked Teiresias—even though I was profoundly stirred" (*Odyssey* 11.87ff.).

mother image is impotent, blind and dumb,[54] with the same phantom quality as the epic narrative when it allows the image to speak. The sacrificial blood is required as a pledge of living memory before the shades can talk, and mythic dumbness can breaks its silence, in however abortive and ephemeral a way. Only when subjectivity gains mastery over itself by acknowledging the nullity of the shades can it partake of the hope of which the phantom images are only an ineffectual promise. The praised land of Odysseus is not the realm of archaic imagery. All the images eventually show Odysseus their real nature as shades in the world of the dead; and their real nature is semblance—illusion. He becomes free of them once he has recognized them as dead with a magisterial gesture of self-preservation has repulsed them from the sacrifice; he will allow only those to approach it who will afford him knowledge of some utility for his life, in which the power of myth still asserts itself only as imagination, as mental imagery. The realm of the dead, where the emasculated powers assemble, is the furthest point from the homeland, and communicates with it only at the farthest possible remove. If we follow Kirchoff in his assumption that Odysseus' visit to the Underworld belongs to the most ancient level of the epic[55]—that of saga—, it is this oldest layer, too, that most decisively features (for example, in the tradition of the visits of Heracles and Orpheus to the Underworld) something extending beyond myth: indeed, the theme of the forcing of the gates of hell, the annulment of death, constitutes the very core of all antimythological thinking. This antimythological element appears in Teiresias' prophecy that it will be possible to appease Poseidon. Odysseus is to carry an oar upon his shoulder and continue to wander until he reaches a people "who do

54. "Over there I see my dead mother's soul. As though speechless, she sits by the blood and does not dare to look at her own son, or to say a single word. Tell me, Lord, how shall I go about letting her know that I am who I am?" (*Odyssey* 11.141ff.).

55. "I cannot help but see the whole of Book II with the exception of a few passages . . . as a displaced fragment of the old *nostos*, and therefore as one of the oldest parts of the poem" (Kirchoff, *Die homerische Odyssee*, Berlin, 1879, p. 226). "Whatever else is original in the myth of Odysseus, the Visit to Death is" (Thomson, *op. cit.*, p. 95).

not know the sea and never eat food seasoned with salt."[56] When he meets another traveler who mentions the winnowing fan he bears on his shoulder, the right spot will have been reached to make the expiatory sacrifice to Poseidon. The core of the prophecy is the mistaking of the oar for a winnowing fan. The Ionians must have found it comic. But this humor, on which expiation is made to depend, is not intended for men but for the angry god Poseidon.[57] The misunderstanding is designed to make the fierce elemental god laugh, so that while he laughs his wrath will disappear. This seems analogous to the neighbor's recommendation in Grimm, when she advises a mother how to get rid of a changeling: "She told her to carry the changeling into the kitchen, to set it on the hearth, and boil water in two eggshells. That would make the changeling laugh, and if the changeling was made to laugh, then its fate was sealed."[58] Even though laughter is still the sign of force, of the breaking out of blind and obdurate nature, it also contains the opposite element —the fact that through laughter blind nature becomes aware of itself as it is, and thereby surrenders itself to the power of destruction. This duality of laughter is akin to that of the name, and perhaps names are no more than frozen laughter, as is evident nowadays in nicknames—the only ones that retain something of the original action of namegiving. Laughter is marked

---

56. *Odyssey* 11.122ff.

57. He was originally the "husband of the earth" (cf. Wilamowitz, *Glaube der Hellenen,* Vol. I, pp. 112ff.) and only later became the god of the sea. Teiresias' prophecy may be a play on his dual nature. It is conceivable that his conciliation by means of an earth sacrifice, far away from the sea, relies on a symbolic restoration of his chthonic power. This restoration is possibly equivalent to the replacement of the maurauding expedition at sea by agriculture: the cults of Poseidon and Demeter were intermixed (cf. Thomson, *op. cit.,* p. 96, footnote).

58. Grimm, *Kinder und Hausmärchen* (Leipzig, n.d.), p. 208. Closely related themes have been handed down from antiquity, especially in connection with Demeter. When she "came to Eleusis in search of her kidnapped daughters," she was "received by Dysaules and his wife Baubo, but in her deep mourning, refused to touch meat or drink. She caused her hostess Baubo to laugh by suddenly raising her skirts and exposing her stomach" (Freud, *Gesammelte Werke,* Vol. X, p. 399. Cf. Salomon Reinach, *Cultes, Mythes et Religions,* Paris, 1912, Vol. IV, pp. 115ff.).

by the guilt of subjectivity, but in the suspension of law which it indicates it also points beyond thralldom. It is a promise of the way home. It is homesickness that gives rise to the adventures through which subjectivity (whose fundamental history is presented in the Odyssey) escapes from the prehistoric world. The quintessential paradox of the epic resides in the fact that the notion of homeland is opposed to myth—which the fascist would falsely present as homeland. Here there is a reminiscence of history, in which the domiciled and settled life, the prerequisite for any homeland, followed the nomadic age. If it is the fixed order of property dependent on the settled life that grounds the human alienation in which originates all homesickness and all longing for the lost primal state of man, it is nevertheless the settled life and fixed property (only in which the notion of a homeland can appear) to which all longing and all homesickness are directed. Novalis' definition, according to which all philosophy is homesickness, holds true only if this longing is not dissolved into the phantasm of a lost remote antiquity, but represents the homeland, nature itself, as wrested from myth. Homeland is the state of having escaped. Therefore the reproach that the Homeric sagas are those which "are departing from the earth" is a guarantee of their truth: "They turn to mankind."[59] The translation of myths into the novel, as in the adventure story, does not so much falsify the myths as sweep myth into time, concealing the abyss that separates it from homeland and expiation. The vengeance wreaked by civilization on the prehistoric world is a fearful one, and makes civilization approximate that very world, as is cruelly instanced in Homer's account of the mutilation of the goatherd Melanthius. The way in which it differs from the latter is not the content of the deeds as narrated. It is the self-consciousness which causes force to desist in the narrative moment. Eloquent discourse itself, language in contradistinction to mythic song, the possibility of retaining in the memory the disaster that has occurred, is the law of Homeric escape, and the reason why the escaping hero is repeatedly introduced as narrator. The cold distancing of narra-

59. Hölderlin, *"Der Herbst," op. cit.,* p. 1066.

tion, which still represents horror as if it were a conversational topic, also allows the horror as such to appear for the first time that in song is solemnly represented as fate. Reticence in narrative, however, is the sudden break, the transformation of what is reported into something long past, by means of which the semblance of freedom glimmers that since then civilization has not wholly succeeded in putting out. In Book 22 of the Odyssey, there is a description of the way in which Odysseus' son punishes the faithless women who had reverted to prostitution. Emotionless, and with an inhuman composure rivaled only by the *impassibilité* of the major nineteenth-century novelists, Homer describes the movement of the nooses and coldly compares the women's appearance as they hang to that of birds caught in a net; the reticence and composure of the narration are the true marks of eloquence. The passage closes with the information that the feet of the row of suspended women "kicked out for a short while, but not for long."[60] The precision of the descriptive artist, which already exhibits the frigidity of anatomy and vivisection,[61] is employed to provide evidence of the dying convulsions of the subjected who, in the name of law and justice, were cast down into that realm from which Odysseus the judge escaped. As a citizen reflecting momentarily upon the nature of hanging, Homer assures himself and his audience (actually readers) that it did not last for long—a moment and then it was all over.[62] But after the "not for long" the inner flow of the narrative is arrested. *Not for long?* The device poses the question, and belies the author's composure. By cut-

60. *Odyssey* 22.473.
61. Wilamowitz is of the opinion that the sentence is "related with relish by the poet" (*Die Heimkehr des Odysseus*, p. 67). Even though the authoritarian philologist is delighted to find that the simile of the bird-net is "just and modern in its appropriateness to the jerking of the hanged women" (*op. cit.*, p. 76), the relish seems to be mostly his own. Wilamowitz's writings are among the most emphatic documents of the German intermingling of barbarism and culture erected on the basis of modern Philhellenism.
62. Gilbert Murray draws attention to the consolatory intention behind these verses. According to his theory, torture scenes have been expurgated from Homer by a civilized censorship. Of these only the deaths of Melanthius and the suitors' mistresses have been retained (*op. cit.*, p. 146).

ting short the account, Homer prevents us from forgetting the victims, and reveals the unutterable eternal agony of the few seconds in which the women struggle with death. No echo of the "not for long" remains except the *Quo usque tandem* that the rhetors of a later period unwittingly devalued by themselves laying claim to the long-suffering attitude in question. In the narrative account of atrocity, however, hope attaches to the fact that it happened a long time ago. Homer offers consolation for the entanglement of prehistory, savagery, and culture by recourse to the once-upon-a-time device. Yet the epic is novel first, and fairy tale after.

EXCURSUS II

JULIETTE
OR ENLIGHTENMENT
AND MORALITY

ENLIGHTENMENT, according to Kant, is ". . . man's emergence from his self-incurred immaturity. Immaturity is the inability to use one's understanding without the guidance of another person."[1] "Understanding without the guidance of another person" is understanding guided by reason. This means no more than that, by virtue of its own consistency, it organizes the individual data of cognition into a system. "Reason has . . . for its object only the understanding and its purposive employment."[2] It makes "a certain collective unity the aim of the operations of the understanding,"[3] and this unity is the system. Its rules are the indications for a hierarchical construction of concepts. For Kant, as for Leibniz and Descartes, rationality consists of "completing the systematical connection, both in ascending to higher genera, and in descending to lower species."[4] The "systematizing" of knowledge is "its coherence according to one principle."[5] In the Enlightenment's interpretation, thinking is the creation of unified, scientific order and the derivation of factual knowledge

1. Kant, *"Beantwortung der Frage: Was ist Aufklärung?" Kants Werke* (Akademie-Ausgabe), Vol. VIII, p. 35.
2. *Kritik der reinen Vernunft (Critique of Pure Reason), ed. cit.,* Vol. III (2nd ed.), p. 427.
3. *Ibid.,* p. 427.
4. *Ibid.,* pp. 435f.
5. *Ibid.,* p. 428.

from principles, whether the latter are elucidated as arbitrarily postulated axioms, innate ideas, or higher abstractions. Logical laws produce the most general relations within the arrangement, and define them. Unity resides in agreement. The resolution of contradiction is the system *in nuce*. Knowledge consists of subsumption under principles. Any other than systematically directed thinking is unoriented or authoritarian. Reason contributes only the idea of systematic unity, the formal elements of fixed conceptual coherence. Every substantial goal which men might adduce as an alleged rational insight is, in the strict Enlightenment sense, delusion, lies or "rationalization," even though individual philosophers try to advance from this conclusion toward the postulate of philanthropic emotion. Reason is the "faculty . . . of deducing the particular from the general."[6] According to Kant, the homogeneity of the general and the particular is guaranteed by the "schematism of pure understanding," or the unconscious operation of the intellectual mechanism which structures perception in accordance with the understanding. The understanding impresses the intelligibility of the matter (which subjective judgment discovers there) on it as an objective quality, before it enters into the ego. Without such a schematism—in short, without intellectual perception—no impression would harmonize with a concept, and no category with an example; and the unity of thought (let alone of system) toward which everything is directed would not prevail. To produce this unity is the conscious task of science. If "all empirical laws . . . are only special determinations of the pure laws of the understanding,"[7] research must always ensure that the principles are always properly linked with factual judgments. "This concurrence of nature with our cognitive faculty is an *a priori* assumption . . . of judgment."[8] It is the "guideline"[9] for organized experience.

The system must be kept in harmony with nature; just as the

6. *Ibid.*, p. 429.
7. *Kritik der reinen Vernunft, ed. cit.*, Vol. IV (1st ed.), p. 93.
8. *Kritik der Urteilskraft (Critique of Judgment), ed. cit.*, Vol. V, p. 185.
9. *Ibid.*, p. 185.

facts are predicted from the system, so they must confirm it
Facts, however, belong to practice; they always characterize the
individual's contact with nature as a social object: experience
is always real action and suffering. In physics, of course, perception—by means of which a theory may be proved—is usually reduced to the electric sparks visible in the experimental
apparatus. Its absence is as a rule without practical consequence,
for it destroys no more than a theory—or possibly the career
of the assistant responsible for setting up the experiment. But
laboratory conditions constitute the exception. Thinking that
does not make system and perception accord conflicts with
more than isolated visual impressions; it conflicts with practice.
The expected event fails to occur, yes, but the unexpected event
does occur: the bridge collapses, the crops wither, or the drug
kills. The spark which most surely indicates the lack of systematic thinking, the violation of logic, is no transient percept,
but sudden death. The system the Enlightenment has in mind
is the form of knowledge which copes most proficiently with
the facts and supports the individual most effectively in the
mastery of nature. Its principles are the principles of self-
preservation. Immaturity is then the inability to survive. The
burgher, in the successive forms of slaveowner, free entrepreneur, and administrator, is the logical subject of the Enlightenment.

The difficulties in the concept of reason caused by the fact
that its subjects, the possessors of that very reason, contradict
one another, are concealed by the apparent clarity of the judgments of the Western Enlightenment. In the *Critique of Pure
Reason*, however, they are expressed in the unclear relation of
the transcendental to the empirical ego, and in the other unresolved contradictions. Kant's concepts are ambiguous. As the
transcendental, supraindividual self, reason comprises the idea
of a free, human social life in which men organize themselves
as the universal subject and overcome the conflict between pure
and empirical reason in the conscious solidarity of the whole.
This represents the idea of true universality: utopia. At the
same time, however, reason constitutes the court of judgment of
calculation, which adjusts the world for the ends of self-preser-

vation and recognizes no function other than the preparation of the object from mere sensory material in order to make it the material of subjugation. The true nature of schematism, of the general and the particular, of concept and individual case reconciled from without, is ultimately revealed in contemporary science as the interest of industrial society. Being is apprehended under the aspect of manufacture and administration. Everything —even the human individual, not to speak of the animal—is converted into the repeatable, replaceable process, into a mere example for the conceptual models of the system. Conflict between administrative, reifying science, between the public mind and the experience of the individual, is precluded by circumstances. The conceptual apparatus determines the senses, even before perception occurs; *a priori,* the citizen sees the world as the matter from which he himself manufactures it. Intuitively, Kant foretold what Hollywood consciously put into practice: in the very process of production, images are pre-censored according to the norm of the understanding which will later govern their apprehension. Even before its occurrence, the perception which serves to confirm the public judgment is adjusted by that judgment. Even if the secret utopia in the concept of reason pointed, despite fortuitous distinctions between individuals, to their common interest, reason—functioning, in compliance with ends, as a mere systematic science—serves to level down that same identical interest. It allows no determination other than the classifications of the societal process to operate. No one is other than what he has come to be: a useful, successful, or frustrated member of vocational and national groups. He is one among many representatives of his geographical, psychological and sociological type. Logic is democratic; in this respect the great have no advantage over the insignificant. The great are classed as the important, and the insignificant as prospective objects for social relief. Science in general relates to nature and man only as the insurance company in particular relates to life and death. Whoever dies is unimportant: it is a question of ratio between accidents and the company's liabilities. Not the individuality but the law of the majority recurs in the formula. The concurrence of the general and the particular is no longer hidden in the one intellect which perceives the particular only as one case of the general, and the general only as the aspect of the particular by which it can be grasped and manipulated. Science itself is not conscious of itself; it is only a tool. Enlightenment, however, is the philosophy which equates the truth with scientific systematization. The attempt to establish this identity, which Kant was still able to undertake with a philosophic intention, led to concepts which have no meaning in a scientific sense, because they are not mere indications for manipulation according to the rules of the game. The notion of the self-understanding of science contradicts the notion of science itself. Kant's work transcends experience as mere operation, and for that reason—in accordance with its own principles —is now condemned by the Enlightenment as dogmatic. With Kant's consequent, full confirmation of the scientific system as the form of truth, thought seals its own nullity, for science is technical practice, as far removed from reflective consideration of its own goal as are other forms of labor under the pressure of the system.

The moral teachings of the Enlightenment bear witness to a hopeless attempt to replace enfeebled religion with some reason for persisting in society when interest is absent. As genuine burghers, the philosophers come to terms with the powers who, in theory, are to be condemned. The theories are firm and consistent, whereas the moral doctrines are propagandist and sentimental (even when they seem rigorous), or else they are mere *coups de main* by reason of the consciousness that morality itself is underivable—as in the case of Kant's recourse to ethical forces as a fact. His attempt (even though more careful than Western philosophy as a whole) to derive the duty of mutual respect from a law of reason finds no support in the *Critique*. It is the conventional attempt of bourgeois thought to ground respect, without which civilization cannot exist, upon something other than material interest and force; it is more sublime and paradoxical than, yet as ephemeral as, any previous attempt. The citizen who would forego profit only on the Kantian motive of respect for the mere form of law would not be enlightened, but superstitious—a fool. The root of Kantian optimism, according to which moral behavior is rational even if the mean and wretched would prevail, is actually an expression of horror at the thought of reversion to barbarism. If (so Kant wrote to Haller) one of these great moral forces of mutual love and respect were to founder, ". . . then nothingness [immorality] would open wide its maw and swallow the whole realm of [moral] virtue as if it were a drop of water."[10] But, according to Kant, in the face of scientific reason moral forces are no less neutral impulses and modes of behavior than the immoral forces into which they suddenly change when directed not to that hidden possibility but to reconciliation with power. Enlightenment expels the distinction from the theory. It treats emotions *"ac si quaestio de lineis, planis aut de corporibus esset."*[11] The totalitarian order has carried this out with all seriousness. Liberated from the control of the same class which tied the nineteenth-century businessman to Kantian respect and mutual love, Fascism (which by its iron discipline saves its subject peoples the trouble of moral feelings) no longer needs to uphold any disciplines. In contradistinction to the categorical imperative and all the more in accordance with pure reason, it treats men as things—as the loci of modes of behavior. The rulers were anxious to protect the bourgeois world against the ocean of open force (which has now really broken into Europe), only so long as the economic concentration had made inadequate progress. Previously, only the poor and savages were exposed to the fury of the capitalist elements. But the totalitarian order gives full rein to calculation and abides by science as such. Its canon is its own brutal efficiency. It was the hand of philosophy that wrote it on the wall—from Kant's *Critique* to Nietzsche's *Genealogy of Morals;* but one man made out the detailed account. The work of the Marquis de Sade portrays "understanding without the guidance of another person": that is, the bourgeois individual freed from tutelage.

Self-preservation is the constitutive principle of science, the soul of the table of categories, even when it is to be deduced

10. *Metaphysische Anfänge der Tugendlehre, ed. cit.,* Vol. VI, p. 449.
11. Spinoza, *Ethica,* Pars III. Praefatio.

idealistically, as with Kant. Even the ego, the synthetic unit of apperception, the instance which Kant calls the highest point, on which the possibility of the logical form of all knowledge necessarily depends,[12] is in fact the product of, as well as the condition for, material existence. Individuals, who have to look after themselves, develop the ego as the instance of the reflective preliminary and general view; it is extended and contracted as the prospects of economic self-sufficiency and productive owner-ship extend and contract from generation to generation. Finally it passes from the dispossessed bourgeoisie to the totalitarian cartel-lords, whose science has become the inclusive concept of the methods of reproduction of the subjugated mass society. Sade erected an early monument to their sense of planning. The conspiracy of the powerholders against the people by means of undeviating organization is as close as the bourgeois republic to the enlightened spirit since Machiavelli and Hobbes. It is inimical to authority only when authority does not have power enough to compel obedience—the force which is no fact. So long as the identity of the user of reason is disregarded, the affinity of reason is as much to force as the mediation; accord-ing to the individual or group situation, it permits peace or war, tolerance or repression. Since it exposes substantial goals as the power of nature over mind, as the erosion of its self-legislation, reason is—by virtue, too, of its very formality—at the service of any natural interest. Thinking becomes an organic medium pure and simple, and reverts to nature. But for the rulers, men become material, just as nature as a whole is material for society. After the short intermezzo of liberalism, in which the bourgeois kept one another in check, domination appears as ar-chaic terror in a fascistically rationalized form. As Francavilla says at the court of King Ferdinand of Naples: "Religious chime-ras must be replaced by the most extreme forms of terror. If the people are freed from fear of a future hell, as soon as it has vanished they will abandon themselves to anything. But if this chimerical fear is replaced by utterly relentless penal laws, which of course apply only to the people, then they alone will

12. *Kritik der reinen Vernunft, ed. cit.,* Vol. III (2nd ed.), p. 109.

provoke unrest in the State; the discontented will be born only into the lowest class. What does the idea of a curb which they never experience themselves mean to the rich, if with this empty semblance they are able to preserve a justice that allows them to crush all those who live under their yoke? You will find no one in that class who would not submit to the worst tyranny so long as all others must suffer it."[13] Reason is the organ of calculation, of planning; it is neutral in regard to ends; its element is coordination. What Kant grounded transcendentally, the affinity of knowledge and planning, which impressed the stamp of inescapable expediency on every aspect of a bourgeois existence that was wholly rationalized, even in every breathing-space, Sade realized empirically more than a century before sport was conceived. The teams of modern sport, whose interaction is so precisely regulated that no member has any doubt about his role, and which provide a reserve for every player, have their exact counterpart in the sexual teams of *Juliette,* which employ every moment usefully, neglect no human orifice, and carry out every function. Intensive, purposeful activity prevails in spirt as in all branches of mass culture, while the inadequately initiated spectator cannot divine the difference in the combinations, or the meaning of variations, by the arbitrarily determined rules. The architectonic structure of the Kantian system, like the gymnastic pyramids of Sade's orgies and the schematized principles of the early bourgeois freemasonry—which has its cynical mirror-image in the strict regimentation of the libertine society of the *120 Journées*—reveals a organization of life as a whole which is deprived of any substantial goal. These arrangements amount not so much to pleasure as to its regimented pursuit—organization—just as in other demythologized epochs (Imperial Rome and the Renaissance, as well as the Baroque) the schema of an activity was more important than its content. In the modern era, enlightenment separated the notions of harmony and fulfillment from their hypostatization in the religious Beyond, and, in the form of systematization, transferred them as criteria to human aspiration. When utopia,

13. *Histoire de Juliette* (Holland, 1797), Vol. V, pp. 319f.

which provided the French Revolution with its content of hope, entered German music and philosophy (effectively and ineffectively), the established civil order wholly functionalized reason, which became a purposeless purposiveness which might thus be attached to all ends. In this sense, reason is planning considered solely as planning. The totalitarian State manipulates the people. Or, as Sade's Francavilla puts it: "The government must control the population, and must possess all the means necessary to exterminate them when afraid of them, or to increase their numbers when that seems desirable. There should never be any counterweight to the justice of government other than that of the interests or passions of those who govern, together with the passions and interests of those who, as we have said, have received from it only so much power as is requisite to reproduce their own."[14] Francavilla indicates the road that imperialism, the most terrible form of the *ratio,* has always taken: "Take its god from the people that you wish to subjugate, and then demoralize it; so long as it worships no other god than you, and has no other morals than your morals, you will always be its master . . . allow it in return the most extreme criminal license; punish it only when it turns upon you."[15]

Since reason posits no substantial goals, all affects are equally removed from its governance, and are purely natural. The principle by which reason is merely set over against all that is unreasonable, is the basis of the true antithesis of enlightenment and mythology. Mythology recognizes spirit only as immersed in nature, as natural power. Like the powers without, inward impulses appear as living powers of divine or demonic origin. Enlightenment, on the other hand, puts back coherence, meaning and life into subjectivity, which is properly constituted only in this process. For subjectivity, reason is the chemical agent which absorbs the individual substance of things and volatilizes them in the mere autonomy of reason. In order to escape the superstitious fear of nature, it wholly transformed objective effective entities and forms into the mere veils of a chaotic mat-

14. *Ibid.,* pp. 322f.
15. *Ibid.,* p. 324.

ter, and anathematized their influence on humanity as slavery, until the ideal form of the subject was no more than unique, unrestricted, though vacuous authority.

All the power of nature was reduced to mere indiscriminate resistance to the abstract power of the subject. The particular mythology which the Western Enlightenment, even in the form of Calvinism, had to get rid of was the Catholic doctrine of the *ordo* and the popular pagan religion which still flourished under it. The goal of bourgeois philosophy was the liberate men from all this. But the liberation went further than its humane progenitors had conceived. The unleashed market economy was both the actual form of reason and the power which destroyed reason. The Romantic reactionaries only expressed what the bourgeois themselves experienced: that in their world freedom tended toward organized anarchy. The Catholic counterrevolution proved itself right as against the Enlightenment, just as the Enlightenment had shown itself to be right in regard to Catholicism. The Enlightenment committed itself to liberalism. If all affects are of equal value, then survival—which anyway governs the form of the system—seems also to be the most probable source of maxims for human conduct. Self-preservation, in fact, was given full rein in the free market economy. Those somber writers of the bourgeois dawn—Machiavelli, Hobbes, Mandeville, and so on—who decried the egotism of the self, acknowledged in so doing that society was the destructive principle, and denounced harmony before it was elevated as the official doctrine by the serene and classical authors. The latter boosted the totality of the bourgeois order as the misery that finally fused both general and particular, society and self, into one. With the development of the economic system in which control of the economic apparatus by private groups divides men, survival as affirmed by reason—the reified drive of the individual bourgeois—was revealed as destructive natural power, no longer to be distinguished from self-destruction. The two were now indissolubly blended. Pure reason became unreason, a faultless and insubstantial mode of procedure. But the utopia which proclaimed reconciliation between nature and the individual emerged together with the

90

revolutionary avant-garde from its concealment in German philosophy, simultaneously irrational and rational, as the idea of the combination of free men, and called down on itself all the wrath of the *ratio*. In society as it is, despite all the wretched moralistic attempts to propagate humanity as the most rational of means, survival remains free from utopia, which is denounced as myth. Among the rulers, cunning self-preservation takes the form of struggle for Fascist power; among individuals, it is expressed as adaptation to injustice at any price. Enlightened reason is as little capable of finding a standard by which to measure any drive in itself, and in comparison with all other drives, as of arranging the universe in spheres. It established natural hierarchy as a reflex of medieval society, and later enterprises are branded as lies in order to indicate a new, objective value ranking. Irrationalism, as it appears in such empty reconstructions, is far from being able to withstand the *ratio*. With Leibniz and Hegel, mainstream philosophy—even in those subjective and objective assertions which only approximate to thought—discovered the claim to truth in emotions, institutions, and works of art, but irrationalism (close in this as in other respects to modern positivism, that last remnant of the Enlightenment) demarcates emotion, like religion and art, from everything deserving of the title of knowledge or cognition. It limits cold reason in favor of immediate living, yet makes this no more than a principle inimical to thought. Under the cover of this enmity, emotion and finally all human expression, even culture as a whole, are withdrawn from thought; thereby, however, they are transformed into a neutralized element of the comprehensive *ratio* of the economic system—itself irrationalized long ago. From the start, it was unable to rely on its own pull, which it enhanced with the cult of feeling. But wherever it has recourse to the emotions, it militates against their very medium, thought, which was always suspicious of this self-alienated reason. The exuberantly tender affection of the lover in the movie strikes a blow against the unmoved theory—a blow continued in that sentimental polemic against thought which presents itself as an attack upon injustice. Though feelings are raised in this way to the level of an ideology, they continue to be despised in reality.

91

When set against the firmament to which ideology transfers them, they still seem rather too vulgar; the effect is to exile them all the more. As a natural impulse, self-preservation has, like all other impulses, a bad conscience; but efficiency and the institutions which meant to serve it—that is, independent mediation, the apparatus, the organization, systematization—like to appear reasonable, both in theory and in practice; and the emotions are made to share in this apparent rationality.

The Enlightenment of modern times advanced from the very beginning under the banner of radicalism; this distinguishes it from any of the earlier stages of demythologization. When a new mode of social life allowed room for a new religion and a new way of thinking, the overthrow of the old classes, tribes, and nations was usually accompanied by that of the old gods. But especially where a nation (the Jews, for example) was brought by its own destiny to change to a new form of social life, the time-honored customs, sacred activities, and objects of worship were magically transformed into heinous crimes and phantoms. Present-day fears and idiosyncracies, derided and execrated character traits, may be deciphered as the marks of the violent onset of this or that stage of progress in human development. From the reflex of disgust at excrement or human flesh to the suspicion of fanaticism, laziness, and poverty, whether intellectual or material, there is a long line of modes of behavior which were metamorphosed from the adequate and necessary into abominations. This is the line both of destruction and of civilization. Each step forward on it represents some progress, a stage of enlightenment. But whereas all earlier changes, from pre-animism to magic, from the matriarchal to a patriarchal culture, from the polytheism of the slaveowners to the Catholic hierarchy, replaced the older mythologies with new —though enlightened—ones, and substituted the god of legions for the Great Mother, the adoration of the Lamb for that of the totem, the brilliance of enlightened reason banished as mythological any form of devotion which claimed to be objective, and grounded in actuality. All previous obligations therefore succumbed to the verdict which pronounced them taboo—not excluding those which were necessary for the existence of the bourgeois order itself. The instrument by means of which the bourgeoisie came to power, the liberation of forces, universal freedom, self-determination—in short, the Enlightenment, itself turned against the bourgeoisie once, as a system of domination, it had recourse to suppression. In accordance with its principle, enlightenment does not stop at the minimum of belief, without which the bourgeois world cannot exist. It does not give domination the reliable service which the old ideologies always allowed it. Its antiauthoritarian tendency, which (though of course only in a subterranean form) still relates to the utopia in the concept of reason, ultimately makes it as inimical to the bourgeoisie as it was to the aristocracy—with which the bourgeoisie is then very soon allied. Finally, the antiauthoritarian principle has to change into its very antithesis—into opposition to reason; the abrogation of everything inherently binding, which it brings about, allows domination to ordain as sovereign and to manipulate whatever bonds and obligations prove appropriate to it. After civil virtue and love of humanity (for which it already had no adequate grounds), philosophy proceeded to proclaim authority and hierarchy as virtues, when the Enlightenment had long posited them as lies. But the Enlightenment possesses no argument against even such a perversion of its proper nature, for the plain truth had no advantage over distortion, and rationalization none over the *ratio,* if they could prove no practical benefit in themselves. With the formalization of reason, to the extent that its preferred function is that of a symbol for neutral procedures, theory itself becomes an incomprehensible concept, and thought appears meaningful only when meaning has been discarded. Once it is harnessed to the dominant mode of production, the Enlightenment—which strives to undermine any order which has become repressive—abrogates itself. This was obvious even in the early attacks of the contemporary Enlightenment on Kant, the universal reducer. Just as Kant's moral philosophy restricted his enlightened critique, in order to preserve the possibility of reason, so—conversely— unreflective enlightened thinking based on the notion of survival always tends to convert into skepticism, in order to make enough room for the existing order.

On the other hand, the work of the Marquis de Sade, like that of Nietzsche, constitutes the intransigent critique of practical reason, in contradistinction to which Kant's critique itself seems a revocation of his own thought. It makes the scientistic the destructive principle. Of course Kant had so far cleansed the moral law within me of all heteronomous belief, that respect for Kant's assurances was a mere natural psychological fact, just as the starry heavens above me were a natural physical fact. Kant himself called it a "fact of reason,"[16] and Leibniz's term for it was *un instinct général de société.*"[17] But facts have no validity when they simply are not there. Sade does not deny their presence. Justine, the virtuous sister, is a martyr for the moral law. Juliette draws the conclusion that the bourgeoisie wanted to ignore: she demonizes Catholicism as the most up-to-date mythology, and with it civilization as a whole. The energies which were devoted to the Blessed Sacrament, are applied to sacrilege instead. But this reversal is merely attributed to society. In all this, Juliette is by no means fanatical, as Catholicism was in the case of the Incas; her procedure is enlightened and efficient as she goes about her work of sacrilege—which the Catholics also retained as an archaic inheritance. The primeval behaviors which civilization had made taboo had led a subterranean existence, having been transformed into destructive tendencies under the stigma of bestiality. Juliette practices them not as natural but as tabooed activities. She compensates the value judgment against them (which was unfounded because all value judgments are unfounded) by its opposite. Even though she repeats the primitive reactions in so doing, they are not really primitive but bestial. Not unlike Merteuil in the *Liaisons Dangeureuses,*[18] Juliette embodies (in psychological terms) neither unsublimated nor regressive libido, but intellectual pleasure in regression—*amor intellectualis diaboli,* the pleasure of attacking civilization with its own weapons. She favors system

16. *Kritik der praktischen Vernunft (Critique of Practical Reason), ed. cit.,* Vol. V, pp. 31, 47, 55, etc.
17. *Nouveaux Essais sur l'Entendement Humain,* Ed. Erdmann (Berlin, 1840), Book 1, cap. 2, p. 215.
18. Cf. Heinrich Mans introduction to the Insel Verlag edition.

and consequence. She is a proficient manipulator of the organ of rational thought. In regard to self-control, her directions are at times related to Kant's as the special application is to its basic proposition: "Therefore virtue, to the extent that it is founded upon inner freedom, also contains an affirmative commandment for men, which is to bring all their abilities and inclinations under its control [i.e., of reason], and therefore under self-control, which prevails over the negative commandment not to be ruled by one's emotions and inclinations [the duty of apathy]; because, unless reason takes the reins of government into its hand, emotions and inclinations will be in control."[19] Juliette preaches on the self-discipline of the criminal: "Work out your plan a few days beforehand; consider all its consequences; be attentive to what might assist you . . . what might betray you, and weigh up all these things with the same callousness you would apply if you were certain to be discovered."[20] The murderer's face must display the greatest calm. ". . . Let your features express calm and equanimity; and try to summon up an extreme degree of callousness . . . if you were not certain that no pangs of conscience would attack you (and you will be so assured only through constant habituation to crime) . . . all your efforts to control your features and gestures would be of no account. . . ."[21] For formalistic reason, freedom from the bite of conscience is as essential as the absence of love or hate. Repentance posits the past (which popular ideology, in contradistinction to the bourgeoisie, always considered null and void) as existent; it is reversion, to prevent which was for bourgeois practice, its only justification. Spinoza echoes the Stoics: "*Poenitentia virtus non est, sive ex ratione non oritur, sed is, quem facti poenitet, bis miser seu impotens est.*"[22] Wholly in the spirit of Francavilla, he then goes on to remark: "*terret vulgus, nisi metuat,*"[23] and therefore asserts (as a good Machiavellian) that humility and repentance, like fear and hope, can be

19. *Metaphysische Anfänge der Tugendlehre, ed. cit.,* Vol. VI, p. 408.
20. *Juliette, ed. cit.,* Vol. IV, p. 58.
21. *Ibid.,* pp. 60f.
22. Spinoza, *Ethica,* Pars IV, Prop. LIV, p. 368.
23. *Ibid.,* Schol.

very useful despite their irrationality. "Apathy (in the form of rigor)," says Kant, "is a necessary presupposition of virtue,"[24] and (not unlike Sade) he distinguishes this "moral apathy" from insensibility in the shape of indifference to sensory stimuli. Enthusiasm is bad. Calmness and decisiveness constitute the strength of virtue. "That is the state of health in the moral life; an emotion, on the other hand, even when awakened by the notion of good, is but a transient brilliance succeeded by languor."[25] Juliette's friend Clairwil affirms the same thing in regard to vice:[26] "My soul is unyielding, and I am far from preferring sensibility to happy indifference, in which I rejoice. Oh Juliette . . . you are probably deluded as to that dangerous sensibility on which so many fools pride themselves." Apathy appears at those turning points of bourgeois history (even in ancient times) when the sovereign historical tendency makes the *pauci beati* aware of their own impotence. Apathy indicates the reversion of individual human spontaneity into the private world which was thereby established as the bourgeois life-form proper. Stoicism (which is the bourgeois philosophy) makes it easier for the privileged, confronted with the suffering of others, to steel themselves to their own threats. It confirms the general by elevating private existence, as a protection from the generality, to the condition of a principle. The bourgeois' private sphere is upper-class cultural material that has lost its status.

Juliette believes in science. She wholly despises any form of worship whose rationality cannot be demonstrated: belief in God and his dead Son, obedience to the Ten Commandments, good rather than evil, not sin but salvation. She is attracted by the reactions proscribed by the legends of civilization. She operates with semantics and logical syntax like the most up-to-date positivism, but does not anticipate this servant of our own administration in directing her linguistic criticism primarily against thought and philosophy; instead, as a child of the aggressive Enlightenment, she fixes upon religion. "A dead god!" she says

24. *Metaphysische Anfänge der Tugendlehre, ed. cit.*, Vol. VI, p. 408.
25. *Ibid.*, p. 409.
26. *Juliette, ed. cit.*, Vol. II, p. 114.

of Christ:[27] "Nothing is more ridiculous than the Catholic dictionary's nonsequacious God = infinite, and death = finite. Idiotic Christians, what are you to do with your dead God?" Her particular passion is to transform what has been damned as devoid of scientific proof into something worth aspiring after, to transform what is acknowledged without evidence into the object of abomination—the transvaluation of all values, the "courage to do what is forbidden"[28] (but without Nietzsche's telltale "Come!", without his biological idealism). "Are pretexts necessary in order to commit a crime?" asks Princess Borghese, Juliette's friend, wholly in Nietzsche's sense.[29] And he proclaims the quintessence of her theory:[30] "The weak and unsuccessful must perish; this is the first proposition of *our* philanthropy. And they should even be helped on their way. What is more injurious than any vice—the compassion of action for all failures and weaklings—Christianity . . ."[31] Christianity, ". . . singularly desirous of subjugating tyrants and forcing them to acknowledge the doctrine of brotherhood . . . takes up the role of the weak; it represents them and has to speak and sound like them . . . We should be persuaded that this bond [of fraternity] was, in truth, proposed by the weak and sanctioned by them when sacerdotal authority happened to fall into their hands."[32] This is the contribution of Noirceuil, Juliette's mentor, to the genealogy of morals. Nietzsche maliciously celebrates the powerful and their cruelty: "exerted without, where the alien world begins," against, that is, everything which does not belong to them. "There they enjoy freedom from any social constraint, and dally in the wilderness to compensate themselves for the tension brought about by long enclosure in the peaceful atmosphere of their society; they return to the guiltlessness of a predatory conscience, as exultant beasts who amble off after,

27. *Juliette, ed. cit.*, Vol. III, p. 282.
28. Nietzsche, *Umwertung aller Werte* (*Transvaluation of All Values*), *Werke* (Kröner), Vol. VIII, p. 213.
29. *Juliette, ed. cit.*, Vol. IV, p. 204.
30. E. Dühren (in *Neue Forschungen*, Berlin, 1904, pp. 453ff.) has referred to the association.
31. Nietzsche, *ed. cit.*, Vol. VIII, p. 218.
32. *Juliette, ed. cit.*, Vol. I, pp. 315f.

say, a frightful sequence of murder, arson, rape, and torture, as if it were all no more than some student's prank, yet convinced that they have provided their bards with something to celebrate for ages to come . . . This 'courage' displayed by superior races, which is outrageous, absurd, and sudden, the very incalculability and improbability of their enterprises . . . their indifference to and contempt for safety, body, life, comfort, their ghastly serenity and profound pleasure in all destruction and in all the debauchery of conquest and cruelty,"[33] this courage that Nietzsche so emphatically describes also captivates Juliette. To "live dangerously" is her mission too: ". . . *oser tout dorénavant sans peur.*"[34] There are the weak and the strong; there are classes, races and nations which rule, and there are those who are defeated. "Where, I ask you," cries Verneuil,[35] "is the mortal stupid enough to swear against all the evidence to the contrary that men are born equal in justice and in fact? Only such an enemy of mankind as Rousseau could assert this paradox, because being so very weak himself he wished to draw down to his level those to whose height he could not ascend. But what impudence, I ask you, could allow the pygmy of four feet two inches to compare himself with the stature that nature has endowed with the strength and form of a Hercules? The fly might as well rank itself with the elephant. Strength, beauty, stature, eloquence: these were the virtues that in the dawn of society proved decisive when authority passed into the rulers' hands." "To require of strength," Nietzsche continues,[36] "that it should *not* assert itself as strength, that it should *not* be a will to conquer, a will to overthrow, a will to be master, a thirst for enmity and resistance and triumph, is as senseless as to demand of weakness that it masquerade as strength."—"How in truth can you require," says Verneuil,[37] "that he who has been endowed by nature with an eminent capacity for crime, whether

33. *Genealogie der Moral (Genealogy of Morals), ed. cit.,* Vol. VII, pp. 321ff.

34. *Juliette, ed. cit.,* Vol. I, p. 300.

35. *Histoire de Justine* (Holland, 1797), Vol. IV, p. 4 (also cited by Dühren, *art. cit.,* p. 452).

36. *Genealogie der Moral, ed. cit.,* Vol. VII. p. 326f.

37. *Justine, ed. cit.,* Vol. IV, p. 7.

by virtue of the superiority of his powers, and the refinement of his physical organs, or through an education conformable to his station or through his riches; how, I repeat, can you require that this individual should have to obey the same law that calls all to virtue or to moderation? Is the law more just when it punishes the two men alike? Is it natural that he whom everything invites to commit evil should be treated exactly as he whom everything drives to behave prudently?"

When the objective systematization of nature has been disposed of as prejudice and myth, nature remains only as a material mass. Nietzsche knows of no law "which we not only acknowledge, but acknowledge as above us."[38] In so far as the understanding, which owes its importance to the yardstick of survival, recognizes a law of existence, it is that of the stronger. Even though the formalism of reason does not allow it to offer a necessary pattern for mankind, it nevertheless enjoys the advantage of actuality as against the untruthful ideology. Nietzsche's theory is that the weak are guilty, for they circumvent the natural law by means of cunning. "The physically disadvantaged are man's greatest enemy, not the evil, and not the 'predators.' Those who are unfortunate, conquered, ruined from the start—they, the weak, are most responsible for the undermining of men's life in common; they are the ones who most effectively embitter and question our trust in life, in men, and in ourselves."[39] They are responsible for the spread of Christianity, which Nietzsche hates and despises no less than Sade. ". . . nature does not actually prescribe any reprisals which the weak may take upon the strong; these reprisals exist in the moral though not in the physical realm; in order to take such reprisals, a weak man must use physical forces he does not possess; he must assume a character with which he is in no way endowed; he must in some way go against nature. But that sage mother's laws do unequivocally stipulate that the mighty injure the feeble, since the mighty can have received their gifts for no other end. Unlike the weak, the strong individual never

38. *Nachlass, ed. cit.*, Vol. XI, p. 214.
39. *Genealogie der Moral, ed. cit.*, Vol. VII, p. 433.

adopts another persona; he merely expresses in action what he has received from nature. Therefore everything he does is natural: his oppression, his violences, his cruelties, his tyrannies, his injustices . . . are as pure as the hand that impressed them in him; and when he exercises all his rights to oppress the weak and to rob them, he does only the most natural thing in the world . . . Therefore we should never have any qualms about what we can snatch from the weak, for it is not we who are criminal in acting thus; rather it is the defensive reaction or vengeance of the weak which qualifies our deeds as criminal."[40] If the weak man defends himself, he does wrong, "in betraying the character of weakness which nature has engraved in him; she created him to be a slave and poor; he will not submit to slavery and poverty: that is his fault."[41] Thus Dorval, the leader of a respectable Parisian gang, expounds for Juliette's benefit the secret credo of all ruling classes, for which, with the addition of the psychology of resentment, Nietzsche reproaches the modern age. Like Juliette, he admires "the terrible beauty of the deed,"[42] even though, as a German professor, he parts company from Sade in rejecting criminals because their egotism "is directed and restricted to such low ends. If the aims are high, then mankind has another yardstick and does not judge 'crime'—even the most frightful means—as such."[43] The enlightened Juliette is still free from this preference for the big thing, which is actually characteristic of the bourgeois world. She finds the racketeer no less agreeable than the minister because his sacrifices are numerically smaller. The German Nietzsche, however, makes beauty dependent on extent; despite all the twilight of the idols, he cannot abandon the idealistic convention which would accept the hanging of a petty thief and elevate imperialistic raids to the level of world-historical missions. By raising the cult of strength to a world-historical doc-

40. *Juliette, ed. cit.,* Vol. I, pp. 208ff.
41. *Ibid.,* pp. 211f.
42. *Jenseits von Gut und Böse* (*Beyond Good and Evil*), *ed. cit.,* Vol. III, p. 100.
43. *Nachlass, ed. cit.,* Vol. XII, p. 108.

trine, German Fascism also took it to an absurd extreme. As a protest against civilization, the masters' morality conversely represents the oppressed. Hatred of atrophied instincts actually denounces the true nature of the task-masters—which comes to light only in their victims. But as a Great Power, or state religion, the masters' morality wholly subscribes to the civilizing powers that be, the compact majority, resentment, and everything that it formerly opposed. The realization of Nietzsche's assertions both refutes them and at the same time reveals their truth, which—despite all his affirmation of life—was inimical to the spirit of reality.

If repentance is senseless, then pity is sin pure and simple. Whoever surrenders to compassion "perverts the general law: whence it results that pity, far from being a virtue, becomes a real vice once it leads us to interfere with an inequality prescribed by nature's laws."[44] Sade and Nietzsche recognized that, after the formalization of reason, pity still remained as, so to speak, the sensual consciousness of the identity of the general and the particular, as naturalized mediation. It constitutes the most compulsive form of prejudice, *"quamvis pietatis specimen prae se ferre videatur,"* as Spinoza says,[45] "for anyone whom neither reason nor compassion moves to help others is justly called inhuman."[46] *Commiseratio* is humanity in a direct form, but at the same time *"mala et inutilis,"*[47] that is, as the opposite of manly prowess which, from the Roman *virtus* by way of the Medicis down to the efficiency required by the Ford family, has always been the only true bourgeois virtue. Clairwil calls compassion womanly and childish, as she boasts of her "stoicism," the "serene command over the emotions" which allows her "to do, and to continue to do, everything without any feeling."[48] ". . . Compassion is nothing less than a virtue; it is a weakness, born of fear and misfortune, a weakness which must above

44. *Juliette, ed. cit.,* Vol. I, p. 313.
45. *Ethica,* Pars. IV, Appendix, Cap. XVI.
46. *Ibid.,* Prop. L. Schol.
47. *Ibid.,* Prop. L.
48. *Juliette, ed. cit.,* Vol. II, p. 125.

all be overcome when one strives to suppress the excessive sensitivity which is irreconcilable with the maxims of philosophy."[49] Woman is the source of "outbreaks of unrestrained compassion."[50] Sade and Nietzsche knew that their doctrine of the sinfulness of compassion was an old bourgeois heritage. Nietzsche refers to all "strong ages," to "superior cultures," and Sade to Aristotle[51] and the Peripatetics.[52] Compassion did not hold out against philosophy. Even Kant himself made no exception in its favor. According to him, it can be "softheartedness" and without the "dignity of virtue."[53] He does not see, however, that the principle of "general benevolence toward the human race,"[54] by which (in contradistinction to Clairwil's rationalism) he seeks to replace compassion, is subject to the same anathema of irrationality as "this benign passion" which can easily lead a man to become "a soft-hearted idler." Enlightenment is not deceived; for enlightenment, the general has no advantage over the particular fact, and all-encompassing love is not superior to limited love. Compassion is disreputable. Like Sade, Nietzsche appeals to the *ars poetica.* "The Greeks, according to Aristotle, suffered from excessive pity: consequently it had to be discharged through tragedy. We can see how dangerous this inclination seemed to them. It is a threat to the state, takes away the necessary rigor and discipline, makes heroes behave like whimpering women, and so on."[55] And Zarathustra preaches thus: "I see so much goodness and so much weakness. So much justice and compassion, so much weakness."[56] In fact, there is an aspect of compassion which conflicts with justice, to which Nietzsche of course allies it. It confirms the rule of inhumanity by the exception which it practices. By reserving the cancellation of injustice to fortuitous love of one's neighbor, compassion accepts that the

49. *Ibid.*
50. *Nietzsche contra Wagner, ed. cit.,* Vol. VIII, p. 204.
51. *Juliette, ed. cit.,* Vol. I, p. 313.
52. *Juliette, ed. cit.,* Vol. II, p. 126.
53. *Beobachtungen über das Gefühl des Schönen und Erhabenen, ed. cit.,* Vol. II, p. 215f.
54. *Ibid.*
55. *Nachlass, ed. cit.,* Vol. XI, pp. 227f.
56. *Also Sprach Zarathustra, ed. cit.,* Vol. VI, p. 248.

law of universal alienation—which it would mitigate—is unalterable. Certainly, as an individual, the compassionate man represents the claim of the generality—that is, to live—against the generality, against nature and society, which deny it. But that unity with the universal, as with the heart, which the individual displays, is shown to be deceptive in his own weakness. It is not the softness but the restrictive element in pity which makes it questionable; for compassion is always inadequate. Just as the stoic indifference from which the bourgeois coldness, the antithesis of compassion, is descended was more loyal to the universal which it rejected than the participant communuality which adapted itself to the world, so those who discredited compassion in fact declared themselves (though negatively) for revolution. The narcissistic distortions of pity, such as the exaltations of the philanthropist and the moral self-awareness of the social welfare worker, are still intensified confirmations of the distinction between rich and poor. Of course, the fact that philosophy carelessly divulged the pleasure of rigor made it accessible to those least prepared to excuse such an avowal. The Fascist masters of this world have transformed the deprecation of compassion into a rejection of political indulgence and into recourse to martial law, in which point they agree with Schopenhauer, the metaphysician of pity. For Schopenhauer, any hope for the establishment of humanity was the fond delusion of a man who had nothing but misfortune to hope for. The enemies of compassion were unwilling to equate man with misfortune. They looked on the existence of misfortune as an outrage. The very sensitivity of their actual impotence could not suffer man to be pitied. In despair, they lent their voices to the celebration of power, but disclaimed allegiance to it in practice —while constructing the very causeways of power.

Goodness and benevolence become sin, whereas domination and oppression become virtue. "All good things were once bad things; every original sin has given birth to an original virtue."[57] In this, Juliette is properly a child of the new age: for the first time she is consciously performing a transvaluation of values.

57. *Genealogie der Moral, ed. cit.,* Vol. VII, p. 421.

When all ideologies have been abrogated, she adopts as her own morality what Christianity—ideologically, if not always in practice—always held to be execrable. As a good philosopher she remains cool and reflective. When Clairwil proposes some sacrilege, she replies: "As soon as we no longer believe in God, my dear . . . the desecrations you call for are no more than vain trifles . . . Perhaps I am more rigid than you; my atheism is whole-hearted. Do not imagine that I need the childish tricks you suggest to strengthen it. I shall take part because they amuse you, but purely for diversion" (the American murderess Annie Henry would have said "just for fun") "and never out of necessity, whether to confirm my way of thinking or to bring others round to it."[58] Her principles prevail. Even injustice, hatred, and destruction are regulated, automatic procedures, since the formalization of reason has caused all goals to lose, as delusion, any claim to necessity and objectivity. Magic is transferred to mere activity, to means—in short, to industry. The formalization of reason is only the intellectual expression of mechanized production. The means is fetishized, and absorbs pleasure. Just as enlightenment in theory turns into illusions with whose ends the old form of domination decked itself out, so enlightenment uses the possibility of abundance to deprive it of its practical basis. Domination survives as an end in itself. in the form of economic power. Indulgence already displays a trace of something outdated and unobjective—like the metaphysics which forbade it. Juliette talks of the motives for crime.[59] She is herself no less ambitious and avaricious than her friend Sbrigani, but she deifies the forbidden. Sbrigani, the man of means and duty, is more progressive: "To enrich ourselves is the point of it all; we are quite guilty if we fall short of this goal. Only when one is well on the way to being rich, is one entitled to reap one's pleasures; until then they must be forgotten." Despite all her rationalism, Juliette is still somewhat superstitious. She sees the childishness of sacrilege, yet in the end derives pleasure from it. But every indulgence betrays an

58. *Juliette, ed. cit.*, Vol. III, pp. 78f.
59. *Juliette, ed. cit.*, Vol. IV, pp. 126f.

idol: pleasure is self-sacrifice to another. Nature does not feature enjoyment as such; natural pleasure does not go beyond the appeasement of need. All pleasure is social—in unsublimated no less than in sublimated emotions. It originates in alienation. Even when the enjoyment lacks any knowledge of the interdiction against which it offends, it owes its origin to civilization, to the fixed order from which it longs to return to nature, against which that very order protects it. Men sense the magic of enjoyment only in that dream which releases them from the pressure of work and the bond which joins the individual to a specific social function and, ultimately, to the self—that dream which leads back to a primeval era without masters and without discipline. The homesickness of man enmeshed in civilization, the "objective despair" of those who were forced to become part of the social order, was the longing from which the affection for gods and demons was bred, and which men worshipped as a transfigured nature. Thought originated in the course of liberation from a terrifying nature, which was finally wholly mastered. Pleasure is, so to speak, nature's vengeance. In pleasure men disavow thought and escape civilization. In the ancient societies festivals offered a communal celebration of this reversion. The primitive orgies are the collective origin of enjoyment. "This interval of universal confusion represented by the festival," says Roger Caillois, "masquerades as the moment in which the world order is abrogated. Therefore all excesses are allowed during it. Your behavior must be contrary to the rules. Everything should be back to front. In the mythic age the course of time was reversed: one was born as an old man, and died a child . . . in this way all those laws which protect the good natural and social order are systematically violated."[60] One surrenders to the glorified primeval powers; but, from the viewpoint of the suspended interdiction, this action seems only dissolute and insane.[61] Only with the firm growth of civilization and enlightenment is the self strong enough and domination secure enough to turn festival into farce. The masters introduce

60. *Théorie de la Fête* (*Nouvelle Revue Française*, Jan. 1940), p. 49.
61. See Caillois, *art. cit.*

the notion of enjoyment as something rational, as a tribute paid to a not yet wholly contained nature; at the same time they try to decontaminate it for their own use, to retain it in their higher form of culture; and administer it sparingly to their subjects where they cannot be wholly deprived of it. Enjoyment becomes the object of manipulation, until, ultimately, it is entirely extinguished in fixed entertainments. The process has developed from the primitive festival to the modern vacation. "As the social organism grows increasingly complex, so it become less prepared to tolerate any arrestation of the conventional course of life. Everything must go on today as it did yesterday and will tomorrow. The general overflow of emotion is no longer possible. The period of license has been individualized. Holidays have replaced the festival."[62] Under Fascism holidays are enhanced by the phony collective euphoria produced by radio, slogans, and benzedrine. Sbrigani anticipates this to some extent. He allows himself some enjoyment, as a sort of vacation *"sur la route de la fortune."* Juliette, on the other hand, keeps to the *Ancien Régime,* and deifies sin. Her libertinage is as marked by Catholicism as the nun's ecstasy is by paganism.

Nietzsche recognizes the still mythic quality of all pleasure. By paying tribute to nature, enjoyment relinquishes the possible, just as compassion renounces the transformation of the whole. Both feature an aspect of resignation. Nietzsche detects it in every nook and cranny—as self-enjoyment in loneliness, as masochism in the depressions of the self-tormentor: "Down with all those who merely enjoy!"[63] Juliette tries to retain enjoyment by rejecting the faithful bourgeois love which is characteristic of the bourgeoisie in the last century as a form of resistance to its own cunning. In love enjoyment was coupled with a deification of man, who vouchsafed it; it was the human emotion proper. Finally it was revoked as a sexually conditioned value judgment. In the pietistic adoration of the lover, as in the boundless admiration he commanded from his sweetheart, the actual slavery of woman was glorified anew. By

62. Caillois, *art. cit.,* pp. 58f.
63. *Nachlass, ed. cit.,* Vol. XII, p. 364.

acknowledging this thralldom, the sexes were eternally reconciled. Woman appeared voluntarily to accept defeat, and man to concede her the victory. In marriage, Christianity transfigured the hierarchy of the sexes, the yoke that the male organization of property had put on the female character, as a union of hearts, thus assuaging the reminiscence of the better past enjoyed by women in pre-patriarchal times. The decay of middle-class possession, the disappearance of the free economic subject, affects the family: it is no longer the formerly landed cell of society, because it no longer constitutes the basis of the citizen's economic existence. Young people no longer have the family as the horizon of their developing lives; the autonomy of the father disappears, and with it resistance to his authority. Before, thralldom in her father's house would awaken an emotion in a girl which seemed to point to freedom, even though it was actually realized either in marriage or somewhere else outside. But now that a girl has the prospect of a job before her, that of love is obstructed. The more universally the modern industrial system requires everyone to bind himself to it, the more everyone who is not part of the ocean of "white trash" into which the unqualified employed and unemployed pour, will tend to become the smalltime expert, the creature who has to fend for himself. As qualified labor, the independence of the entrepreneur (which is of the past) envelops all (including the "professional" woman) as their nature. Men's self-respect grows in proportion to their easy replacement. Nevertheless, there is as little opposition to the family as the leisure relationship with the boy friend is really the way to paradise. Men enter into the rational, calculating relation to their own kind, that in Juliette's enlightened circle has long passed as proverbial. Mind and body are separated in reality, just as the libertines required. "It seems to me," is Noirceuil's rationalistic opinion,[64] "that love and pleasure are very different things . . . for the sentiments of tenderness correspond to the conditions of humor and convenience, but are in no way dependent on the beauty of a neck or a handsomely curved thigh. These objects which, as taste decrees,

64. *Juliette, ed. cit.,* Vol. II, pp. 81f.

effectively arouse our physical emotions, have, I think, no right of access to the intellectual emotions. To put it more explicitly, Bélize is unattractive, forty, has not a whit of elegance about her, not one regular feature, and no grace; yet Bélize has spirit, an admirable nature, a million things which accord with my own feelings and preferences; I shall never wish to sleep with Bélize, but I shall nevertheless continue to love her to distraction. On the other hand, I shall lust after Araminthe, but heartily detest her as soon as the pitch of desire is gone ... ." The unavoidable consequence, already implicit in the Cartesian separation of man into cognitive and extensive substances, is quite explicitly expressed as the destruction of romantic love, which is actually a disguise, a rationalization of physical impulse, "a false and always dangerous metaphysic," as Count Belmor puts it in his long speech on love.[65] Juliette's friends, despite all their libertinage, conceive of sexuality as against tenderness, worldly as against divine love, not just a mite too excessively but as less innocuous than they are. The beauty of a neck and the curve of a thigh do not arouse sexuality as a-historical, purely natural facts, but as images which comprise all social experience. In this experience there survives an intention of something other than nature, of love which is not restricted to sex. Tenderness, however, by far the least physical form, is transformed sexuality; the passing of a hand over a head of hair, a kiss on the forehead, which express the delusion of spiritual love, are pacified forms of the blows and bites of the sex act as performed by Australian aborigines. The separation is an abstract one. Metaphysics, says Belmor, falsifies the facts, and prevents the lover from being seen as he really is: it originates in magic, and serves only to veil and mystify. "And I am not to tear it away from my eyes! That is weakness . . . cowardice. Once the pleasure is past we must analyze this goddess who so dazzled me beforehand."[66] Love itself is an unscientific term: ". . . false definitions always lead us astray," explains Dolmance in the memorable fifth dialogue of the *Philosophie dans le Boudoir*. "The heart—I do not

---

65. *Juliette, ed. cit.*, Vol. III, pp. 172f.
66. *Juliette, ed. cit.*, Vol. III, pp. 176f.

know what it is. I merely use the word for temerity of spirit."[67]
"Let us spend but a moment, as Lucretius says, in the background of life," that is, in cold-blooded analysis, "and we shall
find that neither the elevation of the beloved nor romantic sentiment can resist our analysis . . . it is only the body that I love,
and it is only the body that I lament over, even though I can
have it again at any time."[68] What is true in all this is the insight
into the dissociation of love, the work of progress. This dissociation, which mechanizes pleasure and distorts longing into deceit,
attacks the core of love. By praising genital and perverted sex
to the disadvantage of unnatural, immaterial, and illusionary
sexuality, the libertine throws himself in with that normality
that belittles and diminishes not only the utopian exuberance of
love but its physical pleasure, not only the happiness of the
seventh heaven but that of the immediate reality. The rake without illusions (whom Juliette stands for) transforms himself
with the assistance of sex educators, psychoanalysts, and hor-
mone physiologists into the open and practical man who extends
his attitude to sport and hygiene to his sexual life. Juliette's
critique is discordant, like the Enlightenment itself. In so far as
the flagrant violation of the taboo, which was once allied to the
bourgeois revolution, has not adjusted proficiently to the new
reality, it lives on with sublime love as faith in that now proximate utopia which makes sexual pleasure free for all.

"The ridiculous enthusiasm" which confined us to the specific
individual, and the elevation of woman in love, can be traced
back beyond Christianity to matriarchal stages of society. ". . .
It is certain that our spirit of noble courtship, which ludicrously
makes us pay homage to the object which is made only to satisfy
our need, originated in the reverence which our forefathers
formerly extended to women because of their functions as urban
or rural prophetesses: fear caused men to turn what was once
timidity into a cult; chivalry was nurtured in the womb of superstition. But nature never knew this awe, and it would be a
waste of time to seek it there. The inferiority of this sex in

67. Edition privée par Helpey, p. 267.
68. *Juliette, ed. cit.*, Vol. III, pp. 176f.

respect to our own is far too firmly grounded for it ever to arouse any strong motivation in us that would cause us to pay it respect. The love which arises from this blind awe is, like itself, but a prejudice."[69] Though it may seek a legalistic covering, the social hierarchy is ultimately dependent on force. Mastery over nature is reproduced within humanity. Christian civilization, which allowed the idea of protecting the physically weak to be used for the exploitation of the strong serf, was never able wholly to win over the hearts of the converted nations. The principle of love was too firmly disavowed by the exactness of understanding and the still more precise weapons of the Christian rulers, until Lutheranism extinguished the antithesis of state and doctrine by making the word and the scourge the essence of the Gospel. It directly equated spiritual freedom with the affirmation of actual oppression. Woman, however, is marked out by her weakness; her weakness puts her in the minority, even where women are numerically superior to men. As with the oppressed aboriginal inhabitants in early national states, or the colonial natives whose organization and weapons are primitive compared with those of their conquerors, or the Jews among the "Aryans," women's defenselessness is the legal title of their oppression. Sade provides a formulation for Strindberg's reflections: "We should not doubt that there is as certain and major a difference between man and woman as between man and the apes in the wilderness. We have just as good grounds for denying women a title to be part of our race as we have for refusing to acknowledge the ape as our brother. Examine carefully a naked woman by the side of a man of her age, naked as she is, and the obvious difference (quite apart from sex) in the structure of these two creatures will easily persuade you that the woman is but a lower degree of the man; the differences are equally to be found within, the anatomical differentiation of one from the other when meticulously examined one against the other brings this truth into the light of day."[70] The attempt of Christianity ideologically to compensate the oppression of the one sex by means of reverence for woman, and thus

69. *Ibid.*, pp. 178f.
70. *Ibid.*, pp. 188–89.

to cultivate rather than to suppress the memory of an archaic age, is redeemed by resentment of the ennobled woman and the theoretically emancipated pleasure. The emotion which corresponds to the practice of oppression is contempt, not reverence, and in the centuries of Christianity love for one's neighbor has always concealed a lurking, forbidden though now compulsive, hatred for woman—the object which served repeatedly to recall the fact of futile exertion. This hatred made up for the cult of the Madonna with the persecution of witches—a form of vengeance on the memory of those pre-Christian prophetesses, the lasting afterimage which implicitly called in question the sacralized patriarchal order of domination. Woman arouses the primitive anger of the half-converted man who is required to revere her, just as the weak individual awakens the enmity of the superficially civilized strong man who is supposed to protect him. Sade makes this latent hatred conscious. "I have never believed," says Count Ghigi, the Roman police chief, "that the union of two bodies must always produce a union of two hearts. In this physical conjoining I can see a strong motive for contempt . . . and for aversion, but none for love."[71] And Saint-Fonds, the royal minister, declares when a girl whom he is torturing breaks into tears: "That's how I like women . . . if only I could reduce them all to such a state with a single word!"[72] Man as ruler denies woman the honor of individualization. Socially, the individual is an example of the species, a representative of her sex; and therefore male logic sees her wholly as standing for nature, as the substrate of never-ending subsumption notionally, and of never-ending subjection in reality Woman as an alleged natural being is a product of history, which denaturizes her. But the desperate will to destroy everything that embodies the allurement of nature, the attraction of the physiological, biological, national, and social underdog, shows that Christianity has miscarried. ". . . que ne puis-je, d'un mot, les réduire toutes en cet état!" Wholly to expunge the odious overpowering longing to return to a state of nature is the cruelty produced by an abortive civilization: barbarism, the

71. *Juliette, ed. cit.,* Vol. IV, p. 261.
72. *Juliette, ed. cit.,* Vol. II, p. 273.

other face of culture. ". . . Them all!" Annihilation allows of no exception. The will to destruction is totalitarian. "I go so far," says Juliette to the Pope, "as to wish Tiberius that all mankind had but a single head, that I might have the pleasure of severing it at one blow!"[73] The signs of powerlessness, sudden uncoordinated movements, animal fear, confusion, awaken the thirst for blood. The justification of hatred for woman that represents her as intellectually and physically inferior, and bearing the brand of domination on her forehead, is equally that of hatred for Jews. Women and Jews can be seen not to have ruled for thousands of years. They live, although they could be exterminated; and their fear and weakness, the greater affinity to nature which perennial oppression produces in them, is the very element which gives them life. This enrages the strong, who must pay for their strength with an intense alienation from nature, and must always suppress their fear. They identify themselves with nature when they hear their victims utter over and over again the cry that they dare not themselves emit. "The foolish creatures," says Blammont in *Aline et Valcour*, "how I love to have them struggle in my hands! They are like lambs in the lion's jaws."[74] And in the same letter: "It is just like pillaging a town . . . you have to get control of the heights . . . you establish yourself in all the important points, and then you attack the center without any fear of resistance."[75] What lies below draws the attack upon itself: it is most pleasurable to inflict humiliation where misfortune has already hit hard. The less danger there is for those above, the more refined the pleasure they will derive from the anguish they are about to inflict. Domination comes really into its own principle of discipline when the quarry is cornered and desperate. The fear that no longer threatens the dominator himself explodes in hearty laughter—an expression of the inward obduracy of the individual in himself, who lives his life to the full only in the collective.

Resounding laughter has served to denounce civilization in

73. *Juliette, ed. cit.*, Vol. IV, p. 379.
74. *Aline et Valcour* (Brussels, 1883), Vol. I, p. 58.
75. *Ibid.*, p. 57.

every age. "The most destructive lava which the crater of the human mouth spews out is hilarity," says Victor Hugo in the chapter which bears the title "Human tempests are worse than those of the seas."[76] "One must," says Juliette,[77] "as far as possible allow the weight of one's malice to fall on those in distress; the tears drawn from misery provide a most powerful stimulant for one's nervous energies . . ."[78] Pleasure is joined not with tenderness but with cruelty, and sexual love becomes what, according to Nietzsche,[79] it always was: "in means, war; and, basically, the deadly hatred of the sexes." And zoology tells us that, in the male and female, "love" or sexual attraction were originally and essentially "sadistic," and undoubtedly associated with pain; love is as cruel as hunger.[80] It is as if the final result of civilization were a return to the terrors of nature. That fatal love which Sade highlights, and Nietzsche's ashamedly unashamed magnanimity which would go to any extreme to save the suffering from humiliation: cruelty as greatness, when imagined in play or fancy, deals as harshly with men as German Fascism does in reality. Whereas, however, the unconscious colossus of actuality, anti-individualistic capitalism, proceeds blindly on its course of annihilation, the rebellious though deluded individual is fulfilled by that same fatal love. And so that same icy and perverted love which in the world of things takes the place of straightforward love, is directed against men—who are misused as things. Sickness becomes a symptom of recovery. In the ecstasy of sacrifice delusion recognizes its own humiliation, and becomes equal to the enormity of domination that in real life it is powerless to overcome. In the shape of dread, imagination seeks to resist dread. The Roman proverb which held that harshness is true pleasure expresses the insoluble contradiction of order, which transforms happiness into a travesty of happiness when sanctioning it, and manufactures it when

76. Victor Hugo, *L'Homme qui rit*, Vol. VIII, cap. 7.
77. *Juliette, ed. cit.*, Vol. IV, p. 199.
78. Cf. *Les 120 Journées de Sodome* (Paris, 1935), Vol. II, p. 308.
79. *Der Fall Wagner, ed. cit.*, Vol. VIII, p. 10.
80. R. Briffault, *The Mothers* (New York, 1927), Vol. I, p. 119.

113

proscribing it. In immortalizing this contradiction, Sade and Nietzsche made it a concept.

In the face of the *ratio*, devotion to the object of adoration appears as idolatry. The dissolution of idol worship is a consequence of the interdiction on mythology enacted in Jewish monotheism and carried out by its secularized form, the Enlightenment, in the course of various forms of philosophic attack on changing forms of worship. The decay of the economic reality which was always at the basis of a particular superstition liberated the specific forces of negation. Christianity, however, propagated love—the pure adoration of Jesus. It tried to elevate blind sexual impulse in the sanctification of marriage, just as it attempted to bring the crystalline Law closer to this earth by the device of divine grace. The reconciliation of civilization with nature, which Christianity tried prematurely to contrive by means of its doctrine of the crucified god, remained as alien to Judaism as to the rigorism of the Enlightenment. Moses and Kant did not proclaim feeling, and their cold Law knows neither love nor the stake. Nietzsche's struggle against monotheism hits more profoundly at Christian than at Jewish teaching. Of course he denies the Law, but he is for the "higher self,"[81] not for the natural but the more-than-natural. He wants to replace God by the superman, because monotheism, even in its modified Christian form, can now be seen for what it is. But, just as in the service of this "higher self" the old ascetic ideals are lauded by Nietzsche as self-mastery "for cultivation of supreme power,"[82] so the higher self shows itself to be a desperate attempt to rescue God (who is dead), and a renewal of Kant's effort to transform the divine law into autonomy in order to save European civilization—which gave up the ghost in English skepticism. Kant's principle that "everything is to be done on the basis of the maxim of one's will as one which, while legislating universally, can act with itself as an object"[83] is also the secret of the superman. His will is no less despotic than the categorical imperative. Both principles aim at independence from external

81. *Nachlass, ed. cit.*, Vol. XI, p. 216.
82. *Nachlass, ed. cit.*, Vol. XIV, p. 273.
83. *Grundlegung zur Metaphysik der Sitten, ed. cit.*, Vol. IV, p. 432.

powers, at the unconditioned maturity defined as the essence of enlightenment. But, of course, inasmuch as dread of lies (which even in the best moments Nietzsche still decried as "Don-Quixotery")[84] abrogates the Law through self-legislation and everything becomes as transparent as if it were but one great unveiled superstition, enlightenment itself—and, indeed, truth in any form—becomes an idol; then we see "that even we enlightened of this modern age, we the godless antimetaphysicians, still take *our* fire from the torch lit by a faith that has lived for thousands of years—the Christian belief (which was also the belief of Plato) that God is truth and that truth is divine."[85] Hence science, too, is subject to the critique of metaphysics. The denial of God contains an irremediable contradiction: it negates knowledge itself. Sade did not take Enlightenment thought to this, the point of reversal. For Sade, enlightenment is not so much an intellectual or spiritual as a social phenomenon. He took the dissolution of bonds (which Nietzsche sought idealistically to abrogate by means of the higher self), the critique of solidarity with society, duty, and family,[86] so far as to preach anarchy. His work discloses the mythological character of the principles which religion says are the foundations of civilization: the Decalogue, paternal authority, property. This is the precise reverse of the social theory which Le Play produced a hundred years later.[87] Each of the Ten Commandments is declared null and void by the tribunal of formal reason. They are wholly rejected as ideologies. In answer to Juliette's request,[88] the Pope finds it easier to rationalize unchristian actions than it was ever possible by the light of nature to justify the Christian principles according to which such actions are of the devil. The *"philosophe mitré"* who justifies murder must have recourse to less sophisms than did Maimonides and Aquinas, who condemned it. Roman reason is inclined even more than

84. *Die Fröhliche Wissenschaft (Joyful Wisdom)*, ed. cit., Vol. V, p. 275. Cf. *Genealogie der Moral*, ed. cit., Vol. VII, pp. 267–71.
85. *Die Fröhliche Wissenschaft*, ed. cit.
86. Cf. Nietzsche, *Nachlass*, ed. cit., Vol. XI, p. 216.
87. Cf. Le Play, *Les Ouvriers Européens* (Paris, 1879), Vol. I. See esp. pp. 133ff.
88. *Juliette*, ed. cit., Vol. IV, pp. 303ff.

the god of the Prussians to support the bigger side. But the Law is dethroned; and love, which would humanize the Law, is exposed. Science and industry denounced as metaphysics not merely romantic sexual love, but every kind of universal love, for reason displaces all love: that of woman for man as much as that of the lover for his sweetheart, parental affection as much as that of children for their parents. Blangis declares to the subordinated that even those related to the rulers—their daughters or their wives—will be treated as harshly as the others, nay more harshly, "precisely in order to show you how we despise the bonds you are deluded into thinking we too are held by."[89] The love of woman is dissolved as is that of man. The rules of libertinage, which Saint-Fonds describes to Juliette, are to apply to all women.[90] Dolmance provides the materialistic disenchantment of parental love: "These bonds derive from parents' fear that they will be deserted in their old age; and the degree of care which they show us in our infancy is intended to bring them the same attention in their dotage."[91] Sade's argument is as ancient as bourgeoisie. Even Democritus denounced human parental love as economically founded.[92] But Sade also disenchants exogamy, the foundation of civilization. According to him, there are no rational objections against incest,[93] and the hygienic argument offered against it has finally been retracted by modern science, which has ratified Sade's cool judgment: ". . . there is absolutely no proof that children born of incest tend more than others to be cretins, deaf-mutes, to suffer from rickets, and so forth."[94] The family, held together not by romantic sexual love, but by mother love, which constitutes the ground of all tenderness and social emotions,[95] conflicts with society itself. "Do not think you can make good republicans so

89. *Les 120 Journées de Sodome, ed. cit.,* Vol. I, p. 72.
90. Cf. *Juliette, ed. cit.,* Vol. II, p. 234, note.
91. *La Philosophie dans le Boudoir, ed. cit.,* p. 185.
92. Cf. Democritus (Diels, fragment 278, Berlin, 1912), Vol. II, pp. 117f.
93. *La Philosophie dans le Boudoir, ed. cit.,* p. 242.
94. S. Reinach, "La prohibition de l'inceste et le sentiment de la pudeur," in: *Cultes, Mythes et Religions* (Paris, 1905), Vol. I, p. 157.
95. *La Philosophie dans le Boudoir, ed. cit.,* p. 238.

long as you isolate in your family the children who should belong to the community alone . . . If it is wholly disadvantageous to allow children to imbibe interests from their family circle which are often quite different from those of their country, it is wholly advantageous to separate them from their family."[96] "Conjugal ties" are to be destroyed on social grounds; acquaintance with their faith is to be *"absolument interdite"* to children, who are *"uniquement les enfants de la patrie"*,[97] and anarchy, the individualism which Sade proclaimed in combatting the laws,[98] ends in the absolute rule of the generality, the republic. Just as the overthrown god returns in the form of a tougher idol, so the old bourgeois guardian state returns in the force of the Fascist collective. Sade conceived the full course of the state socialism with whose first steps St. Just and Robespierre tumbled. If the bourgeoisie sent them, its most loyal politicians, to the guillotine, it condemned its most outspoken writer to the hell of the Bibliothèque Nationale. For the *chronique scandaleuse* of Justine and Juliette, with its production-line methods, and its foreshadowing in an eighteenth-century style of the nineteenth-century shockers and twentieth-century mass literature, is the Homeric epic with its last mythological covering removed: the history of thought as an organ of domination. Now, frightened by its own image in its own glass, it discloses the prospect of what lies beyond it. It is not the ideal of a harmonious society—which, for Sade too, glimmered in the future: *"Gardez vos frontières et restez chez vous"*[99]—and not the socialist utopia delineated in the story of Zamé,[100] which makes Sade's work a spur to the salvation of the Enlightenment, but the fact that he did not leave it to the Enlightenment's opponents to make it take fright at its own nature.

Unlike its apologists, the black writers of the bourgeoisie have not tried to ward off the consequences of the Enlightenment by harmonizing theories. They have not postulated that

96. *Ibid.*, pp. 238–49.
97. *Ibid.*,
98. *Juliette, ed. cit.*, Vol. IV, pp. 240–44.
99. *La Philosophie dans le Boudoir, ed. cit.*, p. 263.
100. *Aline et Valcour, ed. cit.*, Vol. II, pp. 181ff.

formalistic reason is more closely allied to morality than to immorality. Whereas the optimistic writers merely disavowed and denied in order to protect the indissoluble union of reason and crime, civil society and domination, the dark chroniclers mercilessly declared the shocking truth. "Heaven vouchsafes these riches to those whose hands are soiled by the murder of wives and children, by sodomy, assassination, prostitution, and atrocities; to reward me for these shameful deeds, it offers me wealth," says Clairwil when summing up her brother's life history.[101] Of course she exaggerates. The justice of bad rule is not quite so consistent as to reward crime alone. But only exaggeration is true. The essential nature of prehistory is the appearance of extreme cruelty in detail. The statistical account of those slain in a pogrom, which includes those mercifully shot, obscures the essence which comes to light only in an exact portrayal of the exception, of the very worst atrocity. A fortunate life in a world of cruelty is shown to be the vicious contradiction it really is in the light of the mere existence of that world. Torture becomes the essential truth, and the happy life vanity. Certainly in the bourgeois era the murder of one's own wife and children, recourse to prostitution and bestiality, happen less to the rulers than to the ruled—who adopted the morals of the masters of earlier times. To that end, when power was at stake, they heaped up mountains of corpses even in later centuries. Compared with the attitude and deeds of the masters under Fascism, in which domination came into its own, the enthusiastic representation of the life of Brisa-Testa (in whom, admittedly, the Fascist countenance can be glimpsed) fades into an innocuous banality. In Sade as in Mandeville, private vice constitutes a predictive chronicle of the public virtues of the totalitarian era. Not to have glossed over or suppressed but to have trumpeted far and wide the impossibility of deriving from reason any fundamental argument against murder fired the hatred which the progressives (and they precisely) still direct against Sade and Nietzsche. They were significantly unlike the logical positivists in taking science at its word. The fact that Sade and

---

101. *Juliette, ed. cit.,* Vol. V, p. 232.

Nietzsche insist on the *ratio* more decisively even than logical positivism, implicitly liberates from its hiding-place the utopia contained in the Kantian notion of reason as in every great philosophy: the utopia of a humanity which, itself no longer distorted, has no further need to distort. Inasmuch as the merciless doctrines proclaim the identity of domination and reason, they are more merciful than those of the moralistic lackeys of the bourgeoisie. "Where do your greatest dangers lie?" was the question Nietzsche once posed himself,[102] and answered thus: "In compassion." With his denial he redeemed the unshakable confidence in man that is constantly betrayed by every form of assurance that seeks only to console.

102. *Die Fröhliche Wissenschaft, ed. cit.,* Vol. V, p. 205.

THE CULTURE INDUSTRY: ENLIGHTENMENT AS MASS DECEPTION

THE sociological theory that the loss of the support of objectively established religion, the dissolution of the last remnants of precapitalism, together with technological and social differentiation or specialization, have led to cultural chaos is disproved every day; for culture now impresses the same stamp on everything. Films, radio and magazines make up a system which is uniform as a whole and in every part. Even the aesthetic activities of political opposites are one in their enthusiastic obedience to the rhythm of the iron system. The decorative industrial management buildings and exhibition centers in authoritarian countries are much the same as anywhere else. The huge gleaming towers that shoot up everywhere are outward signs of the ingenious planning of international concerns, toward which the unleashed entrepreneurial system (whose monuments are a mass of gloomy houses and business premises in grimy, spiritless cities) was already hastening. Even now the older houses just outside the concrete city centers look like slums, and the new bungalows on the outskirts are at one with the flimsy structures of world fairs in their praise of technical progress and their built-in demand to be discarded after a short while like empty food cans. Yet the city housing projects designed to perpetuate the individual as a supposedly independent unit in a small hygienic dwelling make him all the more subservient to his adversary—the absolute power of capitalism. Because the inhabitants, as producers and as consumers, are drawn into the center in search of work and pleasure, all the living units crystallize into well-organized complexes. The striking unity of microcosm and macrocosm presents men with a model of their culture: the false identity of the general and the particular. Under monopoly all mass culture is identical, and the lines of its artificial framework begin to show through. The people at the top are no longer so interested in concealing monopoly: as its violence becomes more open, so its power grows. Movies and radio need no longer pretend to be art. The truth that they are just business is made into an ideology in order to justify the rubbish they deliberately produce. They call themselves industries; and when their directors' incomes are published, any doubt about the social utility of the finished products is removed.

Interested parties explain the culture industry in technological terms. It is alleged that because millions participate in it, certain reproduction processes are necessary that inevitably require identical needs in innumerable places to be satisfied with identical goods. The technical contrast between the few production centers and the large number of widely dispersed consumption points is said to demand organization and planning by management. Furthermore, it is claimed that standards were based in the first place on consumers' needs, and for that reason were accepted with so little resistance. The result is the circle of manipulation and retroactive need in which the unity of the system grows ever stronger. No mention is made of the fact that the basis on which technology acquires power over society is the power of those whose economic hold over society is greatest. A technological rationale is the rationale of domination itself. It is the coercive nature of society alienated from itself. Automobiles, bombs, and movies keep the whole thing together until their leveling element shows its strength in the very wrong which it furthered. It has made the technology of the culture industry no more than the achievement of standardization and mass production, sacrificing whatever involved a distinction between the logic of the work and that of the social system. This is the result not of a law of movement in technology as such but of its function in today's economy. The need which might resist central control has already been suppressed by the control of the individual consciousness. The step from the telephone to the radio has

121

clearly distinguished the roles. The former still allowed the subscriber to play the role of subject, and was liberal. The latter is democratic: it turns all participants into listeners and authoritatively subjects them to broadcast programs which are all exactly the same. No machinery of rejoinder has been devised, and private broadcasters are denied any freedom. They are confined to the apocryphal field of the "amateur," and also have to accept organization from above. But any trace of spontaneity from the public in official broadcasting is controlled and absorbed by talent scouts, studio competitions and official programs of every kind selected by professionals. Talented performers belong to the industry long before it displays them; otherwise they would not be so eager to fit in. The attitude of the public, which ostensibly and actually favors the system of the culture industry, is a part of the system and not an excuse for it. If one branch of art follows the same formula as one with a very different medium and content; if the dramatic intrigue of broadcast soap operas becomes no more than useful material for showing how to master technical problems at both ends of the scale of musical experience—real jazz or a cheap imitation; or if a movement from a Beethoven symphony is crudely "adapted" for a film sound-track in the same way as a Tolstoy novel is garbled in a film script: then the claim that this is done to satisfy the spontaneous wishes of the public is no more than hot air. We are closer to the facts if we explain these phenomena as inherent in the technical and personnel apparatus which, down to its last cog, itself forms part of the economic mechanism of selection. In addition there is the agreement—or at least the determination—of all executive authorities not to produce or sanction anything that in any way differs from their own rules, their own ideas about consumers, or above all themselves.

In our age the objective social tendency is incarnate in the hidden subjective purposes of company directors, the foremost among whom are in the most powerful sectors of industry—steel, petroleum, electricity, and chemicals. Culture monopolies are weak and dependent in comparison. They cannot afford to neglect their appeasement of the real holders of power if their sphere of activity in mass society (a sphere producing a specific type of commodity which anyhow is still too closely bound up with easygoing liberalism and Jewish intellectuals) is not to undergo a series of purges. The dependence of the most powerful broadcasting company on the electrical industry, or of the motion picture industry on the banks, is characteristic of the whole sphere, whose individual branches are themselves economically interwoven. All are in such close contact that the extreme concentration of mental forces allows demarcation lines between different firms and technical branches to be ignored. The ruthless unity in the culture industry is evidence of what will happen in politics. Marked differentiations such as those of A and B films, or of stories in magazines in different price ranges, depend not so much on subject matter as on classifying, organizing, and labeling consumers. Something is provided for all so that none may escape; the distinctions are emphasized and extended. The public is catered for with a hierarchical range of mass-produced products of varying quality, thus advancing the rule of complete quantification. Everybody must behave (as if spontaneously) in accordance with his previously determined and indexed level, and choose the category of mass product turned out for his type. Consumers appear as statistics on research organization charts, and are divided by income groups into red, green, and blue areas; the technique is that used for any type of propaganda.

How formalized the procedure is can be seen when the mechanically differentiated products prove to be all alike in the end. That the difference between the Chrysler range and General Motors products is basically illusory strikes every child with a keen interest in varieties. What connoisseurs discuss as good or bad points serve only to perpetuate the semblance of competition and range of choice. The same applies to the Warner Brothers and Metro Goldwyn Mayer productions. But even the differences between the more expensive and cheaper models put out by the same firm steadily diminish: for automobiles, there are such differences as the number of cylinders, cubic capacity, details of patented gadgets; and for films there are the number of stars, the extravagant use of technology,

123

labor, and equipment, and the introduction of the latest psychological formulas. The universal criterion of merit is the
amount of "conspicuous production," of blatant cash invest-
ment. The varying budgets in the culture industry do not bear
the slightest relation to factual values, to the meaning of the
products themselves. Even the technical media are relentlessly
forced into uniformity. Television aims at a synthesis of radio
and film, and is held up only because the interested parties have
not yet reached agreement, but its consequences will be quite
enormous and promise to intensify the impoverishment of aesthetic matter so drastically, that by tomorrow the thinly veiled
identity of all industrial culture products can come triumphantly
out into the open, derisively fulfilling the Wagnerian dream of
the *Gesamtkunstwerk*—the fusion of all the arts in one work.
The alliance of word, image, and music is all the more perfect
than in *Tristan* because the sensuous elements which all ap-
provingly reflect the surface of social reality are in principle
embodied in the same technical process, the unity of which becomes its distinctive content. This process integrates all the
elements of the production, from the novel (shaped with an eye
to the film) to the last sound effect. It is the triumph of invested capital, whose title as absolute master is etched deep into
the hearts of the dispossessed in the employment line; it is the
meaningful content of every film, whatever plot the production
team may have selected.

The man with leisure has to accept what the culture manufacturers offer him. Kant's formalism still expected a contribution
from the individual, who was thought to relate the varied experiences of the senses to fundamental concepts; but industry
robs the individual of his function. Its prime service to the customer is to do his schematizing for him. Kant said that there
was a secret mechanism in the soul which prepared direct intuitions in such a way that they could be fitted into the system of
pure reason. But today that secret has been deciphered. While
the mechanism is to all appearances planned by those who serve
up the data of experience, that is, by the culture industry, it is
in fact forced upon the latter by the power of society, which

remains irrational, however we may try to rationalize it; and this inescapable force is processed by commercial agencies so that they give an artificial impression of being in command. There is nothing left for the consumer to classify. Producers have done it for him. Art for the masses has destroyed the dream but still conforms to the tenets of that dreaming idealism which critical idealism balked at. Everything derives from consciousness: for Malebranche and Berkeley, from the consciousness of God; in mass art, from the consciousness of the production team. Not only are the hit songs, stars, and soap operas cyclically recurrent and rigidly invariable types, but the specific content of the entertainment itself is derived from them and only appears to change. The details are interchangeable. The short interval sequence which was effective in a hit song, the hero's momentary fall from grace (which he accepts as good sport), the rough treatment which the beloved gets from the male star, the latter's rugged defiance of the spoilt heiress, are, like all the other details, ready-made clichés to be slotted in anywhere; they never do anything more than fulfill the purpose allotted them in the overall plan. Their whole *raison d'être* is to confirm it by being its constituent parts. As soon as the film begins, it is quite clear how it will end, and who will be rewarded, punished, or forgotten. In light music, once the trained ear has heard the first notes of the hit song, it can guess what is coming and feel flattered when it does come. The average length of the short story has to be rigidly adhered to. Even gags, effects, and jokes are calculated like the setting in which they are placed. They are the responsibility of special experts and their narrow range makes it easy for them to be apportioned in the office. The development of the culture industry has led to the predominance of the effect, the obvious touch, and the technical detail over the work itself—which once expressed an idea, but was liquidated together with the idea. When the detail won its freedom, it became rebellious and, in the period from Romanticism to Expressionism, asserted itself as free expression, as a vehicle of protest against the organization. In music the single harmonic effect obliterated the awareness of form as a whole; in painting the individual color was stressed at the expense of pictorial composition; and in the novel psychology became more important than structure. The totality of the culture industry has put an end to this. Though concerned exclusively with effects, it crushes their insubordination and makes them subserve the formula, which replaces the work. The same fate is inflicted on whole and parts alike. The whole inevitably bears no relation to the details—just like the career of a successful man into which everything is made to fit as an illustration or a proof, whereas it is nothing more than the sum of all those idiotic events. The so-called dominant idea is like a file which ensures order but not coherence. The whole and the parts are alike; there is no antithesis and no connection. Their prearranged harmony is a mockery of what had to be striven after in the great bourgeois works of art. In Germany the graveyard stillness of the dictatorship already hung over the gayest films of the democratic era.

The whole world is made to pass through the filter of the culture industry. The old experience of the movie-goer, who sees the world outside as an extension of the film he has just left (because the latter is intent upon reproducing the world of everyday perceptions), is now the producer's guideline. The more intensely and flawlessly his techniques duplicate empirical objects, the easier it is today for the illusion to prevail that the outside world is the straightforward continuation of that presented on the screen. This purpose has been furthered by mechanical reproduction since the lightning takeover by the sound film.

Real life is becoming indistinguishable from the movies. The sound film, far surpassing the theater of illusion, leaves no room for imagination or reflection on the part of the audience, who is unable to respond within the structure of the film, yet deviate from its precise detail without losing the thread of the story; hence the film forces its victims to equate it directly with reality. The stunting of the mass-media consumer's powers of imagination and spontaneity does not have to be traced back to any psychological mechanisms; he must ascribe the loss of those attributes to the objective nature of the products themselves, especially to the most characteristic of them, the sound film. They are so designed that quickness, powers of observation, and

126

experience are undeniably needed to apprehend them at all; yet sustained thought is out of the question if the spectator is not to miss the relentless rush of facts. Even though the effort required for his response is semi-automatic, no scope is left for the imagination. Those who are so absorbed by the world of the movie—by its images, gestures, and words—that they are unable to supply what really makes it a world, do not have to dwell on particular points of its mechanics during a screening. All the other films and products of the entertainment industry which they have seen have taught them what to expect; they react automatically. The might of industrial society is lodged in men's minds. The entertainments manufacturers know that their products will be consumed with alertness even when the customer is distraught, for each of them is a model of the huge economic machinery which has always sustained the masses, whether at work or at leisure—which is akin to work. From every sound film and every broadcast program the social effect can be inferred which is exclusive to none but is shared by all alike. The culture industry as a whole has molded men as a type unfailingly reproduced in every product. All the agents of this process, from the producer to the women's clubs, take good care that the simple reproduction of this mental state is not nuanced or extended in any way.

The art historians and guardians of culture who complain of the extinction in the West of a basic style-determining power are wrong. The stereotyped appropriation of everything, even the inchoate, for the purposes of mechanical reproduction surpasses the rigor and general currency of any "real style," in the sense in which cultural *cognoscenti* celebrate the organic precapitalist past. No Palestrina could be more of a purist in eliminating every unprepared and unresolved discord than the jazz arranger in suppressing any development which does not conform to the jargon. When jazzing up Mozart he changes him not only when he is too serious or too difficult but when he harmonizes the melody in a different way, perhaps more simply, than is customary now. No medieval builder can have scrutinized the subjects for church windows and sculptures more suspiciously than the studio hierarchy scrutinizes a work by Balzac

127

or Hugo before finally approving it. No medieval theologian could have determined the degree of the torment to be suffered by the damned in accordance with the *ordo* of divine love more meticulously than the producers of shoddy epics calculate the torture to be undergone by the hero or the exact point to which the leading lady's hemline shall be raised. The explicit and implicit, exoteric and esoteric catalog of the forbidden and tolerated is so extensive that it not only defines the area of freedom but is all-powerful inside it. Everything down to the last detail is shaped accordingly. Like its counterpart, avant-garde art, the entertainment industry determines its own language, down to its very syntax and vocabulary, by the use of anathema. The constant pressure to produce new effects (which must conform to the old pattern) serves merely as another rule to increase the power of the conventions when any single effect threatens to slip through the net. Every detail is so firmly stamped with sameness that nothing can appear which is not marked at birth, or does not meet with approval at first sight. And the star performers, whether they produce or reproduce, use this jargon as freely and fluently and with as much gusto as if it were the very language which it silenced long ago. Such is the ideal of what is natural in this field of activity, and its influence becomes all the more powerful, the more technique is perfected and diminishes the tension between the finished product and everyday life. The paradox of this routine, which is essentially travesty, can be detected and is often predominant in everything that the culture industry turns out. A jazz musician who is playing a piece of serious music, one of Beethoven's simplest minuets, syncopates it involuntarily and will smile superciliously when asked to follow the normal divisions of the beat. This is the "nature" which, complicated by the ever-present and extravagant demands of the specific medium, constitutes the new style and is a "system of non-culture, to which one might even concede a certain 'unity of style' if it really made any sense to speak of stylized barbarity."[1]

The universal imposition of this stylized mode can even go

1. Nietzsche, *Unzeitgemässe Betrachtungen, Werke,* Vol. I (Leipzig, 1917), p. 187.

beyond what is quasi-officially sanctioned or forbidden; today a hit song is more readily forgiven for not observing the 32 beats or the compass of the ninth than for containing even the most clandestine melodic or harmonic detail which does not conform to the idiom. Whenever Orson Welles offends against the tricks of the trade, he is forgiven because his departures from the norm are regarded as calculated mutations which serve all the more strongly to confirm the validity of the system. The constraint of the technically-conditioned idiom which stars and directors have to produce as "nature" so that the people can appropriate it, extends to such fine nuances that they almost attain the subtlety of the devices of an avant-garde work as against those of truth. The rare capacity minutely to fulfill the obligations of the natural idiom in all branches of the culture industry becomes the criterion of efficiency. What and how they say it must be measurable by everyday language, as in logical positivism. The producers are experts. The idiom demands an astounding productive power, which it absorbs and squanders. In a diabolical way it has overreached the culturally conservative distinction between genuine and artificial style. A style might be called artificial which is imposed from without on the refractory impulses of a form. But in the culture industry every element of the subject matter has its origin in the same apparatus as that jargon whose stamp it bears. The quarrels in which the artistic experts become involved with sponsor and censor about a lie going beyond the bounds of credibility are evidence not so much of an inner aesthetic tension as of a divergence of interests. The reputation of the specialist, in which a last remnant of objective independence sometimes finds refuge, conflicts with the business politics of the Church, or the concern which is manufacturing the cultural commodity. But the thing itself has been essentially objectified and made viable before the established authorities began to argue about it. Even before Zanuck acquired her, Saint Bernadette was regarded by her latter-day hagiographer as brilliant propaganda for all interested parties. That is what became of the emotions of the character. Hence the style of the culture industry, which no longer has to test itself against any refractory material, is also the negation of style. The reconciliation of the general and particular, of the rule and the specific demands of the subject matter, the achievement of which alone gives essential, meaningful content to style, is futile because there has ceased to be the slightest tension between opposite poles: these concordant extremes are dismally identical; the general can replace the particular, and vice versa.

Nevertheless, this caricature of style does not amount to something beyond the genuine style of the past. In the culture industry the notion of genuine style is seen to be the aesthetic equivalent of domination. Style considered as mere aesthetic regularity is a romantic dream of the past. The unity of style not only of the Christian Middle Ages but of the Renaissance expresses in each case the different structure of social power, and not the obscure experience of the oppressed in which the general was enclosed. The great artists were never those who embodied a wholly flawless and perfect style, but those who used style as a way of hardening themselves against the chaotic expression of suffering, as a negative truth. The style of their works gave what was expressed that force without which life flows away unheard. Those very art forms which are known as classical, such as Mozart's music, contain objective trends which represent something different to the style which they incarnate. As late as Schönberg and Picasso, the great artists have retained a mistrust of style, and at crucial points have subordinated it to the logic of the matter. What Dadaists and Expressionists called the untruth of style as such triumphs today in the sung jargon of a crooner, in the carefully contrived elegance of a film star, and even in the admirable expertise of a photograph of a peasant's squalid hut. Style represents a promise in every work of art. That which is expressed is subsumed through style into the dominant forms of generality, into the language of music, painting, or words, in the hope that it will be reconciled thus with the idea of true generality. This promise held out by the work of art that it will create truth by lending new shape to the conventional social forms is as necessary as it is hypocritical. It unconditionally posits the real forms of life as it is by suggesting that fulfillment lies in their aesthetic derivatives. To this extent the claim of art is always ideology too. However, only in this confronta-

130

tion with tradition of which style is the record can art express suffering. That factor in a work of art which enables it to transcend reality certainly cannot be detached from style; but it does not consist of the harmony actually realized, of any doubtful unity of form and content, within and without, of individual and society; it is to be found in those features in which discrepancy appears: in the necessary failure of the passionate striving for identity. Instead of exposing itself to this failure in which the style of the great work of art has always achieved self-negation, the inferior work has always relied on its similarity with others —on a surrogate identity.

In the culture industry this imitation finally becomes absolute. Having ceased to be anything but style, it reveals the latter's secret: obedience to the social hierarchy. Today aesthetic barbarity completes what has threatened the creations of the spirit since they were gathered together as culture and neutralized. To speak of culture was always contrary to culture. Culture as a common denominator already contains in embryo that schematization and process of cataloging and classification which bring culture within the sphere of administration. And it is precisely the industrialized, the consequent, subsumption which entirely accords with this notion of culture. By subordinating in the same way and to the same end all areas of intellectual creation, by occupying men's senses from the time they leave the factory in the evening to the time they clock in again the next morning with matter that bears the impress of the labor process they themselves have to sustain throughout the day, this subsumption mockingly satisfies the concept of a unified culture which the philosophers of personality contrasted with mass culture.

And so the culture industry, the most rigid of all styles, proves to be the goal of liberalism, which is reproached for its lack of style. Not only do its categories and contents derive from liberalism—domesticated naturalism as well as operetta and revue —but the modern culture monopolies form the economic area in which, together with the corresponding entrepreneurial types, for the time being some part of its sphere of operation survives, despite the process of disintegration elsewhere. It is still possible to make one's way in entertainment, if one is not too obstinate about one's own concerns, and proves appropriately pliable. Anyone who resists can only survive by fitting in. Once his particular brand of deviation from the norm has been noted by the industry, he belongs to it as does the land-reformer to capitalism. Realistic dissidence is the trademark of anyone who has a new idea in business. In the public voice of modern society accusations are seldom audible; if they are, the perceptive can already detect signs that the dissident will soon be reconciled. The more immeasurable the gap between chorus and leaders, the more certainly there is room at the top for everybody who demonstrates his superiority by well-planned originality. Hence, in the culture industry, too, the liberal tendency to give full scope to its able men survives. To do this for the efficient today is still the function of the market, which is otherwise proficiently controlled; as for the market's freedom, in the high period of art as elsewhere, it was freedom for the stupid to starve. Significantly, the system of the culture industry comes from the more liberal industrial nations, and all its characteristic media, such as movies, radio, jazz, and magazines, flourish there. Its progress, to be sure, had its origin in the general laws of capital. Gaumont and Pathé, Ullstein and Hugenberg followed the international trend with some success; Europe's economic dependence on the United States after war and inflation was a contributory factor. The belief that the barbarity of the culture industry is a result of "cultural lag," of the fact that the American consciousness did not keep up with the growth of technology, is quite wrong. It was pre-Fascist Europe which did not keep up with the trend toward the culture monopoly. But it was this very lag which left intellect and creativity some degree of independence and enabled its last representatives to exist—however dismally. In Germany the failure of democratic control to permeate life had led to a paradoxical situation. Many things were exempt from the market mechanism which had invaded the Western countries. The German educational system, universities, theaters with artistic standards, great orchestras, and museums enjoyed protection. The political powers, state and

municipalities, which had inherited such institutions from abso-
lutism, had left them with a measure of the freedom from the
forces of power which dominates the market, just as princes and
feudal lords had done up to the nineteenth century. This
strengthened art in this late phase against the verdict of supply
and demand, and increased its resistance far beyond the actual
degree of protection. In the market itself the tribute of a quality for which no use had been found was turned into purchasing
power; in this way, respectable literary and music publishers
could help authors who yielded little more in the way of profit
than the respect of the connoisseur. But what completely fet-
tered the artist was the pressure (and the accompanying drastic
threats), always to fit into business life as an aesthetic expert.
Formerly, like Kant and Hume, they signed their letters "Your
most humble and obedient servant," and undermined the foundations of throne and altar. Today they address heads of government by their first names, yet in every artistic activity they
are subject to their illiterate masters. The analysis Tocqueville
offered a century ago has in the meantime proved wholly accurate. Under the private culture monopoly it is a fact that
"tyranny leaves the body free and directs its attack at the soul.
The ruler no longer says: You must think as I do or die. He
says: You are free not to think as I do; your life, your property,
everything shall remain yours, but from this day on you are a
stranger among us."[2] Not to conform means to be rendered
powerless, economically and therefore spiritually—to be "self-
employed." When the outsider is excluded from the concern, he
can only too easily be accused of incompetence. Whereas today
in material production the mechanism of supply and demand is
disintegrating, in the superstructure it still operates as a check
in the rulers' favor. The consumers are the workers and employees, the farmers and lower middle class. Capitalist production so confines them, body and soul, that they fall helpless victims to what is offered them. As naturally as the ruled always
took the morality imposed upon them more seriously than did
the rulers themselves, the deceived masses are today captivated

2. Alexis de Tocqueville, *De la Démocratie en Amérique*, Vol. II
(Paris, 1864), p. 151.

by the myth of success even more than the successful are. Immovably, they insist on the very ideology which enslaves them. The misplaced love of the common people for the wrong which is done them is a greater force than the cunning of the authorities. It is stronger even than the rigorism of the Hays Office, just as in certain great times in history it has inflamed greater forces that were turned against it, namely, the terror of the tribunals. It calls for Mickey Rooney in preference to the tragic Garbo, for Donald Duck instead of Betty Boop. The industry submits to the vote which it has itself inspired. What is a loss for the firm which cannot fully exploit a contract with a declining star is a legitimate expense for the system as a whole. By craftily sanctioning the demand for rubbish it inaugurates total harmony. The connoisseur and the expert are despised for their pretentious claim to know better than the others, even though culture is democratic and distributes its privileges to all. In view of the ideological truce, the conformism of the buyers and the effrontery of the producers who supply them prevail. The result is a constant reproduction of the same thing.

A constant sameness governs the relationship to the past as well. What is new about the phase of mass culture compared with the late liberal stage is the exclusion of the new. The machine rotates on the same spot. While determining consumption it excludes the untried as a risk. The movie-makers distrust any manuscript which is not reassuringly backed by a bestseller. Yet for this very reason there is never-ending talk of ideas, novelty, and surprise, of what is taken for granted but has never existed. Tempo and dynamics serve this trend. Nothing remains as of old; everything has to run incessantly, to keep moving. For only the universal triumph of the rhythm of mechanical production and reproduction promises that nothing changes, and nothing unsuitable will appear. Any additions to the well-proven culture inventory are too much of a speculation. The ossified forms—such as the sketch, short story, problem film, or hit song—are the standardized average of late liberal taste, dictated with threats from above. The people at the top in the culture agencies, who work in harmony as only one manager can with another, whether he comes from the rag trade or from college, have long since reorganized and rationalized the objective spirit. One might think that an omnipresent authority had sifted the material and drawn up an official catalog of cultural commodities to provide a smooth supply of available mass-produced lines. The ideas are written in the cultural firmament where they had already been numbered by Plato—and were indeed numbers, incapable of increase and immutable.

Amusement and all the elements of the culture industry existed long before the latter came into existence. Now they are taken over from above and brought up to date. The culture industry can pride itself on having energetically executed the previously clumsy transposition of art into the sphere of consumption, on making this a principle, on divesting amusement of its obtrusive naïvetés and improving the type of commodities. The more absolute it became, the more ruthless it was in forcing every outsider either into bankruptcy or into a syndicate, and became more refined and elevated—until it ended up as a synthesis of Beethoven and the Casino de Paris. It enjoys a double victory: the truth it extinguishes without it can reproduce at will as a lie within. "Light" art as such, distraction, is not a decadent form. Anyone who complains that it is a betrayal of the ideal of pure expression is under an illusion about society. The purity of bourgeois art, which hypostasized itself as a world of freedom in contrast to what was happening in the material world, was from the beginning bought with the exclusion of the lower classes—with whose cause, the real universality, art keeps faith precisely by its freedom from the ends of the false universality. Serious art has been withheld from those for whom the hardship and oppression of life make a mockery of seriousness, and who must be glad if they can use time not spent at the production line just to keep going. Light art has been the shadow of autonomous art. It is the social bad conscience of serious art. The truth which the latter necessarily lacked because of its social premises gives the other the semblance of legitimacy. The division itself is the truth: it does at least express the negativity of the culture which the different spheres constitute. Least of all can the antithesis be reconciled by absorbing light into serious art, or vice versa. But that is what the culture industry attempts.

135

The eccentricity of the circus, peepshow, and brothel is as embarrassing to it as that of Schönberg and Karl Kraus. And so the jazz musician Benny Goodman appears with the Budapest string quartet, more pedantic rhythmically than any philharmonic clarinettist, while the style of the Budapest players is as uniform and sugary as that of Guy Lombardo. But what is significant is not vulgarity, stupidity, and lack of polish. The culture industry did away with yesterday's rubbish by its own perfection, and by forbidding and domesticating the amateurish, although it constantly allows gross blunders without which the standard of the exalted style cannot be perceived. But what is new is that the irreconcilable elements of culture, art and distraction, are subordinated to one end and subsumed under one false formula: the totality of the culture industry. It consists of repetition. That its characteristic innovations are never anything more than improvements of mass reproduction is not external to the system. It is with good reason that the interest of innumerable consumers is directed to the technique, and not to the contents—which are stubbornly repeated, outworn, and by now half-discredited. The social power which the spectators worship shows itself more effectively in the omnipresence of the stereotype imposed by technical skill than in the stale ideologies for which the ephemeral contents stand in.

Nevertheless the culture industry remains the entertainment business. Its influence over the consumers is established by entertainment; that will ultimately be broken not by an outright decree, but by the hostility inherent in the principle of entertainment to what is greater than itself. Since all the trends of the culture industry are profoundly embedded in the public by the whole social process, they are encouraged by the survival of the market in this area. Demand has not yet been replaced by simple obedience. As is well known, the major reorganization of the film industry shortly before World War I, the material prerequisite of its expansion, was precisely its deliberate acceptance of the public's needs as recorded at the box-office—a procedure which was hardly thought necessary in the pioneering days of the screen. The same opinion is held today by the captains of the film industry, who take as their criterion the more or less phenomenal song hits but wisely never have recourse to the judgment of truth, the opposite criterion. Business is their ideology. It is quite correct that the power of the culture industry resides in its identification with a manufactured need, and not in simple contrast to it, even if this contrast were one of complete power and complete powerlessness. Amusement under late capitalism is the prolongation of work. It is sought after as an escape from the mechanized work process, and to recruit strength in order to be able to cope with it again. But at the same time mechanization has such power over a man's leisure and happiness, and so profoundly determines the manufacture of amusement goods, that his experiences are inevitably after-images of the work process itself. The ostensible content is merely a faded foreground; what sinks in is the automatic succession of standardized operations. What happens at work, in the factory, or in the office can only be escaped from by approximation to it in one's leisure time. All amusement suffers from this incurable malady. Pleasure hardens into boredom because, if it is to remain pleasure, it must not demand any effort and therefore moves rigorously in the worn grooves of association. No independent thinking must be expected from the audience: the product prescribes every reaction: not by its natural structure (which collapses under reflection), but by signals. Any logical connection calling for mental effort is painstakingly avoided. As far as possible, developments must follow from the immediately preceding situation and never from the idea of the whole. For the attentive movie-goer any individual scene will give him the whole thing. Even the set pattern itself still seems dangerous, offering some meaning—wretched as it might be—where only meaninglessness is acceptable. Often the plot is maliciously deprived of the development demanded by characters and matter according to the old pattern. Instead, the next step is what the script writer takes to be the most striking effect in the particular situation. Banal though elaborate surprise interrupts the story-line. The tendency mischievously to fall back on pure nonsense, which was a legitimate part of popular art, farce and clowning, right up to Chaplin and the Marx Brothers, is most obvious in the unpretentious kinds. This ten-

137

dency has completely asserted itself in the text of the novelty song, in the thriller movie, and in cartoons, although in films :.::ing Greer Garson and Bette Davis the unity of the socio-psychological case study provides something approximating a claim to a consistent plot. The idea itself, together with the objects of comedy and terror, is massacred and fragmented. Novelty songs have always existed on a contempt for meaning which, as predecessors and successors of psychoanalysis, they reduce to the monotony of sexual symbolism. Today detective and adventure films no longer give the audience the opportunity to experience the resolution. In the non-ironic varieties of the genre, it has also to rest content with the simple horror of situations which have almost ceased to be linked in any way.

Cartoons were once exponents of fantasy as opposed to rationalism. They ensured that justice was done to the creatures and objects they electrified, by giving the maimed specimens a second life. All they do today is to confirm the victory of technological reason over truth. A few years ago they had a consistent plot which only broke up in the final moments in a crazy chase, and thus resembled the old slapstick comedy. Now, however, time relations have shifted. In the very first sequence a motive is stated so that in the course of the action destruction can get to work on it: with the audience in pursuit, the protagonist becomes the worthless object of general violence. The quantity of organized amusement changes into the quality of organized cruelty. The self-elected censors of the film industry (with whom it enjoys a close relationship) watch over the unfolding of the crime, which is as drawn-out as a hunt. Fun replaces the pleasure which the sight of an embrace would allegedly afford, and postpones satisfaction till the day of the pogrom. In so far as cartoons do any more than accustom the senses to the new tempo, they hammer into every brain the old lesson that continuous friction, the breaking down of all individual resistance, is the condition of life in this society. Donald Duck in the cartoons and the unfortunate in real life get their thrashing so that the audience can learn to take their own punishment.

The enjoyment of the violence suffered by the movie character turns into violence against the spectator, and distraction into exertion. Nothing that the experts have devised as a stimulant must escape the weary eye; no stupidity is allowed in the face of all the trickery; one has to follow everything and even display the smart responses shown and recommended in the film. This raises the question whether the culture industry fulfills the function of diverting minds which it boasts about so loudly. If most of the radio stations and movie theaters were closed down, the consumers would probably not lose so very much. To walk from the street into the movie theater is no longer to enter a world of dream; as soon as the very existence of these institutions no longer made it obligatory to use them, there would be no great urge to do so. Such closures would not be reactionary machine wrecking. The disappointment would be felt not so much by the enthusiasts as by the slow-witted, who are the ones who suffer for everything anyhow. In spite of the films which are intended to complete her integration, the housewife finds in the darkness of the movie theater a place of refuge where she can sit for a few hours with nobody watching, just as she used to look out of the window when there were still homes and rest in the evening. The unemployed in the great cities find coolness in summer and warmth in winter in these temperature-controlled locations. Otherwise, despite its size, this bloated pleasure apparatus adds no dignity to man's lives. The idea of "fully exploiting" available technical resources and the facilities for aesthetic mass consumption is part of the economic system which refuses to exploit resources to abolish hunger.

The culture industry perpetually cheats its consumers of what it perpetually promises. The promissory note which, with its plots and staging, it draws on pleasure is endlessly prolonged; the promise, which is actually all the spectacle consists of, is illusory: all it actually confirms is that the real point will never be reached, that the diner must be satisfied with the menu. In front of the appetite stimulated by all those brilliant names and images there is finally set no more than a commendation of the depressing everyday world it sought to escape. Of course works of art were not sexual exhibitions either. However, by representing deprivation as negative, they retracted, as it were, the prostitution of the impulse and rescued by mediation what was denied. The secret of aesthetic sublimation is its representation of fulfillment as a broken promise. The culture industry does not sublimate; it represses. By repeatedly exposing the objects of desire, breasts in a clinging sweater or the naked torso of the athletic hero, it only stimulates the unsublimated forepleasure which habitual deprivation has long since reduced to a masochistic semblance. There is no erotic situation which, while insinuating and exciting, does not fail to indicate unmistakably that things can never go that far. The Hays Office merely confirms the ritual of Tantalus that the culture industry has established anyway. Works of art are ascetic and unashamed; the culture industry is pornographic and prudish. Love is downgraded to romance. And, after the descent, much is permitted; even license as a marketable speciality has its quota bearing the trade description "daring." The mass production of the sexual automatically achieves its repression. Because of his ubiquity, the film star with whom one is meant to fall in love is from the outset a copy of himself. Every tenor voice comes to sound like a Caruso record, and the "natural" faces of Texas girls are like the successful models by whom Hollywood has typecast them. The mechanical reproduction of beauty, which reactionary cultural fanaticism wholeheartedly serves in its methodical idolization of individuality, leaves no room for that unconscious idolatry which was once essential to beauty. The triumph over beauty is celebrated by humor—the *Schadenfreude* that every successful deprivation calls forth. There is laughter because there is nothing to laugh at. Laughter, whether conciliatory or terrible, always occurs when some fear passes. It indicates liberation either from physical danger or from the grip of logic. Conciliatory laughter is heard as the echo of an escape from power; the wrong kind overcomes fear by capitulating to the forces which are to be feared. It is the echo of power as something inescapable. Fun is a medicinal bath. The pleasure industry never fails to prescribe it. It makes laughter the instrument of the fraud practised on happiness. Moments of happiness are without laughter; only operettas and films portray sex to the accompaniment of resounding laughter. But Baude-laire is as devoid of humour as Hölderlin. In the false society laughter is a disease which has attacked happiness and is draw-ing it into its worthless totality. To laugh at something is always to deride it, and the life which, according to Bergson, in laugh-ter breaks through the barrier, is actually an invading barbaric life, self-assertion prepared to parade its liberation from any scruple when the social occasion arises. Such a laughing audi-ence is a parody of humanity. Its members are monads, all dedicated to the pleasure of being ready for anything at the ex-pense of everyone else. Their harmony is a caricature of soli-darity. What is fiendish about this false laughter is that it is a compelling parody of the best, which is conciliatory. Delight is austere: *res severa verum gaudium*. The monastic theory that not asceticism but the sexual act denotes the renunciation of attainable bliss receives negative confirmation in the gravity of the lover who with foreboding commits his life to the fleeting moment. In the culture industry, jovial denial takes the place of the pain found in ecstasy and in asceticism. The supreme law is that they shall not satisfy their desires at any price; they must laugh and be content with laughter. In every product of the culture industry, the permanent denial imposed by civiliza-tion is once again unmistakably demonstrated and inflicted on its victims. To offer and to deprive them of something is one and the same. This is what happens in erotic films. Precisely be-cause it must never take place, everything centers upon copula-tion. In films it is more strictly forbidden for an illegitimate relationship to be admitted without the parties being punished than for a millionaire's future son-in-law to be active in the labor movement. In contrast to the liberal era, industrialized as well as popular culture may wax indignant at capitalism, but it cannot renounce the threat of castration. This is fundamental. It outlasts the organized acceptance of the uniformed seen in the films which are produced to that end, and in reality. What is decisive today is no longer puritanism, although it still asserts itself in the form of women's organizations, but the necessity inherent in the system not to leave the customer alone, not for a moment to allow him any suspicion that resistance is possible.

141

The principle dictates that he should be shown all his needs as capable of fulfillment, but that those needs should be so pre-determined that he feels himself to be the eternal consumer, the object of the culture industry. Not only does it make him believe that the deception it practices is satisfaction, but it goes further and implies that, whatever the state of affairs, he must put up with what is offered. The escape from everyday drudgery which the whole culture industry promises may be compared to the daughter's abduction in the cartoon: the father is holding the ladder in the dark. The paradise offered by the culture industr¨ is the same old drudgery. Both escape and elopement are pre-designed to lead back to the starting point. Pleasure promotes the resignation which it ought to help to forget.

Amusement, if released from every restraint, would not only be the antithesis of art but its extreme role. The Mark Twain absurdity with which the American culture industry flirts at times might be a corrective of art. The more seriously the latter regards the incompatibility with life, the more it resembles the seriousness of life, its antithesis; the more effort it devotes to developing wholly from its own formal law, the more effort it demands from the intelligence to neutralize its burden. In some revue films, and especially in the grotesque and the fun-nies, the possibility of this negation does glimmer for a few mo-ments. But of course it cannot happen. Pure amusement in its consequence, relaxed self-surrender to all kinds of associations and happy nonsense, is cut short by the amusement on the mar-ket: instead, it is interrupted by a surrogate overall meaning which the culture industry insists on giving to its products, and yet misuses as a mere pretext for bringing in the stars. Biog-raphies and other simple stories patch the fragments of non-sense into an idiotic plot. We do not have the cap and bells of the jester but the bunch of keys of capitalist reason, which even screens the pleasure of achieving success. Every kiss in the revue film has to contribute to the career of the boxer, or some hit song expert or other whose rise to fame is being glorified. The deception is not that the culture industry supplies amusement but that it ruins the fun by allowing business considerations to involve it in the ideological clichés of a culture in the process of self-liquidation. Ethics and taste cut short unrestrained amusement as "naïve"—naïveté is thought to be as bad as intellectualism—and even restrict technical possibilities. The culture industry is corrupt; not because it is a sinful Babylon but because it is a cathedral dedicated to elevated pleasure. On all levels, from Hemingway to Emil Ludwig, from Mrs. Miniver to the Lone Ranger, from Toscanini to Guy Lombardo, there is untruth in the intellectual content taken ready-made from art and science. The culture industry does retain a trace of something better in those features which bring it close to the circus, in the self-justifying and nonsensical skill of riders, acrobats and clowns, in the "defense and justification of physical as against intellectual art."[3] But the refuges of a mindless artistry which represents what is human as opposed to the social mechanism are being relentlessly hunted down by a schematic reason which compels everything to prove its significance and effect. The consequence is that the nonsensical at the bottom disappears as utterly as the sense in works of art at the top.

The fusion of culture and entertainment that is taking place today leads not only to a depravation of culture, but inevitably to an intellectualization of amusement. This is evident from the fact that only the copy appears: in the movie theater, the photograph; on the radio, the recording. In the age of liberal expansion, amusement lived on the unshaken belief in the future: things would remain as they were and even improve. Today this belief is once more intellectualized; it becomes so faint that it loses sight of any goal and is little more than a magic-lantern show for those with their backs to reality. It consists of the meaningful emphases which, parallel to life itself, the screen play puts on the smart fellow, the engineer, the capable girl, ruthlessness disguised as character, interest in sport, and finally automobiles and cigarettes, even where the entertainment is not put down to the advertising account of the immediate producers but to that of the system as a whole. Amusement itself becomes an ideal, taking the place of the higher things of which it completely deprives the masses by repeating them in a manner even more

3. Frank Wedekind, *Gesammelte Werke,* Vol. IX (Munich, 1921), p. 426.

stereotyped than the slogans paid for by advertising interests. Inwardness, the subjectively restricted form of truth, was always more at the mercy of the outwardly powerful than they imagined. The culture industry turns it into an open lie. It has now become mere twaddle which is acceptable in religious bestsellers, psychological films, and women's serials as an embarrassingly agreeable garnish, so that genuine personal emotion in real life can be all the more reliably controlled. In this sense amusement carries out that purgation of the emotions which Aristotle once attributed to tragedy and Mortimer Adler now allows to movies. The culture industry reveals the truth about catharsis as it did about style.

The stronger the positions of the culture industry become, the more summarily it can deal with consumers' needs, producing them, controlling them, disciplining them, and even withdrawing amusement: no limits are set to cultural progress of this kind. But the tendency is immanent in the principle of amusement itself, which is enlightened in a bourgeois sense. If the need for amusement was in large measure the creation of industry, which used the subject as a means of recommending the work to the masses—the oleograph by the dainty morsel it depicted, or the cake mix by a picture of a cake—amusement always reveals the influence of business, the sales talk, the quack's spiel. But the original affinity of business and amusement is shown in the latter's specific significance: to defend society. To be pleased means to say Yes. It is possible only by insulation from the totality of the social process, by desensitization and, from the first, by senselessly sacrificing the inescapable claim of every work, however inane, within its limits to reflect the whole. Pleasure always means not to think about anything, to forget suffering even where it is shown. Basically it is helplessness. It is flight; not, as is asserted, flight from a wretched reality, but from the last remaining thought of resistance. The liberation which amusement promises is freedom from thought and from negation. The effrontery of the rhetorical question, "What do people want?" lies in the fact that it is addressed—as if to reflective individuals—to those very people who are deliberately to be deprived

144

of this individuality. Even when the public does—exceptionally—rebel against the pleasure industry, all it can muster is that feeble resistance which that very industry has inculcated in it. Nevertheless, it has become increasingly difficult to keep people in this condition. The rate at which they are reduced to stupidity must not fall behind the rate at which their intelligence is increasing. In this age of statistics the masses are too sharp to identify themselves with the millionaire on the screen, and too slow-witted to ignore the law of the largest number. Ideology conceals itself in the calculation of probabilities. Not everyone will be lucky one day—but the person who draws the winning ticket, or rather the one who is marked out to do so by a higher power—usually by the pleasure industry itself, which is represented as unceasingly in search of talent. Those discovered by talent scouts and then publicized on a vast scale by the studio are ideal types of the new dependent average. Of course, the starlet is meant to symbolize the typist in such a way that the splendid evening dress seems meant for the actress as distinct from the real girl. The girls in the audience not only feel that they could be on the screen, but realize the great gulf separating them from it. Only one girl can draw the lucky ticket, only one man can win the prize, and if, mathematically, all have the same chance, yet this is so infinitesimal for each one that he or she will do best to write it off and rejoice in the other's success, which might just as well have been his or hers, and somehow never is. Whenever the culture industry still issues an invitation naïvely to identify, it is immediately withdrawn. No one can escape from himself any more. Once a member of the audience could see his own wedding in the one shown in the film. Now the lucky actors on the screen are copies of the same category as every member of the public, but such equality only demonstrates the insurmountable separation of the human elements. The perfect similarity is the absolute difference. The identity of the category forbids that of the individual cases. Ironically, man as a member of a species has been made a reality by the culture industry. Now any person signifies only those attributes by which he can replace everybody else: he is interchangeable, a copy. As an individual he is completely expendable and utterly

145

insignificant, and this is just what he finds out when time deprives him of this similarity. This changes the inner structure of the religion of success—otherwise strictly maintained. Increasing emphasis is laid not on the path *per aspera ad astra* (which presupposes hardship and effort), but on winning a prize. The element of blind chance in the routine decision about which song deserves to be a hit and which extra a heroine is stressed by the ideology. Movies emphasize chance. By stopping at nothing to ensure that all the characters are essentially alike, with the exception of the villain, and by excluding non-conforming faces (for example, those which, like Garbo's, do not look as if you could say "Hello sister!" to them), life is made easier for movie-goers at first. They are assured that they are all right as they are, that they could do just as well and that nothing beyond their powers will be asked of them. But at the same time they are given a hint that any effort would be useless because even bourgeois luck no longer has any connection with the calculable effect of their own work. They take the hint. Fundamentally they all recognize chance (by which one occasionally makes his fortune) as the other side of planning. Precisely because the forces of society are so deployed in the direction of rationality that anyone might become an engineer or manager, it has ceased entirely to be a rational matter who the one will be in whom society will invest training or confidence for such functions. Chance and planning become one and the same thing, because, given men's equality, individual success and failure—right up to the top—lose any economic meaning. Chance itself is planned, not because it affects any particular individual but precisely because it is believed to play a vital part. It serves the planners as an alibi, and makes it seem that the complex of transactions and measures into which life has been transformed leaves scope for spontaneous and direct relations between man. This freedom is symbolized in the various media of the culture industry by the arbitrary selection of average individuals. In a magazine's detailed accounts of the modestly magnificent pleasure-trips it has arranged for the lucky person, preferably a stenotypist (who has probably won the competition because of her contacts with local bigwigs), the powerlessness of all is re-

146

flected. They are mere matter—so much so that those in control can take someone up into their heaven and throw him out again: his rights and his work count for nothing. Industry is interested in people merely as customers and employees, and has in fact reduced mankind as a whole and each of its elements to this all-embracing formula. According to the ruling aspect at the time, ideology emphasizes plan or chance, technology or life, civilization or nature. As employees, men are reminded of the rational organization and urged to fit in like sensible people. As customers, the freedom of choice, the charm of novelty, is demonstrated to them on the screen or in the press by means of the human and personal anecdote. In either case they remain objects.

The less the culture industry has to promise, the less it can offer a meaningful explanation of life, and the emptier is the ideology it disseminates. Even the abstract ideals of the harmony and beneficence of society are too concrete in this age of universal publicity. We have even learned how to identify abstract concepts as sales propaganda. Language based entirely on truth simply arouses impatience to get on with the business deal it is probably advancing. The words that are not means appear senseless; the others seem to be fiction, untrue. Value judgments are taken either as advertising or as empty talk. Accordingly ideology has been made vague and noncommittal, and thus neither clearer nor weaker. Its very vagueness, its almost scientific aversion from committing itself to anything which cannot be verified, acts as an instrument of domination. It becomes a vigorous and prearranged promulgation of the status quo. The culture industry tends to make itself the embodiment of authoritative pronouncements, and thus the irrefutable prophet of the prevailing order. It skilfully steers a winding course between the cliffs of demonstrable misinformation and manifest truth, faithfully reproducing the phenomenon whose opaqueness blocks any insight and installs the ubiquitous and intact phenomenon as ideal. Ideology is split into the photograph of stubborn life and the naked lie about its meaning—which is not expressed but suggested and yet drummed in. To demonstrate its divine nature, reality is always repeated in a purely

147

cynical way. Such a photological proof is of course not stringent, but it is overpowering. Anyone who doubts the power of monotony is a fool. The culture industry refutes the objection made against it just as well as that against the world which it impartially duplicates. The only choice is either to join in or to be left behind: those provincials who have recourse to eternal beauty and the amateur stage in preference to the cinema and the radio are already—politically—at the point to which mass culture drives its supporters. It is sufficiently hardened to deride as ideology, if need be, the old wish-fulfillments, the father-ideal and absolute feeling. The new ideology has as its objects the world as such. It makes use of the worship of facts by no more than elevating a disagreeable existence into the world of facts in representing it meticulously. This transference makes existence itself a substitute for meaning and right. Whatever the camera reproduces is beautiful. The disappointment of the prospect that one might be the typist who wins the world trip is matched by the disappointing appearance of the accurately photographed areas which the voyage might include. Not Italy is offered, but evidence that it exists. A film can even go so far as to show the Paris in which the American girl thinks she will still her desire as a hopelessly desolate place, thus driving her the more inexorably into the arms of the smart American boy she could have met at home anyhow. That this goes on, that, in its most recent phase, the system itself reproduces the life of those of whom it consists instead of immediately doing away with them, is even put down to its credit as giving it meaning and worth. Continuing and continuing to join in are given as justification for the blind persistence of the system and even for its immutability. What repeats itself is healthy, like the natural or industrial cycle. The same babies grin eternally out of the magazines; the jazz machine will pound away for ever. In spite of all the progress in reproduction techniques, in controls and the specialities, and in spite of all the restless industry, the bread which the culture industry offers man is the stone of the stereotype. It draws on the life cycle, on the well-founded amazement that mothers, in spite of everything, still go on bearing children and that the wheels still do not grind to a halt. This serves to confirm the immutability of circumstances. The ears of corn blowing in the wind at the end of Chaplin's *The Great Dictator* give the lie to the anti-Fascist plea for freedom. They are like the blond hair of the German girl whose camp life is photographed by the Nazi film company in the summer breeze. Nature is viewed by the mechanism of social domination as a healthy contrast to society, and is therefore denatured. Pictures showing green trees, a blue sky, and moving clouds make these aspects of nature into so many cryptograms for factory chimneys and service stations. On the other hand, wheels and machine components must seem expressive, having been degraded to the status of agents of the spirit of trees and clouds. Nature and technology are mobilized against all opposition; and we have a falsified memento of liberal society, in which people supposedly wallowed in erotic plush-lined bedrooms instead of taking open-air baths as in the case today, or experiencing breakdowns in prehistoric Benz models instead of shooting off with the speed of a rocket from A (where one is anyhow) to B (where everything is just the same). The triumph of the gigantic concern over the initiative of the entrepreneur is praised by the culture industry as the persistence of entrepreneurial initiative. The enemy who is already defeated, the thinking individual, is the enemy fought. The resurrection in Germany of the anti-bourgeois "Haus Sonnenstösser," and the pleasure felt when watching *Life with Father,* have one and the same meaning.

In one respect, admittedly, this hollow ideology is in deadly earnest: everyone is provided for. "No one must go hungry or thirsty; if anyone does, he's for the concentration camp!" This joke from Hitler's Germany might shine forth as a maxim from above all the portals of the culture industry. With sly naïveté, it presupposes the most recent characteristic of society: that it can easily find out who its supporters are. Everybody is guaranteed formal freedom. No one is officially responsible for what he thinks. Instead everyone is enclosed at an early age in a system of churches, clubs, professional associations, and other such concerns, which constitute the most sensitive instrument of social control. Anyone who wants to avoid ruin must see that he is not found wanting when weighed in the scales of this apparatus. Otherwise he will lag behind in life, and finally perish. In every career, and especially in the liberal professions, expert knowledge is linked with prescribed standards of conduct; this can easily lead to the illusion that expert knowledge is the only thing that counts. In fact, it is part of the irrational planning of this society that it reproduces to a certain degree only the lives of its faithful members. The standard of life enjoyed corresponds very closely to the degree to which classes and individuals are essentially bound up with the system. The manager can be relied upon, as can the lesser employee Dagwood—as he is in the comic pages or in real life. Anyone who goes cold and hungry, even if his prospects were once good, is branded. He is an outsider; and, apart from certain capital crimes, the most mortal of sins is to be an outsider. In films he sometimes, and as an exception, becomes an original, the object of maliciously indulgent humor; but usually he is the villain, and is identified as such at first appearance, long before the action really gets going: hence avoiding any suspicion that society would turn on those of good will. Higher up the scale, in fact, a kind of welfare state is coming into being today. In order to keep their own positions, men in top posts maintain the economy in which a highly-developed technology has in principle made the masses redundant as producers. The workers, the real bread-winners, are fed (if we are to believe the ideology) by the managers of the economy, the fed. Hence the individual's position becomes precarious. Under liberalism the poor were thought to be lazy; now they are automatically objects of suspicion. Anybody who is not provided for outside should be in a concentration camp, or at any rate in the hell of the most degrading work and the slums. The culture industry, however, reflects positive and negative welfare for those under the administrators' control as direct human solidarity of men in a world of the efficient. No one is forgotten; everywhere there are neighbors and welfare workers, Dr. Gillespies and parlor philosophers whose hearts are in the right place and who, by their kind intervention as of man to man, cure individual cases of socially-perpetuated distress—always provided that there is no obstacle in the personal depravity of the unfortunate. The promotion of a friendly atmosphere as advised by management experts and adopted by every factory to increase output, brings even the last private impulse under social control precisely because it seems to relate men's circumstances directly to production, and to reprivatize them. Such spiritual charity casts a conciliatory shadow onto the products of the culture industry long before it emerges from the factory to invade society as a whole. Yet the great benefactors of mankind, whose scientific achievements have to be written up as acts of sympathy to give them an artificial human interest, are substitutes for the national leaders, who finally decree the abolition of sympathy and think they can prevent any recurrence when the last invalid has been exterminated.

By emphasizing the "heart of gold," society admits the suffering it has created: everyone knows that he is now helpless in the system, and ideology has to take this into account. Far from concealing suffering under the cloak of improvised fellowship, the culture industry takes pride in looking it in the face like a man, however great the strain on self-control. The pathos of composure justifies the world which makes it necessary. That is life—very hard, but just because of that so wonderful and so healthy. This lie does not shrink from tragedy. Mass culture deals with it, in the same way as centralized society does not abolish the suffering of its members but records and plans it. That it is why it borrows so persistently from art. This provides the tragic substance which pure amusement cannot itself supply, but which it needs if it is somehow to remain faithful to the principle of the exact reproduction of phenomena. Tragedy made into a carefully calculated and accepted aspect of the world is a blessing. It is a safeguard against the reproach that truth is not respected, whereas it is really being adopted with cynical regret. To the consumer who—culturally—has seen better days it offers a substitute for long-discarded profundities. It provides the regular movie-goer with the scraps of culture he must have for prestige. It comforts all with the thought that a tough, genuine human fate is still possible, and that it must at all costs be represented uncompromisingly. Life in all the aspects which ideology today sets out to duplicate shows up all

151

the more gloriously, powerfully and magnificently, the more it is redolent of necessary suffering. It begins to resemble fate. Tragedy is reduced to the threat to destroy anyone who does not cooperate, whereas its paradoxical significance once lay in a hopeless resistance to mythic destiny. Tragic fate becomes just punishment, which is what bourgeois aesthetics always tried to turn it into. The morality of mass culture is the cheap form of yesterday's children's books. In a first-class production, for example, the villainous character appears as a hysterical woman who (with presumed clinical accuracy) tries to ruin the happiness of her opposite number, who is truer to reality, and herself suffers a quite untheatrical death. So much learning is of course found only at the top. Lower down less trouble is taken. Tragedy is made harmless without recourse to social psychology. Just as every Viennese operetta worthy of the name had to have its tragic finale in the second act, which left nothing for the third except to clear up misunderstandings, the culture industry assigns tragedy a fixed place in the routine. The well-known existence of the recipe is enough to allay any fear that there is no restraint on tragedy. The description of the dramatic formula by the housewife as "getting into trouble and out again" embraces the whole of mass culture from the idiotic women's serial to the top production. Even the worst ending which began with good intentions confirms the order of things and corrupts the tragic force, either because the woman whose love runs counter to the laws of the game plays with her death for a brief spell of happiness, or because the sad ending in the film all the more clearly stresses the indestructibility of actual life. The tragic film becomes an institution for moral improvement. The masses, demoralized by their life under the pressure of the system, and who show signs of civilization only in modes of behavior which have been forced on them and through which fury and recalcitrance show everywhere, are to be kept in order by the sight of an inexorable life and exemplary behavior. Culture has always played its part in taming revolutionary and barbaric instincts. Industrial culture adds its contribution. It shows the condition under which this merciless life can be lived at all. The individual who is thoroughly weary must use his weariness as energy for his surrender to the collective power which wears him out. In films, those permanently desperate situations which crush the spectator in ordinary life somehow become a promise that one can go on living. One has only to become aware of one's own nothingness, only to recognize defeat and one is one with it all. Society is full of desperate people and therefore a prey to rackets. In some of the most significant German novels of the pre-Fascist era such as Döblin's *Berlin Alexanderplatz* and Fallada's *Kleiner Mann, Was Nun,* this trend was as obvious as in the average film and in the devices of jazz. What all these things have in common is the self-derision of man. The possibility of becoming a subject in the economy, an entrepreneur or a proprietor, has been completely liquidated. Right down to the humblest shop, the independent enterprise, on the management and inheritance of which the bourgeois family and the position of its head had rested, became hopelessly dependent. Everybody became an employee; and in this civilization of employees the dignity of the father (questionable anyhow) vanishes. The attitude of the individual to the racket, business, profession or party, before or after admission, the Führer's gesticulations before the masses, or the suitor's before his sweetheart, assume specifically masochistic traits. The attitude into which everybody is forced in order to give repeated proof of his moral suitability for this society reminds one of the boys who, during tribal initiation, go round in a circle with a stereotyped smile on their faces while the priest strikes them. Life in the late capitalist era is a constant initiation rite. Everyone must show that he wholly identifies himself with the power which is belaboring him. This occurs in the principle of jazz syncopation, which simultaneously derides stumbling and makes it a rule. The eunuch-like voice of the crooner on the radio, the heiress's smooth suitor, who falls into the swimming pool in his dinner jacket, are models for those who must become whatever the system wants. Everyone can be like this omnipotent society; everyone can be happy, if only he will capitulate fully and sacrifice his claim to happiness. In his weakness society recognizes its strength, and gives him some of it. His defenselessness makes him reliable. Hence tragedy is discarded. Once the opposition

153

of the individual to society was its substance. It glorified "the bravery and freedom of emotion before a powerful enemy, an exalted affliction, a dreadful problem."[4] Today tragedy has melted away into the nothingness of that false identity of society and individual, whose terror still shows for a moment in the empty semblance of the tragic. But the miracle of integration, the permanent act of grace by the authority who receives the defenseless person—once he has swallowed his rebelliousness —signifies Fascism. This can be seen in the humanitarianism which Döblin uses to let his Biberkopf find refuge, and again in socially-slanted films. The capacity to find refuge, to survive one's own ruin, by which tragedy is defeated, is found in the new generation; they can do any work because the work process does not let them become attached to any. This is reminiscent of the sad lack of conviction of the homecoming soldier with no interest in the war, or of the casual laborer who ends up by joining a paramilitary organization. This liquidation of tragedy confirms the abolition of the individual.

In the culture industry the individual is an illusion not merely because of the standardization of the means of production. He is tolerated only so long as his complete identification with the generality is unquestioned. Pseudo individuality is rife: from the standardized jazz improvization to the exceptional film star whose hair curls over her eye to demonstrate her originality. What is individual is no more than the generality's power to stamp the accidental detail so firmly that it is accepted as such. The defiant reserve or elegant appearance of the individual on show is mass-produced like Yale locks, whose only difference can be measured in fractions of millimeters. The peculiarity of the self is a monopoly commodity determined by society; it is falsely represented as natural. It is no more than the moustache, the French accent, the deep voice of the woman of the world, the Lubitsch touch: finger prints on identity cards which are otherwise exactly the same, and into which the lives and faces of every single person are transformed by the power of the gener-

4. Nietzsche, *Götzendämmerung, Werke,* Vol. VIII, p. 136.

ality. Pseudo individuality is the prerequisite for comprehending tragedy and removing its poison: only because individuals have ceased to be themselves and are now merely centers where the general tendencies meet, is it possible to receive them again, whole and entire, into the generality. In this way mass culture discloses the fictitious character of the "individual" in the bourgeois era, and is merely unjust in boasting on account of this dreary harmony of general and particular. The principle of individuality was always full of contradiction. Individuation has never really been achieved. Self-preservation in the shape of class has kept everyone at the stage of a mere species being. Every bourgeois characteristic, in spite of its deviation and indeed because of it, expressed the same thing: the harshness of the competitive society. The individual who supported society bore its disfiguring mark; seemingly free, he was actually the product of its economic and social apparatus. Power based itself on the prevailing conditions of power when it sought the approval of persons affected by it. As it progressed, bourgeois society did also develop the individual. Against the will of its leaders, technology has changed human beings from children into persons. However, every advance in individuation of this kind took place at the expense of the individuality in whose name it occurred, so that nothing was left but the resolve to pursue one's own particular purpose. The bourgeois whose existence is split into a business and a private life, whose private life is split into keeping up his public image and intimacy, whose intimacy is split into the surly partnership of marriage and the bitter comfort of being quite alone, at odds with himself and everybody else, is already virtually a Nazi, replete both with enthusiasm and abuse; or a modern city-dweller who can now only imagine friendship as a "social contact": that is, as being in social contact with others with whom he has no inward contact. The only reason why the culture industry can deal so successfully with individuality is that the latter has always reproduced the fragility of society. On the faces of private individuals and movie heroes put together according to the patterns on magazine covers vanishes a pretense in which no one now believes; the popularity of the hero models comes partly from a

155

secret satisfaction that the effort to achieve individuation has at last been replaced by the effort to imitate, which is admittedly more breathless. It is idle to hope that this self-contradictory, disintegrating "person" will not last for generations, that the system must collapse because of such a psychological split, or that the deceitful substitution of the stereotype for the individual will of itself become unbearable for mankind. Since Shakespeare's *Hamlet,* the unity of the personality has been seen through as a pretense. Synthetically produced physiognomies show that the people of today have already forgotten that there was ever a notion of what human life was. For centuries society has been preparing for Victor Mature and Mickey Rooney. By destroying they come to fulfill.

The idolization of the cheap involves making the average the heroic. The highest-paid stars resemble pictures advertising unspecified proprietary articles. Not without good purpose are they often selected from the host of commercial models. The prevailing taste takes its ideal from advertising, the beauty in consumption. Hence the Socratic saying that the beautiful is the useful has now been fulfilled—ironically. The cinema makes propaganda for the culture combine as a whole; on radio, goods for whose sake the cultural commodity exists are also recommended individually. For a few coins one can see the film which cost millions, for even less one can buy the chewing gum whose manufacture involved immense riches—a hoard increased still further by sales. *In absentia,* but by universal suffrage, the treasure of armies is revealed, but prostitution is not allowed inside the country. The best orchestras in the world—clearly not so—are brought into your living room free of charge. It is all a parody of the never-never land, just as the national society is a parody of the human society. You name it, we supply it. A man up from the country remarked at the old Berlin Metropol theater that it was astonishing what they could do for the money; his comment has long since been adopted by the culture industry and made the very substance of production. This is always coupled with the triumph that it is possible; but this, in large measure, is the very triumph. Putting on a show means showing everybody what there is, and what can be achieved.

Even today it is still a fair, but incurably sick with culture. Just as the people who had been attracted by the fairground barkers overcame their disappointment in the booths with a brave smile, because they really knew in advance what would happen, so the movie-goer sticks knowingly to the institution. With the cheapness of mass-produce luxury goods and its complement, the universal swindle, a change in the character of the art commodity itself is coming about. What is new is not that it is a commodity, but that today it deliberately admits it is one; that art renounces its own autonomy and proudly takes its place among consumption goods constitutes the charm of novelty. Art as a separate sphere was always possible only in a bourgeois society. Even as a negation of that social purposiveness which is spreading through the market, its freedom remains essentially bound up with the premise of a commodity economy. Pure works of art which deny the commodity society by the very fact that they obey their own law were always wares all the same. In so far as, until the eighteenth century, the buyer's patronage shielded the artist from the market, they were dependent on the buyer and his objectives. The purposelessness of the great modern work of art depends on the anonymity of the market. Its demands pass through so many intermediaries that the artist is exempt from any definite requirements—though admittedly only to a certain degree, for throughout the whole history of the bourgeoisie his autonomy was only tolerated, and thus contained an element of untruth which ultimately led to the social liquidation of art. When mortally sick, Beethoven hurled away a novel by Sir Walter Scott with the cry: "Why, the fellow writes for money," and yet proved a most experienced and stubborn businessman in disposing of the last quartets, which were a most extreme renunciation of the market; he is the most outstanding example of the unity of those opposites, market and independence, in bourgeois art. Those who succumb to the ideology are precisely those who cover up the contradiction instead of taking it into the consciousness of their own production as Beethoven did: he went on to express in music his anger at losing a few pence, and derived the metaphysical *Es Muss Sein* (which attempts an aesthetic banishment

157

of the pressure of the world by taking it into itself) from the housekeeper's demand for her monthly wages. The principle of idealistic aesthetics—purposefulness without a purpose—reverses the scheme of things to which bourgeois art conforms socially: purposelessness for the purposes declared by the market. At last, in the demand for entertainment and relaxation, purpose has absorbed the realm of purposelessness. But as the insistence that art should be disposable in terms of money becomes absolute, a shift in the internal structure of cultural commodities begins to show itself. The use which men in this antagonistic society promise themselves from the work of art is itself, to a great extent, that very existence of the useless which is abolished by complete inclusion under use. The work of art, by completely assimilating itself to need, deceitfully deprives men of precisely that liberation from the principle of utility which it should inaugurate. What might be called use value in the reception of cultural commodities is replaced by exchange value; in place of enjoyment there are gallery-visiting and factual knowledge: the prestige seeker replaces the connoisseur. The consumer becomes the ideology of the pleasure industry, whose institutions he cannot escape. One simply "has to" have seen *Mrs. Miniver,* just as one "has to" subscribe to *Life* and *Time*. Everything is looked at from only one aspect: that it can be used for something else, however vague the notion of this use may be. No object has an inherent value; it is valuable only to the extent that it can be exchanged. The use value of art, its mode of being, is treated as a fetish; and the fetish, the work's social rating (misinterpreted as its artistic status) becomes its use value—the only quality which is enjoyed. The commodity function of art disappears only to be wholly realized when art becomes a species of commodity instead, marketable and interchangeable like an industrial product. But art as a type of product which existed to be sold and yet to be unsaleable is wholly and hypocritically converted into "unsaleability" as soon as the transaction ceases to be the mere intention and becomes its sole principle. No tickets could be bought when Toscanini conducted over the radio; he was heard without charge, and every sound of the symphony was accompanied, as it were, by the sublime puff that the symphony was not interrupted by any advertising: "This concert is brought to you as a public service." The illusion was made possible by the profits of the united automobile and soap manufacturers, whose payments keep the radio stations going—and, of course, by the increased sales of the electrical industry, which manufactures the radio sets. Radio, the progressive latecomer of mass culture, draws all the consequences at present denied the film by its pseudo-market. The technical structure of the commercial radio system makes it immune from liberal deviations such as those the movie industrialists can still permit themselves in their own sphere. It is a private enterprise which really does represent the sovereign whole and is therefore some distance ahead of the other individual combines. Chesterfield is merely the nation's cigarette, but the radio is the voice of the nation. In bringing cultural products wholly into the sphere of commodities, radio does not try to dispose of its culture goods themselves as commodities straight to the consumer. In America it collects no fees from the public, and so has acquired the illusory form of disinterested, unbiased authority which suits Fascism admirably. The radio becomes the universal mouthpiece of the Führer; his voice rises from street loud-speakers to resemble the howling of sirens announcing panic—from which modern propaganda can scarcely be distinguished anyway. The National Socialists knew that the wireless gave shape to their cause just as the printing press did to the Reformation. The metaphysical charisma of the Führer invented by the sociology of religion has finally turned out to be no more than the omnipresence of his speeches on the radio, which are a demoniacal parody of the omnipresence of the divine spirit. The gigantic fact that the speech penetrates everywhere replaces its content, just as the benefaction of the Toscanini broadcast takes the place of the symphony. No listener can grasp its true meaning any longer, while the Führer's speech is lies anyway. The inherent tendency of radio is to make the speaker's word, the false commandment, absolute. A recommendation becomes an order. The recommendation of the same commodities under different proprietary names, the scientifically based praise of the laxative in the announcer's smooth

159

voice between the overture from *La Traviata* and that from *Rienzi* is the only thing that no longer works, because of its silliness. One day the edict of production, the actual advertisement (whose actuality is at present concealed by the pretense of a choice) can turn into the open command of the Führer. In a society of huge Fascist rackets which agree among themselves what part of the social product should be allotted to the nation's needs, it would eventually seem anachronistic to recommend the use of a particular soap powder. The Führer is more up-to-date in unceremoniously giving direct orders for both the holocaust and the supply of rubbish.

Even today the culture industry dresses works of art like political slogans and forces them upon a resistant public at reduced prices; they are as accessible for public enjoyment as a park. But the disappearance of their genuine commodity character does not mean that they have been abolished in the life of a free society, but that the last defense against their reduction to culture goods has fallen. The abolition of educational privilege by the device of clearance sales does not open for the masses the spheres from which they were formerly excluded, but, given existing social conditions, contributes directly to the decay of education and the progress of barbaric meaninglessness. Those who spent their money in the nineteenth or the early twentieth century to see a play or to go to a concert respected the performance as much as the money they spent. The bourgeois who wanted to get something out of it tried occasionally to establish some rapport with the work. Evidence for this is to be found in the literary "introductions" to works, or in the commentaries on *Faust*. These were the first steps toward the biographical coating and other practices to which a work of art is subjected today. Even in the early, prosperous days of business, exchange-value did carry use value as a mere appendix but had developed it as a prerequisite for its own existence; this was socially helpful for works of art. Art exercised some restraint on the bourgeois as long as it cost money. That is now a thing of the past. Now that it has lost every restraint and there is no need to pay any money, the proximity of art to those who are exposed to it completes the alienation and assimilates one to the other under the banner of triumphant objectivity. Criticism and respect disappear in the culture industry; the former becomes a mechanical expertise, the latter is succeeded by a shallow cult of leading personalities. Consumers now find nothing expensive. Nevertheless, they suspect that the less anything costs, the less it is being given them. The double mistrust of traditional culture as ideology is combined with mistrust of industrialized culture as a swindle. When thrown in free, the now debased works of art, together with the rubbish to which the medium assimilates them, are secretly rejected by the fortunate recipients, who are supposed to be satisfied by the mere fact that there is so much to be seen and heard. Everything can be obtained. The screenos and vaudevilles in the movie theater, the competitions for guessing music, the free books, rewards and gifts offered on certain radio programs, are not mere accidents but a continuation of the practice obtaining with culture products. The symphony becomes a reward for listening to the radio, and—if technology had its way—the film would be delivered to people's homes as happens with the radio. It is moving toward the commercial system. Television points the way to a development which might easily enough force the Warner Brothers into what would certainly be the unwelcome position of serious musicians and cultural conservatives. But the gift system has already taken hold among consumers. As culture is represented as a bonus with undoubted private and social advantages, they have to seize the chance. They rush in lest they miss something. Exactly what, is not clear, but in any case the only ones with a chance are the participants. Fascism, however, hopes to use the training the culture industry has given these recipients of gifts, in order to organize them into its own forced battalions.

Culture is a paradoxical commodity. So completely is it subject to the law of exchange that it is no longer exchanged; it is so blindly consumed in use that it can no longer be used. Therefore it amalgamates with advertising. The more meaningless the latter seems to be under a monopoly, the more omnipotent it becomes. The motives are markedly economic. One could certainly live without the culture industry, therefore it necessarily

161

creates too much satiation and apathy.) In itself, it has few resources itself to correct this. Advertising is its elixir of life. But as its product never fails to reduce to a mere promise the enjoyment which it promises as a commodity, it eventually coincides with publicity, which it needs because it cannot be enjoyed. In a competitive society, advertising performed the social service of informing the buyer about the market; it made choice easier and helped the unknown but more efficient supplier to dispose of his goods. Far from costing time, it saved it. Today, when the free market is coming to an end, those who control the system are entrenching themselves in it. It strengthens the firm bond between the consumers and the big combines. Only those who can pay the exorbitant rates charged by the advertising agencies, chief of which are the radio networks themselves; that is, only those who are already in a position to do so, or are co-opted by the decision of the banks and industrial capital, can enter the pseudo-market as sellers. The costs of advertising, which finally flow back into the pockets of the combines, make it unnecessary to defeat unwelcome outsiders by laborious competition. They guarantee that power will remain in the same hands—not unlike those economic decisions by which the establishment and running of undertakings is controlled in a totalitarian state. Advertising today is a negative principle, a blocking device: everything that does not bear its stamp is economically suspect. Universal publicity is in no way necessary for people to get to know the kinds of goods—whose supply is restricted anyway. It helps sales only indirectly. For a particular firm, to phase out a current advertising practice constitutes a loss of prestige, and a breach of the discipline imposed by the influential clique on its members. In wartime, goods which are unobtainable are still advertised, merely to keep industrial power in view. Subsidizing ideological media is more important than the repetition of the name. Because the system obliges every product to use advertising, it has permeated the idiom—the "style"—of the culture industry. Its victory is so complete that it is no longer evident in the key positions: the huge buildings of the top men, floodlit stone advertisements, are free of advertising; at most they exhibit on the rooftops, in monumental brilliance and without any self-glorification, the firm's initials. But, in contrast, the nineteenth-century houses, whose architecture still shamefully indicates that they can be used as a consumption commodity and are intended to be lived in, are covered with posters and inscriptions from the ground right up to and beyond the roof: until they become no more than backgrounds for bills and sign-boards. Advertising becomes art and nothing else, just as Goebbels—with foresight—combines them: *l'art pour l'art*, advertising for its own sake, a pure representation of social power. In the most influential American magazines, *Life* and *Fortune*, a quick glance can now scarcely distinguish advertising from editorial picture and text. The latter features an enthusiastic and gratuitous account of the great man (with illustrations of his life and grooming habits) which will bring him new fans, while the advertisement pages use so many factual photographs and details that they represent the ideal of information which the editorial part has only begun to try to achieve. The assembly-line character of the culture industry, the synthetic, planned method of turning out its products (factory-like not only in the studio but, more or less, in the compilation of cheap biographies, pseudodocumentary novels, and hit songs) is very suited to advertising: the important individual points, by becoming detachable, interchangeable, and even technically alienated from any connected meaning, lend themselves to ends external to the work. The effect, the trick, the isolated repeatable device, have always been used to exhibit goods for advertising purposes, and today every monster close-up of a star is an advertisement for her name, and every hit song a plug for its tune. Advertising and the culture industry merge technically as well as economically. In both cases the same thing can be seen in innumerable places, and the mechanical repetition of the same culture product has come to be the same as that of the propaganda slogan. In both cases the insistent demand for effectiveness makes technology into psycho-technology, into a procedure for manipulating men. In both cases the standards are the striking yet familiar, the easy yet catchy, the skillful yet simple; the object is to overpower the customer, who is conceived as absent-minded or resistant.

163

By the language he speaks, he makes his own contribution to culture as publicity. The more completely language is lost in the announcement, the more words are debased as substantial vehicles of meaning and become signs devoid of quality; the more purely and transparently words communicate what is intended, the more impenetrable they become. The demythologization of language, taken as an element of the whole process of enlightenment, is a relapse into magic. Word and essential content were distinct yet inseparable from one another. Concepts like melancholy and history, even life, were recognized in the word, which separated them out and preserved them. Its form simultaneously constituted and reflected them. The absolute separation, which makes the moving accidental and its relation to the object arbitrary, puts an end to the superstitious fusion of word and thing. Anything in a determined literal sequence which goes beyond the correlation to the event is rejected as unclear and as verbal metaphysics. But the result is that the word, which can now be only a sign without any meaning, becomes so fixed to the thing that it is just a petrified formula. This affects language and object alike. Instead of making the object experiential, the purified word treats it as an abstract instance, and everything else (now excluded by the demand for ruthless clarity from expression—itself now banished) fades away in reality. A left-half at football, a black-shirt, a member of the Hitler Youth, and so on, are no more than names. If before its rationalization the word had given rise to lies as well as to longing, now, after its rationalization, it is a straitjacket for longing more even than for lies. The blindness and dumbness of the data to which positivism reduces the world pass over into language itself, which restricts itself to recording those data. Terms themselves become impenetrable; they obtain a striking force, a power of adhesion and repulsion which makes them like their extreme opposite, incantations. They come to be a kind of trick, because the name of the prima donna is cooked up in the studio on a statistical basis, or because a welfare state is anathematized by using taboo terms such as "bureaucrats" or "intellectuals," or because base practice uses the name of the country as a charm. In general, the name—to which magic most easily attaches—is undergoing a chemical change: a metamorphosis into capricious, manipulable designations, whose effect is admittedly now calculable, but which for that very reason is just as despotic as that of the archaic name. First names, those archaic remnants, have been brought up to date either by stylization as advertising trade-marks (film stars' surnames have become first names), or by collective standardization. In comparison, the bourgeois family name which, instead of being a trade-mark, once individualized its bearer by relating him to his own past history, seems antiquated. It arouses a strange embarrassment in Americans. In order to hide the awkward distance between individuals, they call one another "Bob" and "Harry," as interchangeable team members. This practice reduces relations between human beings to the good fellowship of the sporting community and is a defense against the true kind of relationship. Signification, which is the only function of a word admitted by semantics, reaches perfection in the sign. Whether folksongs were rightly or wrongly called upper-class culture in decay, their elements have only acquired their popular form through a long process of repeated transmission. The spread of popular songs, on the other hand, takes place at lightning speed. The American expression "fad," used for fashions which appear like epidemics—that is, inflamed by highly-concentrated economic forces—designated this phenomenon long before totalitarian advertising bosses enforced the general lines of culture. When the German Fascists decide one day to launch a word—say, "intolerable"— over the loudspeakers the next day the whole nation is saying "intolerable." By the same pattern, the nations against whom the weight of the German "blitzkrieg" was thrown took the word into their own jargon. The general repetition of names for measures to be taken by the authorities makes them, so to speak, familiar, just as the brand name on everybody's lips increased sales in the era of the free market. The blind and rapidly spreading repetition of words with special designations links advertising with the totalitarian watchword. The layer of experience which created the words for their speakers has been removed; in this swift appropriation language acquires the coldness which until now it had only on

165

billboards and in the advertisement columns of newspapers. Innumerable people use words and expressions which they have either ceased to understand or employ only because they trigger off conditioned reflexes; in this sense, words are trade-marks which are finally all the more firmly linked to the things they denote, the less their linguistic sense is grasped. The minister for mass education talks incomprehendingly of "dynamic forces," and the hit songs unceasingly celebrate "reverie" and "rhapsody," yet base their popularity precisely on the magic of the unintelligible as creating the thrill of a more exalted life. Other stereotypes, such as memory, are still partly comprehended, but escape from the experience which might allow them content. They appear like enclaves in the spoken language. On the radio of Flesch and Hitler they may be recognized from the affected pronunciation of the announcer when he says to the nation, "Good night, everybody!" or "This is the Hitler Youth," and even intones "the Führer" in a way imitated by millions. In such clichés the last bond between sedimentary experience and language is severed which still had a reconciling effect in dialect in the nineteenth century. But in the prose of the journalist whose adaptable attitude led to his appointment as an all-German editor, the German words become petrified, alien terms. Every word shows how far it has been debased by the Fascist pseudo-folk community. By now, of course, this kind of language is already universal, totalitarian. All the violence done to words is so vile that one can hardly bear to hear them any longer. The announcer does not need to speak pompously; he would indeed be impossible if his inflection were different from that of his particular audience. But, as against that, the language and gestures of the audience and spectators are colored more strongly than ever before by the culture industry, even in fine nuances which cannot yet be explained experimentally. Today the culture industry has taken over the civilizing inheritance of the entrepreneurial and frontier democracy—whose appreciation of intellectual deviations was never very finely attuned. All are free to dance and enjoy themselves, just as they have been free, since the historical neutralization of religion, to join any of the innumerable sects. But freedom to choose an ideology—since ideology always reflects economic coercion—everywhere proves to be freedom to choose what is always the same. The way in which a girl accepts and keeps the obligatory date, the inflection on the telephone or in the most intimate situation, the choice of words in conversation, and the whole inner life as classified by the now somewhat devalued depth psychology, bear witness to man's attempt to make himself a proficient apparatus, similar (even in emotions) to the model served up by the culture industry. The most intimate reactions of human beings have been so thoroughly reified that the idea of anything specific to themselves now persists only as an utterly abstract notion: personality scarcely signifies anything more than shining white teeth and freedom from body odor and emotions. The triumph of advertising in the culture industry is that consumers feel compelled to buy and use its products even though they see through them.

ELEMENTS
OF ANTI-SEMITISM:

The Limits of Enlightenment

I.

FOR some people today anti-Semitism involves the destiny of mankind; for others it is a mere pretext. The Fascists do not view the Jews as a minority but as an opposing race, the embodiment of the negative principle. They must be exterminated to secure happiness for the world. At the other extreme we have the theory that the Jews have no national or racial characteristics and simply form a group through their religious opinions and tradition. It is claimed that only the Jews of Eastern Europe have Jewish characteristics, and then only if they have not been fully assimilated. Neither doctrine is wholly true or wholly false.

The first is true to the extent that Fascism has made it true. The Jews today are the group which calls down upon itself, both in theory and in practice, the will to destroy born of a false social order. They are branded as absolute evil by those who are absolutely evil, and are now in fact the chosen race. Whereas there is no longer any need for economic domination, the Jews are marked out as the absolute object of domination pure and simple. No one tells the workers, who are the ultimate target, straight to their face—for very good reasons; and the Negroes are to be kept where they belong: but the Jews must be wiped from the face of the earth, and the call to destroy them like vermin finds an echo in the heart of every budding fascist throughout the world. The portrait of the Jews that the nationalists offer to the world is in fact their own self-portrait. They long for total possession and unlimited power, at any price. They transfer their guilt for this to the Jews, whom as masters they despise and crucify, repeating *ad infinitum* a sacrifice which they cannot believe to be effective.

The other, liberal, theory is true as an idea. It contains the image of a society in which irrational anger no longer exists and seeks for outlets. But since the liberal theory assumes that unity among men is already in principle established, it serves as an apologia for existing circumstances. The attempt to avert the extreme threat by a minorities policy and a democratic strategy is ambiguous, like the defensive stance of the last liberal citizens. Their impotence attracts the enemy of impotence. The existence and way of life of the Jews throw into question the generality with which they do not conform. The inflexible adherence to their own order of life has brought the Jews into an uncertain relationship with the dominant order. They expected to be protected without themselves being in command. Their relationship with the ruling nations was one of greed and fear. But the arrivistes who crossed the gulf separating them from the dominant mode of life lost that cold, stoic character which society still makes a necessity. The dialectical link between enlightenment and domination, and the dual relationship of progress to cruelty and liberation which the Jews sensed in the great philosophers of the Enlightenment and the democratic, national movements are reflected in the very essence of those assimilated. The enlightened self-control with which the assimilated Jews managed to forget the painful memories of domination by others (a second circumcision, so to speak) led them straight from their own, long-suffering community into the modern bourgeoisie, which was moving inexorably toward reversion to cold repression and reorganization as a pure "race." But race is not a naturally special characteristic, as the folk mystics would have it. It is a reduction to the natural, to sheer force, to that stubborn particularity which in the status quo constitutes the generality. Today race has become the self-assertion of the bourgeois individual integrated within a barbaric collective. The harmony of society which the liberal Jews believed in turned against them in the form of the harmony of a national community. They thought that anti-Semitism would distort that order which in reality cannot exist without distorting men. The persecution of the Jews, like any other form of persecution, is inseparable from that system of order. However successfully it may at times be concealed, force is the essential nature of this order—and we are witnessing its naked truth today.

II.

Anti-Semitism as a national movement was always based on an urge which its instigators held against the Social Democrats: the urge for equality. Those who have no power to command must suffer the same fate as ordinary people. The covetous mobs— wherever they appeared—have always been aware deep down that ultimately all they would get out of it themselves would be the pleasure of seeing others robbed of all they possessed. The "Aryanization" of Jewish property brought scarcely more benefit to the masses in the Third Reich than the Cossacks got out of the miserable loot they carried away from the burning ghettos. The true advantage lay in half-understood ideology. The fact that the demonstration of its economic uselessness tends to increase rather than to lessen the attraction of the nationalistic panacea, points to its true nature: it does not help men but panders to their urge to destroy. The true benefit for the *Volksgenosse* lies in collective approval of his anger. The smaller the actual advantage are, the more stubbornly he supports the movement against his better judgment. Anti-Semitism has proved immune to the argument of inadequate "profitability." It is a luxury for the masses.

It is an obvious asset to the ruling clique. It is used as a diversion, a cheap means of corruption and an intimidating example. The respectable rackets support it, and the low ones practice it. But the form of the social and individual spirit reflected in anti-Semitism—the prehistorical and historical connections which it cannot escape—remains obscured. If a malady which is so deep-rooted in civilization has no known justification, the individual would not nationalize it even if he were as well-intentioned as the victims themselves. All the rational, economic, and political explanations and counter-arguments—however accurate they may be in part—cannot provide a justification, because the rationality associated with domination is also based on suffering. Attacking or defending blindly, the persecutor and his victim belong to the same sphere of evil. Anti-Semitic behavior is generated in situations where blinded men robbed of their subjectivity are set loose as subjects. For those involved, their actions are murderous and therefore senseless reflexes, as behaviorists note—without providing an interpretation. Anti-Semitism is a deeply imprinted schema, a ritual of civilization; the pogroms are the true ritual murders. They demonstrate the impotence of sense, significance, and ultimately of truth—which might hold them within bounds. The idle occupation of killing confirms the stubbornness of the life to which one has to conform, and to resign oneself.

It is the blindness and lack of purpose of anti-Semitism which lends a measure of truth to the explanation that it is an outlet. Anger is discharged on defenseless victims. And since the victims are interchangeable according to circumstances—gypsies, Jews, Protestants, Catholics, and so on—any one of them may take the place of the murderers, with the same blind lust for blood, should they be invested with the title of the norm. There is no genuine anti-Semitism, and certainly no such thing as a born anti-Semite. The adults to whom the cry for the blood of Jews has become second nature do not know the reason why any more than the young people who are called upon to spill that blood. Those in command who know the reasons do not hate the Jews and do not love their own followers. But the hatred felt by the led, who can never be satisfied economically or sexually, knows no bounds. Their hatred cannot be worked off because it can never be fulfilled. The organized murderers are inspired by a kind of dynamic idealism. They set out to plunder, and construct a complicated ideology to that end, with illogical claims to be the saviors of the family, the fatherland, and mankind. But since they remain dupes (as they have already secretly realized) their wretched national motive—loot—which they tried to rationalize is undermined, and their motiva-

171

tion becomes honest in its own way. The dark impulse which from the outset was closer to them than reason takes full possession of them. The rational island is overwhelmed and the desperate now appear simply as the defenders of truth, the renewers of the earth who still have to reform the last remaining corner. Every living thing becomes material for their vile task, which is now unflinching. Action becomes an autonomous end in itself, and disguises its own purposelessness. Anti-Semitism must now be total; from the outset there has always been an intimate link between anti-Semitism and totality. Blindness is all-embracing because it comprehends nothing.

Liberalism had allowed the Jews property, but no power to command. The rights of man were designed to promise happiness even to those without power. Because the cheated masses feel that this promise in general remains a lie as long as there are still classes, their anger is aroused. They feel mocked. They must suppress the very possibility and idea of that happiness, the more relevant it becomes. Wherever it seems to have been achieved despite its fundamental denial, they have to repeat the suppression of their own longing. Everything which gives occasion for such repetition, however unhappy it may be in itself— Ahasver or Mignon, alien things which are reminders of the promised land, or beauty which recalls sex, or the proscribed animal which is reminiscent of promiscuity—draws upon itself that destructive lust of civilized men who could never fulfill the process of civilization. Those who spasmodically dominate nature see in a tormented nature a provocative image of powerless happiness. The thought of happiness without power is unbearable because it would then be true happiness. The illusory conspiracy of corrupt Jewish bankers financing Bolshevism is a sign of innate impotence, just as the good life is a sign of happiness. The image of the intellectual is in the same category: he appears to think—a luxury which the others cannot afford—and he does not manifest the sweat of toil and physical effort. Bankers and intellectuals, money and mind, the exponents of circulation, form the impossible ideal of those who have been maimed by domination, an image used by domination to perpetuate itself.

172

III.

Modern society, in which primitive religious feelings and new forms of religion as well as the heritage of revolution are sold on the open market, in which the Fascist leaders bargain over the land and life of nations behind locked doors while the habituated public sit by their radio sets and work out the cost; a society in which the word which it unmasks is thereby legitimized as a component part of a political racket: this society, in which politics is not only a business but business the whole of politics, is gripped by a holy anger over the retarded commercial attitudes of the Jews and classifies them as materialists, and hucksters who must give way to the new race of men who have elevated business into an absolute.

Bourgeois anti-Semitism has a specific economic reason: the concealment of domination in production. In earlier ages the rulers were directly repressive and not only left all the work to the lower classes but declared work to be a disgrace, as it always was under domination; and in a mercantile age, the industrial boss is an absolute monarch. Production attracts its own courtiers. The new rulers simply took off the bright garb of the nobility and donned civilian clothing. They declared that work was not degrading, so as to control the others more rationally. They claimed to be creative workers, but in reality they were still the grasping overlords of former times. The manufacturer took risks and acted like a banker or commercial wizard. He calculated, arranged, bought and sold. On the market he competed for the profit corresponding to his own capital. He seized all he could, not only on the market but at the very source: as a representative of his class he made sure that his workers did not sell him short with their labor. The workers had to supply the maximum amount of goods. Like Shylock, the bosses demand their pound of flesh. They owned the machines and materials, and therefore compelled others to produce for them. They called themselves producers, but secretly everyone knew the truth. The productive work of the capitalist, whether he

173

justifies his profit by means of gross returns as under liberalism, or by his director's salary as today, is an ideology cloaking the real nature of the labor contract and the grasping character of the economic system.

And so people shout: Stop thief!—but point at the Jews. They are the scapegoats not only for individual maneuvers and machinations but in a broader sense, inasmuch as the economic injustice of the whole class is attributed to them. The manufacturer keeps an eye on his debtors, the workers, in the factory and makes sure that they have performed well before he pays them their money. They realize the true position when they stop to think what they can buy with this money. The smallest magnate can dispose of a quantity of services and goods which were available to no ruler in the past; but the workers receive a bare minimum. It is not enough actually to experience how few goods they can buy on the market; the salesmen continue to advertise the merits of things which they cannot afford. The relationship between wages and prices shows what is kept from the workers. With their wages they accept the principle of settlement of all their demands. The merchant presents them with the bill which they have signed away to the manufacturer. The merchant is the bailiff of the whole system and takes the hatred of others upon himself. The responsibility of the circulation sector for exploitation is a socially necessary pretense.

The Jews were not the sole owners of the circulation sector. But they had been active in it for so long that they mirrored in their own ways the hatred they had always borne. Unlike their Aryan colleagues, they were still largely denied access to the origins of surplus value. It was a long time before, with difficulty, they were allowed to own the means of production. Admittedly, in the history of Europe and even under the German emperors, baptized Jews were allowed high positions in industry and in the administration. But they had to justify themselves with twice the usual devotion, diligence, and stubborn self-denial. They were only allowed to retain their positions if by their behavior they tacitly accepted or confirmed the verdict pronounced on other Jews: that was the purpose of baptism. No matter how many great achievements the Jews were responsible for, they could not be absorbed into the European nations; they were not allowed to put down roots and so they were dismissed as rootless. At best the Jews were protected and dependent on emperors, princes or the absolute state. But the rulers themselves all had an economic advantage over the remainder of the population. To the extent that they could use the Jews as intermediaries, they protected them against the masses who had to pay the price of progress. The Jews were the colonizers for progress. From the time when, in their capacity as merchants, they helped to spread Roman civilization throughout Gentile Europe, they were the representatives—in harmony with their patriarchal religion—of municipal, bourgeois and, finally, industrial conditions. They carried capitalist ways of life to various countries and drew upon themselves the hatred of all who had to suffer under capitalism. For the sake of the economic progress which is now proving their downfall, the Jews were always a thorn in the side of the craftsmen and peasants who were declassed by capitalism. They are now experiencing to their own cost the exclusive, particularist character of capitalism. Those who always wanted to be first have been left far behind. Even the Jewish president of an American entertainment trust lives hopelessly on the defensive in his cocoon of cash. The kaftan was a relic of ancient middle-class costume. Today it indicates that its wearer has been cast onto the periphery of a society which, though completely enlightened, still wishes to lay the ghosts of its distant past. Those who proclaimed individualism, abstract justice, and the notion of the person are now degraded to the condition of a species. Those who are never allowed to enjoy freely the civil rights which should allow them human dignity are referred to, without distinction, as "the Jew." Even in the nineteenth century the Jews remained dependent on an alliance with the central power. General justice protected by the state was the pledge of their security, and the law of exception a specter held out before them. The Jews remained objects, at the mercy of others, even when they insisted on their rights. Commerce was not their vocation but their fate. The Jews constituted the trauma of the knights of industry who had to pretend to be creative, while the claptrap

175

of anti-Semitism announced a fact for which they secretly despised themselves; their anti-Semitism is self-hatred, the bad conscience of the parasite.

IV.

The nationalist brand of anti-Semitism ignores religious considerations and asserts that the purity of the race and the nation is at stake. The nationalists realize that men have long since ceased to bother about their eternal salvation. Today the average believer is as cunning as a cardinal in former times. It is impossible to arouse the feelings of the masses today by suggesting that the Jews are obstinate unbelievers. But it is difficult to eliminate completely the religious hostility which encouraged Christians to persecute the Jews for two thousand years. The eagerness with which the anti-Semite denies his religious tradition tends to prove that it remains as deep-seated within him as profane idiosyncrasy once was in the zealots of the faith. Religion was subsumed, and not abolished, when it became a cultural commodity. The alliance between enlightenment and domination has cut the link between the aspect of truth in religion and the consciousness, and has retained only the objectified forms of religion. This is a dual benefit for the Fascists: uncontrolled longing is channelled into nationalistic rebellion, and the descendants of the evangelistic fanatics are turned—like Wagner's knight of the Holy Grail—into sworn members of blood brotherhoods and elite guards; religion as an institution is partly embodied in the system and partly converted into mass culture. The fanatical faith of the leader and his followers is no different from that for which men were once willing to submit to the stake; only the content has changed. But the hatred for all who do not share the faith remains. Anti-Semitism is all that the German Christians have retained of the religion of love.

Christianity is not merely regression behind Judaism. In making the transition from the henotheistic to the universal form, the God of Christianity has not completely discarded the features of the natural demon. The horror which stems from ancient pre-animist days is translated from nature into the notion of the absolute self which, as its creator and overlord, completely subjugates nature. In all the indescribable power and splendor which so alienates him from us, the absolute individual is still conceivable by virtue of the universalizing association with supreme, transcendental being. God as spirit is a principle at the opposite pole to nature; it not only represents the blind natural cycle like the mythical gods but can liberate us from this cycle. But the abstract and remote character of this spirit has also increased the horror of the incommensurable manifest in it; and the *I am,* which tolerates no opposition, exceeds in its inescapable force the more blind, but therefore more equivocal assumption of an anonymous fate. The god of Judaism demands his due and calls to reckoning those who do not give it. He entangles his creatures in the net of guilt and merit. Christianity, on the other hand, has emphasized the concept of grace, which is already present in Judaism in the covenant between God and men and in the messianic promise. It has lessened the horror of the absolute by allowing the creature to find his own reflection in the deity: the representative of God is called by a human name and dies a human death. His message is: Do not be afraid; the Law is secondary to faith; love, the only commandment, is greater than all majesty.

But, through the same factors by which Christianity carries on the interdiction on natural religion, it again stresses idolatry, though in a spiritualized form. To the precise degree that the absolute is made to approximate to the finite, the finite is absolutized. Christ, the spirit become flesh, is the deified sorcerer. Man's self-reflection in the absolute, the humanization of God by Christ, is the *proton pseudos.* Progress beyond Judaism is coupled with the assumption that the man Jesus has become God. The reflective aspect of Christianity, the intellectualization of magic, is the root of evil. That which appears to the spirit as natural being is claimed instead to be spiritual being. The spirit consists precisely in developing a contradiction of such pretense on the part of the finite. A bad conscience recommends the prophet as a symbol and the practice of magic as metamorphosis. Christianity becomes a religion, in a certain sense

177

the only religion, establishing intellectual links with the intellectually suspect, and creating a special sphere of culture. Like the great Asian systems, as a faith, pre-Christian Judaism was hardly distinguishable from national life and the general drive toward self-preservation. The pagan ritual of sacrifice was not simply transformed into the cult or attitude of mind; its new form went on to determine the labor process. Sacrifice is rationalized on this basis. The taboo becomes the rational organization of the labor process. It ordains the pattern of war and peace, seedtime and harvest, the preparation of food and the slaughtering of animals. Whereas the rules do not arise from rational reflection, rationality arises from the rules. Among primitive peoples, the attempt to overcome immediate fear led to the organized ritual and became the sanctified rhythm of family and national life in Judaism. The priests were appointed to see that the customs were followed. Their function in the order of domination was apparent in theocratic practice; Christianity, however, wanted to remain spiritual even when it tended toward domination. It broke with the idea of self-preservation by the ultimate sacrifice, that of the man-god, but by that very action handed over devalued existence to profane use: the law of Moses was abolished but that which was Caesar's was rendered unto Caesar and that which was God's unto God. Worldly authority is confirmed or usurped, and the Christian faith acquires the rights on salvation. The instinct of self-preservation must be overcome by imitating Christ. Sacrificial love is stripped of naïveté and isolated from natural love, then set down as merit. The love mediated through devotion is said to be direct, reconciling nature and the supernatural. But here lies the falsehood: in the deceptively positive meaning given to self-denial.

The sense is false because the Church lives by the fact that men see the path to redemption in respect for its doctrine (whether it demands good works, as in the Catholic, or faith, as in the Protestant version), although it cannot guarantee the ultimate objective. The fact that the spiritual promise of salvation is not binding—this Jewish, negative component of Christian doctrine which relativizes magic and finally the Church—is quietly accepted by the naïve believer, for whom Christianity or supernaturalism becomes a magic ritual, a natural religion. He believes only by forgetting his faith. He persuades himself that he enjoys knowledge and certainty, as if he were an astrologer or spiritualist. This is not necessarily worse than spiritualized theology. The old Italian woman who in simple faith lights a candle to Saint Gennaro to protect her soldier grandson is perhaps closer to the truth than the popes and archdeacons who—unstained by idolatry—bless the weapons against which Saint Gennaro is powerless. But to the simple, religion itself becomes a substitute for religion. This fact has been half recognized since the early days of Christianity, but only the paradoxical Christians, the anti-official philosophers, from Pascal by way of Lessing and Kierkegaard to Barth, made it the cornerstone of their theology. With their new-found awareness they were not only radical but patient. But the others, who rejected this knowledge and persuaded themselves with a heavy conscience that Christianity was their own sure possession, had to affirm their eternal salvation as against the worldly damnation of all those who did not make the dull sacrifice of reason. This is the religious origin of anti-Semitism. The adherents of the religion of the Father are hated by those who support the religion of the Son—hated as those who know better. It is the hostility to spirit of the spirit, grown obdurate in the conviction of salvation. For Christian anti-Semites, truth is the stumbling-block, truth which resists evil without rationalizing it, and clings to the idea of undeserved salvation against all the rules of life and salvation which are supposed to ensure that blessed state. Anti-Semitism is meant to confirm that the ritual of faith and history is right by executing it on those who deny its justice.

V.

"I can't stand you—don't forget that," says Siegfried to Mime, who wants his love. The old answer of all the anti-Semites is an appeal to idiosyncracy. The emancipation of society from anti-Semitism depends on whether the content of the idiosyncracy is elevated into a concept and becomes aware of its own futility. But idiosyncracy inheres in the particular. The general, that which fits into the functional context of society, is considered to be natural. But nature which has not been transformed through the channels of conceptual order into something purposeful, the grating sound of a stylus moving over a slate, the *haut goût* which recalls filth and decomposition, the sweat which appears on the brow of the busy man—everything which has failed to keep up, or which infringes the commandments which are the sedimented progress of the centuries—has a penetrating effect; it arouses disgust.

The motives to which idiosyncracy appeals recall the ultimate origins. They produce moments of biological prehistory: danger signs which make the hair stand on end and the heart stop beating. In idiosyncracy, individual organs escape from the control of the subject, and independently obey fundamental biological stimuli. The ego which experiences such reactions—for instance, cutaneous or muscular torpor, or stiffness of joints—is not wholly in control of itself. For a few moments these reactions effect an adaptation to circumambient, motionless nature. But as the animate approaches the inanimate, and the more highly-developed form of life comes closer to nature, it is alienated from it, since inanimate nature, which life in its most vigorous form aspires to become, is capable only of wholly external, spatial, relationships. Space is absolute alienation. When men try to become like nature they harden themselves against it. Protection as fear is a form of mimicry. The reflexes of stiffening and numbness in humans are archaic schemata of the urge to survive: by adaptation to death, life pays the toll of its continued existence.

Civilization has replaced the organic adaptation to others and mimetic behavior proper, by organized control of mimesis, in the magical phase; and, finally, by rational practice, by work, in the historical phase. Uncontrolled mimesis is outlawed. The angel with the fiery sword who drove man out of paradise and onto the path of technical progress is the very symbol of that progress. For centuries, the severity with which the rulers prevented their own followers and the subjugated masses from reverting to mimetic modes of existence, starting with the religious prohibition on images, going on to the social banishment of actors and gypsies, and leading finally to the kind of teaching which does not allow children to behave as children, has been the condition for civilization. Social and individual education confirms men in the objectivizing behavior of workers and protects them from reincorporation into variety of circumambient nature. All devotion and all deflection has a touch of mimicry about it. The ego has been formed in resistance to this mimicry. In the constitution of the ego reflective mimesis becomes controlled reflection. "Recognition in the concept," the absorption of the different by the same, takes the place of physical adaptation to nature. But the situation in which equality is established, the direct equality of mimesis and the mediated equality of synthesis, the adaptation to the condition of the object in the blind course of life, and the comparison of the objectified thing in scientific concept formation, is still the state of terror. Society continues threatening nature as the lasting, organized compulsion which is reproduced in individuals as rational self-preservation and rebounds on nature as social dominance over it. Science is repetition, refined into observed regularity, and preserved in stereotypes. The mathematical formula is regression handled consciously, just as the magic ritual used to be; it is the most sublimated manifestation of mimicry. Technology no longer completes the approximation to death for the sake of survival by physical imitation of external nature, as was the case with magic, but by automation of the mental processes, by converting them into blind cycles. With its triumph human statements become both controllable and inevitable. All that remains of the adaptation to nature is the obduracy against nature. Today protective and repellent coloring is that blind domination of nature which is identical with far-sighted expediency.

In the bourgeois mode of production, the indelible mimetic heritage of all practical experience is consigned to oblivion. The pitiless prohibition of regression becomes mere fate; the denial is now so complete that it is no longer conscious. Those blinded by civilization experience their own tabooed mimetic features only in certain gestures and behavior patterns which they encounter in others and which strike them as isolated remnants, as embarrassing rudimentary elements that survive in the rationalized environment. What seems repellently alien is in fact all too familiar:[1] the infectious gestures of direct contacts suppressed by civilization, for instance, touch, soothing, snuggling up, coaxing. We are put off by the old-fashioned nature of these impulses. They seem to translate long verified human relations back into individual power relations: in trying to influence the purchaser by flattery, the debtor by threats and the creditor by entreaty. Every non-manipulated expression seems to be the grimace which the manipulated expression always was—in the movies, in lynch law, or in speeches by Hitler. However, undisciplined mimicry is the brand of the old form of domination, engraved in the living substance of the dominated and passed down by a process of unconscious imitation in infancy from generation to generation, from the down-at-heel Jew to the rich banker. This mimicry arouses anger because, in the face of the new conditions of production, it displays the old fear which, in order to survive those conditions, must be forgotten. True, personal anger in the civilized man is roused by the constraining situation: by the anger of the tormentor and of the tormented, who are indistinguishable in their grimace. The impotent semblance is answered by deadly reality, the game by seriousness.

The grimace seems forced, mere pretense, because it expresses aversion and disinclination rather than perform a useful function. It appears to escape the seriousness of existence by acknowledging it but refusing to be muzzled by it: it is dishonest. But expressiveness is the painful echo of a superior power, of force, voiced in a complaint. It is always exaggerated, however honest it may be, since the whole world seems to be enclosed in every plaintive note—as in every work of art. Only achievement is appropriate. Only activity, not mimesis, can detract from suffering. But its consequence is the unmoving and unmoved countenance which, with the end of this age, finally degenerates into the "baby face" of practical men, politicians, priests, managing directors, and racketeers.

1. Cf. Freud, *Das Unheimliche, Gesammelte Werke,* Vol. II, pp. 254, 259 etc.

The howling voice of Fascist orators and camp commandants shows the other side of the same social condition. The yell is as cold as business. They both expropriate the sounds of natural complaint and make them elements of their technique. Their bellow has the same significance for the pogrom as the noise generator in the German flying bomb: the terrible cry which announces terror is simply turned on. The cry of pain of the victim who first called violence by its name, the mere word to designate the victim (Frenchman, Negro, or Jew), generates despair in the persecuted who must react violently. The victims are the false counterparts of the dread mimesis. They reproduce the insatiability of the power which they fear. Everything must be used and all must obey. The mere existence of the other is a provocation. Every "other" person who "doesn't know his place" must be forced back within his proper confines—those of unrestricted terror. Anyone who seeks refuge must be prevented from finding it; those who express ideas which all long for, peace, a home, freedom—the nomads and players—have always been refused a homeland. Whatever a man fears, that he suffers. Even the last resting place is emptied of peace. The destruction of cemeteries is not a mere excess of anti-Semitism—it is anti-Semitism in its essence. The outlawed naturally arouse the desire to outlaw others. Violence is even inflamed by the marks which violence has left on them. Anything which just wants to vegetate must be rooted out. In the chaotic net regulated escape reactions of the lower animals, in the convolutions of the sudden swarm, and the convulsive gestures of the martyred, we see the mimetic impulse which can never be completely destroyed. In the death struggle of the creature, at the opposite pole from freedom, freedom still shines out irresistibly as the thwarted destiny of matter. It is opposed by the idiosyncracy which claims anti-Semitism as its motive.

The mental energy harnessed by political anti-Semitism is this rationalized idiosyncracy. All the pretexts over which the Führer and his followers reach agreement, imply surrender to the mimetic attraction without any open infringement of the reality principle—honorably, so to speak. They cannot stand the Jews, yet imitate them.

183

There is no anti-Semite who does not basically want to imitate his mental image of a Jew, which is composed of mimetic cyphers: the argumentative movement of a hand, the musical voice painting a vivid picture of things and feelings irrespective of the real content of what is said, and the nose—the physiognomic *principium individuationis,* symbol of the specific character of an individual, described between the lines of his countenance. The multifarious nuances of the sense of smell embody the archetypal longing for the lower forms of existence, for direct unification with circumambient nature, with the earth and mud. Of all the senses, that of smell—which is attracted without objectifying—bears clearest witness to the urge to lose oneself in and become the "other." As perception and the perceived—both are united—smell is more expressive than the other senses. When we see we remain what we are; but when we smell we are taken over by otherness. Hence the sense of smell is considered a disgrace in civilization, the sign of lower social strata, lesser races and base animals. The civilized individual may only indulge in such pleasure if the prohibition is suspended by rationalization in the service of real or apparent practical ends. The prohibited impulse may be tolerated if there is no doubt that the final aim is its elimination—this is the case with jokes or fun, the miserable parody of fulfillment. As a despised and despising characteristic, the mimetic function is enjoyed craftily. Anyone who seeks out "bad" smells, in order to destroy them, may imitate sniffing to his heart's content, taking unrationalized pleasure in the experience. The civilized man "disinfects" the forbidden impulse by his unconditional identification with the authority which has prohibited it; in this way the action is made acceptable. If he goes beyond the permitted bounds, laughter ensues. This is the schema of the anti-Semitic reaction. Anti-Semites gather together to celebrate the moment when authority permits what is usually forbidden, and become a collective only in that common purpose. There rantings are organized laughter. The more terrible their accusations and threats and the greater their anger, the more compelling their scorn. Anger, scorn, and embittered imitation are actually the same thing. The purpose

184

of the Fascist formula, the ritual discipline, the uniforms, and the whole apparatus, which is at first sight irrational, is to allow mimetic behavior. The carefully thought out symbols (which are proper to every counterrevolutionary movement), the skulls and disguises, the barbaric drum beats, the monotonous repetition of words and gestures, are simply the organized imitation of magic practices, the mimesis of mimesis. The leader with his contorted face and the charisma of approaching hysteria take command. The leader acts as a representative; he portrays what is forbidden to everyone else in actual life. Hitler can gesticulate like a clown, Mussolini strike false notes like a provincial tenor, Goebbels talk endlessly like a Jewish agent whom he wants murdered, and Coughlin preach love like the savior whose crucifixion he portrays—all for the sake of still more bloodshed. Fascism is also totalitarian in that it seeks to make the rebellion of suppressed nature against domination directly useful to domination.

This machinery needs the Jews. Their artificially heightened prominence acts on the legitimate son of the gentile civilization like a magnetic field. The gentile sees equality, humanity, in his difference from the Jew, but this induces a feeling of antagonism and alien being. And so impulses which are normally taboo and conflict with the requirements of the prevailing form of labor are transformed into conforming idiosyncracies. The economic position of the Jews, the last defrauded frauds of liberalistic ideology, affords them no secure protection. Since they are so eminently fitted to generate these mental induction currents, they serve such functions involuntarily. They share the fate of the rebellious nature as which Fascism uses them: they are employed blindly yet perspicaciously. It matters little whether the Jews as individuals really do still have those mimetic features which awaken the dread malady, or whether such features are suppressed. Once the wielders of economic power have overcome their fear of the Fascist administrators, the Jews automatically stand out as the disturbing factor in the harmony of the national society. They are abandoned by domination when its progressive alienation from nature makes it revert to mere

185

nature. The Jews as a whole are accused of participating in forbidden magic and bloody ritual. Disguised as accusation, the subconscious desire of the aboriginal inhabitants to return to the mimetic practice of sacrifice finds conscious fulfillment. When all the horror of prehistory which has been overlaid with civilization is rehabilitated as rational interest by projection onto the Jews, there is no restriction. The horror can be carried out in practice, and its practical implementation goes beyond the evil content of the projection. The fantasies of Jewish crimes, infanticide and sadistic excess, poisoning of the nation, and international conspiracy, accurately define the anti-Semitic dream, but remain far behind its actualization. Once things have reached this stage, the mere word "Jew" appears as the bloody grimace reflected in the swastika flag with its combination of death's head and shattered cross. The mere fact that a person is called a Jew is an invitation forcibly to make him over into a physical semblance of that image of death and distortion.

Civilization is the victory of society over nature which changes everything into pure nature. The Jews themselves have taken part in this process for thousands of years—with enlightenment as with cynicism. The oldest surviving patriarchate, the incarnation of monotheism, they transformed taboos into civilizing maxims when others still clung to magic. The Jews seemed to have succeeded where Christianity failed: they defused magic by its own power—turned against itself as ritual service of God. They did not eliminate adaptation to nature, but converted it into a series of duties in the form of ritual. They have retained the aspect of expiation, but have avoided the reversion to mythology which symbolism implies. And so they are thought to lag behind advanced civilization and yet to be too far ahead of it: they are both clever and stupid, similar and dissimilar. They are declared guilty of something which they, as the first burghers, were the first to overcome: the lure of base instincts, reversion to animality and to the ground, the service of images. Because they invented the concept of kosher meat, they are persecuted as swine. The anti-Semites make themselves the executors of the Old Testament: they want the Jews who have eaten of the tree of knowledge to return unto dust.

VI.

Anti-Semitism is based on a false projection. It is the counterpart of true mimesis, and fundamentally related to the repressed form; in fact, it is probably the morbid expression of repressed mimesis. Mimesis imitates the environment, but false projection makes the environment like itself. For mimesis the outside world is a model which the inner world must try to conform to: the alien must become familiar; but false projection confuses the inner and outer world and defines the most intimate experiences as hostile. Impulses which the subject will not admit as his own even though they are most assuredly so, are attributed to the object—the prospective victim. The actual paranoiac has no choice but to obey the laws of his sickness. But in Fascism this behavior is made political; the object of the illness is deemed true to reality; and the mad system becomes the reasonable norm in the world and deviation from it a neurosis. The mechanism which the totalitarian order uses is as old as civilization. The same sexual impulses which the human species suppressed have survived and prevailed—in individuals and in nations—by way of the mental conversion of the ambient world into a diabolical system. The blind murderer has always seen his victim as a persecutor against whom he must defend himself, and the strongest and wealthiest individuals have always felt their weakest neighbors to be an intolerable threat before they fell upon them to destroy them. Rationalization was a pretense, but at the same time inescapable. The person chosen as an enemy was already seen as an enemy. The disturbance lies in the failure of sensory impressions is a legacy of our animal prehistory, a extraneous share in the projected material.

In a certain sense all perception is projection. The projection of sensory impressions is a legacy of our animal prehistory, an mechanism for self-preservation and obtaining food, an extension of the combative impulse with which the higher animals—with pleasure or pain—reacted to movements, irrespective of the intentions of the object. In human beings projection has been automatized, like other attack and defense behaviors which have become reflexes. And so man's world of objects is built up as a product of that "hidden art in the depths of the human soul whose true movements we shall never fully grasp from nature and expose for all to see."[2] The system of things, the fixed universal order of which science is merely an abstract expression, is—if we apply the Kantian critique of cognition anthropologically—the unconscious product of the animal organ in the struggle for existence, of automatic projection. But in human society, where affective and intellectual life are differentiated with the formation of the individual, the latter requires an increasingly firm control over projection; he must learn at one and the same time to refine and inhibit it. By learning to distinguish between his own and extraneous thoughts and feelings under the force of economic necessity, a distinction is made between without and within, the possibility of distancing and identifying, self-awareness and the conscience. Further consideration is necessary to understand the controlled projection, and the way in which it is deformed into false projection—which is part of the essence of anti-Semitism.

The physiological theory of perception, which was despised by philosophers since Kant as naïvely realistic and as a vicious circle, explains the perceptual world as the plane mirror reflection—controlled by the intellect—of data which the brain receives from actual objects. In this view, the received impressions are ordered by understanding—by the "intellect." While the Gestalt psychologists insist that the physiological substance not only receives "point" impressions but "ready-made" structures, Schopenhauer and von Helmholtz—in spite of, or even because of, the vicious circle—knew more about the limited relationship between subject and object than the official conception of the neo-psychological or neo-Kantian school: the perceptual image contains concepts and judgments. Between the true object and the undisputed data of the senses, between within and without, there is a gulf which the subject must bridge at his own risk. In order to reflect the thing as it is, the subject must return to it more than he receives from it. The subject

2. Kant, *Kritik der reinen Vernunft*, 2nd ed., *Werke*, Vol. III, pp. 180f.

creates the world outside himself from the traces which it leaves in his senses: the unity of the thing in its manifold characteristics and states; and he therefore constitutes the "I" retrospectively by learning to grant a synthetic unity not only to the external impressions, but to the internal impressions which gradually separate off from them. The real ego is the most recent constant product of projection. In a process which could only be completed historically with the developed powers of the human physiological constitution, it developed as a unified and at the same time eccentric function. Even as an independently objectified ego, it is only equivalent to the significance of the world of objects for it. The inner depth of the subject consists in nothing other than the delicacy and wealth of the external world of perceptions. If the links are broken, the ego calcifies. If it proceeds positivistically: merely recording given facts without giving anything in return, it shrinks to a point; and if it idealistically creates the world from its own groundless basis, it plays itself out in dull repetition. In both cases it gives up the spirit. Only in that mediation by which the meaningless sensation brings a thought to the full productivity of which it is capable, while on the other hand the thought abandons itself without reservation to the predominant impression, is that pathological loneliness which characterizes the whole of nature overcome. The possibilities of reconciliation appears not in certainty unaffected by thought, in the preconceptual unity of perception and object, but in their considered opposition. The distinction is made in the subject, which has the external world in its own consciousness and yet recognizes it as something other. Therefore reflection, the life of reason, takes place as conscious projection.

The morbid aspect of anti-Semitism is not projective behavior as such, but the absence from it of reflection. When the subject is no longer able to return to the object what he has received from it, he becomes poorer rather than richer. He loses the reflection in both directions: since he no longer reflects the object, he ceases to reflect upon himself, and loses the ability to differentiate. Instead of the voice of conscience, he hears other voices; instead of examining himself in order to decipher the protocol of its own lust for power, it attributes the "Protocols of the Elders of Zion" to others. It overflows and fades away at one and the same time. It invests the outer world boundlessly with its own content; but it invests it in fact with the void: with an overstatement of mere means, relations, machinations, and dark practice without the perspective of thought. Domination itself, which, even as absolute rule, is only a means, becomes its own purpose and extraneous purpose in uninhibited projection; indeed, it becomes purpose as such. When the individual is diseased, the heightened intellectual apparatus of man works against men again, like the blind hostile organ of animal prehistory as which—in terms of the human species—it has never ceased to fight the rest of nature. Just as, since his coming up, man as a species has always confronted other species as the highest evolutionary and therefore most fearsome distinctive power, and just as within mankind the more advanced races have confronted the more primitive and the technically better equipped have destroyed the slower, so the sick individual is able to confront other individuals with a lust for power and persecution. In both cases the subject is the central factor and the world is simply an opportunity for his madness; the world becomes the weak or all-powerful total concept of all that is projected onto it. The resistance of which the paranoiac individual incessantly complains is the consequence of the lack of resistance, the vacuum which he generates around himself. He cannot stop. The idea which finds no firm hold in reality, insists, and becomes an *idée fixe*.

Since the paranoiac perceives the world about him only as it corresponds to his blind purposes, he can only repeat his own self which is denatured into an abstract mania. The naked pattern of power as such, which dominates all around it as well as its own decomposing ego, seizes all that is offered to it and incorporates it, without reference to its specific nature, into its mythic fabric. The closed circle of eternal sameness becomes a substitute for omnipotence. It is as though the serpent which said to the first men "you will be as God" had redeemed its promise in the paranoiac. He makes everything in his own image. He seems to need no living being, yet demands that all serve him. His will permeates the universe and everything must relate to him. His systems know no gaps. As an astrologer he endows the stars with powers which lead to the ruin of the unheeding—either in the preclinical stage of external relations or in the clinical stage of his own ego. As a philosopher he makes world history the executor of inescapable catastrophes and declines. As the perfect madman or absolutely rational individual, he destroys his opponents by individual acts of terror or by the carefully conceived strategy of extermination. In this way he succeeds. Just as women adore the unmoved paranoiac, so nations genuflect before totalitarian Fascism. In the devotees themselves, paranoia is rendered unto the paranoiac as to a demon; qualms of conscience are offered to the man without conscience, to whom they owe their thanks. They follow a man who looks through them, who take them not as individuals but as material for any purpose. These women have made the occupation of large or small positions of power into their religion—have made themselves the evil objects which society considers them to be. The gaze which reminds them of freedom must strike them as the gaze of the naïve seducer. Their world is turned inside out. But at the same time they know, like the old gods who feared the gaze of their faithful, that death lurks behind the veil. The non-paranoiac, trusting gaze reminds them of the spirit which has died within them because they see outside only the sheer means of self-preservation. Contact of this kind fills them with shame and anger. But the madman does not contact them even when he looks them in the eyes as their Führer. He simply inflames them. The proverbial gaze into their eyes does not preserve their individuality. It merely fixes others and commands unilateral loyalties by pointing the way to the windowless monadic confines of their own personality. It does not arouse the conscience but calls for responsibility. The penetrating and distant gaze, the hypnotic and the distinterested look, are of the same type; in both cases the subject is extinguished. Because such gazes lack reflection those who do not think are electrified by them. They are betrayed. Women are rejected and the nation is burnt out. The madman remains a mocking image of divine power. Just as his sovereign gestures

191

completely lack any creative power in reality, so, like the devil, he is without the attributes of the principle which he usurps: conscious love and peaceful freedom. He is evil, driven by compulsion, and as weak as his strength. If it is said that divine power attracts creation, satanic power likewise draws everything into its own impotence. This is the secret of its domination. The compulsively projecting self can project only its own unhappiness—from the very basis of which it is cut off by reason of its lack of reflective thought. The products of false projection, the stereotype is of thought and reality, are therefore the products of evil. For the ego which sinks into the meaningless abyss of itself, objects become allegories of destruction which contain the meaning of its own downfall.

The psychoanalytical theory of morbid projection views it as consisting of the transference of socially taboo impulses from the subject to the object. Under the pressure of the super-ego, the ego projects the aggressive wishes which originate from the id (and are so intense as to be dangerous even to the id), as evil intentions onto the outside world, and manages to work them out as abreaction on the outside world; either in fantasy by identification with the supposed evil, or in reality by supposed self-defense. The forbidden action which is converted into aggression is generally homosexual in nature. Through fear of castration, obedience to the father is taken to the extreme of an anticipation of castration in conscious emotional approximation to the nature of a small girl, and actual hatred of the father is suppressed. In paranoia, this hatred leads to a castration wish as a generalized urge to destruction. The sick individual regresses to the archaic nondifferentiation of love and domination. He is concerned with physical proximity, seizure—relationship at all costs. Since he cannot allow himself the pleasure of following his own instincts, he attacks other individuals in envy or persecution just as the repressed bestialist hunts or torments an animal. The drawing power comes from an all-too thorough bond or is established spontaneously; it may be exerted by the great—as on the assassins of presidents—or by the lowliest, as in a genuine pogrom. The objects of fixation can be substituted like father figures in childhood. The delusion of reference strikes out all around without any true reference. Pathological projection is a desperate effort of the ego whose stimulus barrier—according to Freud—is much weaker inwardly than outwardly. Under the pressure of pent-up homosexual aggression, the mental mechanism forgets its most recent phylogenetic achievement, self-perception, and experiences this aggression as the enemy in the world in order to be more equal to it.

But this pressure lies heavy on the healthy process of cognition as a factor of its unreflecting and aggressive naïveté. Whenever intellectual energies are intentionally concentrated on the world outside; wherever we are involved in persecuting, fixing, and seizing, in those functions which have been intellectualized from the primitive suppression of the animal nature into scientific methods of controlling nature, the subjective process is easily overlooked in the schematization, and the system is asserted to be the thing itself. Objectifying (like sick) thought contains the despotism of the subjective purpose which is hostile to the thing and forgets the thing itself, thus committing the mental act of violence which is later put into practice. The unconditional realism of civilized humanity, which culminates in Fascism, is a special case of paranoiac delusion which dehumanizes nature and finally the nations themselves. Paranoia takes root in that abyss of uncertainty which every objectifying act must bridge. Because there can be no absolutely convincing argument against materially false judgments, the distorted perception in which they appear cannot be cured. Every perception contains unconsciously conceptual elements, just as every judgment contains unclarified phenomenalistic components. Because truth implies imagination, it can happen that distorted personalities take the truth for fantasy and the illusion for truth. The distorted individual draws on the element of imagination residing in truth by constantly seeking to expose it. Democratically, he insists on equal rights for his delusion because in fact truth too is not stringent. Even when the bourgeois admits that the anti-Semite is in the wrong, he still demands that the victim be shown to be guilty too. Hitler demands justification for mass murder in the name of the legal principle of sovereign national rights, which tolerates any act of violence in another country.

193

Like every paranoiac individual he profits from the hypocritical identification of truth with sophistry; the division between the two is overlooked, however strict it may be. Perception is only possible if the thing is perceived as something definite, e.g., as an example of a species. Perception is directness at one remove, reflection in the seductive power of sensuality. By it, the subjective is blindly transferred by it into the apparent obviousness of the object. Only the self-conscious labor of thought can escape from this hallucinatory power, and philosophy from the idealism of Leibniz and Hegel. When thought in the process of cognition identifies as conceptual the conceptual elements which are directly posited in perception and hence so compelling, it progressively draws them back into the subject and rids them of perceptive power. In this process each previous stage, including that of science, appears as perception by comparison with philosophy, as an alienated phenomenon which is marked by unrecognized intellectual elements; it is part of the pathology character of cognition to stop there, without negation. The naïve devotee of absolutes, however universally active he may be, is a victim of the dazzling power of false immediacy.

But this dazzle is a constitutive element of all judgment, a necessary illusion. Every judgment, even a negative one, asserts and assumes. However much a judgment may seek to overcome its own isolation and relativity for the purpose of self-correction, it must still assert its own content (however carefully formulated the latter may be) as something which is not merely isolated and relative. This is its essential nature as judgment. Truth, unlike probability, has no gradations. The negating step beyond the individual judgment, which saves its truth, is only possible if it accepted its own truth and was so to speak paranoiac in character. True madness lies primarily in immutability, in the inability of the thought to participate in the negativity in which thought—in contradistinction to fixed judgment—comes into its own. The paranoiac insistence on rationality, the poor infinity of an unchanging judgment, reveals a lack of sequacious thought. Instead of thinking out the inadequacies of the absolute claim, and thus qualifying his judgment more proficiently, the paranoiac insists on the unchanging element. Instead of going further by penetrating into the heart of the matter, the entire process of thought serves the hopeless purpose of particularized judgment.

The irresistibility of this judgment is the same as its unbroken positivity, and the weakness of the paranoiac individual is that of thought itself. Reflection, which in a healthy person breaks the power of immediacy, is never so compelling as the illusion which it dispels. As a negative, considered movement which is not directed in a straight line, it lacks the brutality inherent in positive movement. If the mental energy of paranoia originates in that libidinal dynamism exposed by psychoanalysis, its objective immunity is rooted in that ambiguity which cannot be detached from the objectifying act; its hallucinatory power will have been originally the decisive factor In the language of selection theory, one might assert that during the development of the human sensory apparatus, those individuals survived in whom the power of the projection mechanisms extended furthest into the rudimentary logical capacities or was the least impaired by all-too early stirrings of reflective thought. As today practical scientific enterprises require an unimpaired faculty of definition —the capability of arresting thought at a point determined by the needs of society, and of defining an area which is then minutely examined without going beyond it, so the paranoiac cannot transcend a complex of interests delimited by his psychological fate. His discernment is used up in the circle drawn by the fixed idea, just as human ingenuity is liquidated in the area determined for it by technical civilization. Paranoia is the dark side of cognition.

The tendency to false projection is so fatefully present in the spirit that this isolated pattern of self-preservation threatens to dominate everything which extends beyond it: all culture. False projection usurps the kingdom of freedom and education. Paranoia is the symptom of the half-educated man. For him, all words become part of the delusive system, of the attempt to possess through the mind everything for which experience is inadequate, to force meaning upon the world which makes him meaningless; but at the same time to defame the spirit and experience from which he is excluded and to attribute to them the

195

guilt of the society which excludes him. Half-education, which (unlike a complete lack of education) hypostasizes limited knowledge as the truth, cannot stand the now intolerable gulf between within and without, between individual fate and the social law, appearance and essence. This suffering contains an element of truth by comparison with the mere acceptance of the status quo to which the superior nationality has sworn allegiance. In a stereotyped manner, half-education reaches out in its fear for the formula which is best suited to it in order soon to provide a rationale for evil which has already occurred, or to prophesy catastrophe—which is sometimes disguised as regeneration. The explanation in which the wish of the individual appears as an objective force is always as external and void of meaning as the isolated occurrence itself; it is both foolish and sinister. Today the obscurantist systems do just what the satanic myth of official religion did for men in the Middle Ages: they provide an arbitrary meaning for the external world interpreted by the solitary paranoiac in a private manner, which is shared by no one and therefore appears totally mad. Hence the fatal conventicles and panaceas which claim to be scientific and at the same time are remote from thought: theosophy, numerology, natural healing, eurhythmics, vegetarianism, yoga, and innumerable other sects, competing and interchangeable, all with their own academies, hierarchies, and special jargons, the fetishized forms of science and religion. Once education held them to be apocryphal and unrespectable. But today, when education is dying out for economic reasons, there are innumerable new conditions for mass paranoia. The former systems of belief which were adopted nationally as closed paranoiac forms had wider meshes. Because of their rational design and precision they left room—in the upward direction, at least—for education and intellect, whose concept was their own medium. To some extent they counteracted paranoia. Freud goes so far—and he is right—as to call neuroses "asocial forms" which try to achieve with private means something which developed in society through collective labor.[3] The systems of faith retain some-

3. Freud, *Totem und Tabu, Gesammelte Werke,* Vol. I, p. 91.

thing of that collectivity which protects individuals against illness. Illness is socialized: in the intoxication of joint ecstasy, as community, blindness becomes a move of reference and the paranoiac mechanism is rendered controllable without losing the possibility of horror or fright. Perhaps this was one of the great contributions of religion to the preservation of the species. The paranoiac forms of consciousness tend toward the formation of alliances, parties, and rackets. Their members are afraid of believing in their delusion on their own. Projecting their madness, they see conspiracy and proselytism everywhere. The established group always adopts a paranoiac attitude to others. The great empires and even organized humanity as such are not more advanced than headhunters in this respect. Those excluded against their own will from other men know, just like those who through longing for mankind cut themselves off from others, that the pathological relationship was strengthened by their persecution. The normal member of society dispels his own paranoia by participating in the collective form, and clings passionately to the objectivized, collective and confirmed forms of delusion. The *horror vacui* with which they subscribe to their leagues welds them together and lends them an almost irresistible force.

Cultural education spread with bourgeois property. It forced paranoia into the dark corners of society and the soul. But since the real emancipation of mankind did not take place with the enlightenment of the mind, education itself became diseased. The greater the distance between the educated consciousness and social reality, the more it was itself exposed to the process of reification. Culture became wholly a commodity disseminated as information without permeating the individuals who acquired it. Thought became restricted to the acquisition of isolated facts. Conceptual relationships were rejected as uncomfortable and useless effort. The aspect of development in thought, all that is genetic and intensive in it, is forgotten and leveled down to the immediately given, to the extensive. Today the order of life allows no room for the ego to draw spiritual or intellectual conclusions. The thought which leads to knowledge is neutralized and used as a mere qualification on specific labor markets and

197

to heighten the commodity value of the personality. And so that self-examination of the mind which works against paranoia is defeated. Finally, under the conditions of modern capitalism, half-education has become objective spirit. In the totalitarian phase of domination, it calls upon the provincial charlatans of politics, and with them the system of delusion as the *ultima ratio:* forcing it upon the majority of the ruled, who are already deadened by the culture industry. The contradictions of rule can be seen through by the healthy consciousness so easily today that it takes a diseased mind to keep them alive. Only those who suffer from a delusion of persecution accept the persecution to which domination must necessarily lead, inasmuch as they are allowed to persecute others.

In Fascism, the conscience is taken care of; the responsibility for wife and children so carefully nurtured by bourgeois civilization is replaced by the constant necessity for the individual to obey the rules. Unlike the assumptions of Dostoevsky and the German apostles of inwardness, the conscience consisted in the devotion of the ego to the substantial outside world, in the ability to take into account the true interests of others. This ability is the capacity for reflection as the penetration of receptivity and imagination. When the big industrial interests incessantly eliminate the economic basis for moral decision, partly by eliminating the independent economic subject, partly by taking over the self-employed tradesmen, and partly by transforming the works into objects in trade unions, reflective thought must also die out. The soul, as the possibility of self-comprehending guilt, is destroyed. There is no object left for the conscience because the responsibility of the individual for himself and his family is replaced by his contribution to the apparatus, even if the old moral assumptions are retained. There is no longer an internal, instinctive or motivational conflict to form a basis for the development of the tribunal of conscience. Instead of the internalization of the social command which not only made it more binding and at the same time more open, but emancipated it from society and even turned it against the latter, there is an immediate and direct identification with stereotyped value scales. The exemplary German woman who has monopolized the female character and the true German male who has done the same in his own regard—as well as similar versions in other countries—are archetypes of conforming asocial beings. In spite of, and because of, the evident evil nature of domination, the latter has become so supremely powerful that each individual in his impotence can exorcize his fate only by blind obedience.

In this state of power it remains for chance as directed by the Party to determine where the desperate aim of self-preservation should project the guilt of its own horror. The Jews seem ready-made for such projection. The sphere of circulation in which they occupied their positions of economic power is shrinking. The liberalistic form of enterprise still allowed the splintered centers of wealth to enjoy a certain political influence. But now the emancipated interests are delivered up to the great concentrations of capital which have grown beyond competition and become fused with the apparatus of the state. No matter what the Jews as such may be like, their image, as that of the defeated people, has the features to which totalitarian domination must be completely hostile: happiness without power, wages without work, a home without frontiers, religion without myth. These characteristics are hated by the rulers because the ruled secretly long to possess them. The rulers are only safe as long as the people they rule turn their longed-for goals into hated forms of evil. This they manage to do by pathological projection, since even hatred leads to unification with the object—in destruction. This is the negative aspect of reconciliation. Reconciliation is the highest notion of Judaism, and expectation is its whole meaning. The paranoiac reaction arises from inability to expect. The anti-Semites try to realize their negative absolute by their own power, and change the world into the hell which they always thought it was. The change depends on whether the ruled see and control themselves in the face of absolute madness and call a halt to it. If thought is liberated from domination and if violence is abolished, the long absent idea is liable to develop that Jews too are human beings. This development would represent the step out of an anti-Semitic society which drives Jews and others to madness, and into the human society. This step

199

would also fulfill the Fascist lie, but in contradicting it: the Jewish question would prove in fact to be the turning point of history. By overcoming that sickness of the mind which thrives on the ground of self-assertion untainted by reflective thought, mankind would develop from a set of opposing races to the species which, even as nature, is more than mere nature. Individual and social emancipation from domination is the counter-movement to false projection, and no Jew would then resemble the senseless evil visited upon him as upon all persecuted beings, be they animals or men.

VII.

But there are no more anti-Semites. In their most recent form they were liberals who wanted to assert their antiliberal opinions. The classic conservative distance between the nobility or the officer class and the Jews was merely reactionary at the end of the nineteenth century. The Ahlwardts and Knuppelkunzes were the up-to-date figures. They already had as their followers the sort of people who later sided with the Führer, and they were supported by all the bad characters and confused minds throughout the country. If anti-Semitic ideas were voiced, they were felt to be bourgeois and revolutionary at one and the same time. The nationalistic ranting was still a distortion of civil liberty. The beer-cellar politics of the anti-Semites revealed the lie rooted in the German liberalism on which they thrived and which they finally destroyed. Even if they made their own mediocrity a pretext for attacking the Jews which already contained the seeds of universal murder, they were still sufficiently realistic economically to weigh up the risks of the Third Reich against the advantages of an inimical form of tolerance. Anti-Semitism was still a theme open to subjective choice. The decision related specifically to it. Acceptance of the "folk" theory did, however, include the whole vocabulary of chauvinism. Anti-Semitic judgments have always born witness to stereotyped thought. Today this is all that remains. A choice is still made, but only between totalities. Anti-Semitic psychology has been replaced by mere acceptance of the whole Fascist ticket, the slogans of aggressive big business. Just as on the voting papers of the mass party the elector is given names by the party machine to vote for *en bloc,* the basic ideological elements are coded on a few lists. If one opts for one of them one opts for the lot, or allows one's individual position to appear as futile as the dissenting votes on polling day in comparison with the vast statistics of the mammoth parties. Anti-Semitism has virtually ceased to be an independent impulse and is now a plank in the platform. Anyone who gives a chance to Fascism, subscribes to the destruction of the trade unions and the crusade against Bolshevism; he automatically subscribes too to the destruction of the Jews. The conviction of the anti-Semites—however artificial it may be—has been absorbed in the predetermined and subjectless reflexes of a political party. If the masses accept the reactionary ticket which contains an anti-Semitic component they are obeying social mechanisms in which the experiences of individual persons with individual Jews play no part. It has in fact been found that anti-Semitism has as much chance in areas where there are no Jews as it does, say, in Hollywood. Experience is replaced by clichés, and the imagination active in experience by eager acceptance. The members of all social strata must swallow their dose of directive knowledge or face rapid decline. They have to know all about the latest airplane in the same way as they must subscribe to one of the specified tribunals of power.

In the world of mass series production, stereotypes replace individual categories. Judgments are no longer based on a genuine synthesis but on blind subsumption. At an earlier stage of history judgments were based on hasty distinctions which gave impetus to the process, and in the meantime exchange, circulation and legal precedents and convention have contributed their share. The process of judgment passed through the stage of weighing up the relative merits of individual cases, which gave the subject some measure of protection against brutal identification with the predicate. In late industrial society, there is a regression to illogical judgment. When Fascism replaced involved legal procedures by an accelerated form of judgment and retribution, the up-to-date were economically prepared for this new development; they had learned to see things through the conceptual models, the *termini technici*, which remain as the iron ration when language disintegrates. The perceiver is no longer present in the process of perception. He no longer uses the active passivity of cognition in which the categorial components can be appropriately formed from a conventionally pre-shaped "given," and the "given" formed anew from these elements, so that justice is done to the perceived object. In the sphere of the social sciences, and in the world of individual experience, blind observation and empty concepts are grouped together rigidly and without mediation. In the age of three hundred key words, the ability to make the effort required by judgment disappears, and the distinction between truth and falsehood is removed. To the extent that thought in a highly specialized form still appears as part of the professional equipment for certain branches of divided labor, it is treated suspiciously as an antiquated luxury— "armchair thinking." People have to *do* things—accomplish something. As the development of technology makes physical work more and more superfluous, the latter is more energetically elevated into a model of intellectual work—which must not be tempted to draw the appropriate conclusions. This is the secret of the stultification on which anti-Semitism thrives. If, even within the framework of logic, the concept encounters the particular only on an external plane, everything which stands for difference in society is threatened. Everyone is either a friend or an enemy; there are no half measures. The lack of concern for the subject makes things easy for administration. Ethnic groups are forced to move to a different region; individuals are branded as Jews and sent to the gas chamber.

The indifferent attitude to the individual expressed in logic draws the necessary conclusions from the economic process. The individual has become an obstacle to production. The gap between technical and human development, the cultural lag highlighted by sociologists, is beginning to disappear. Economic rationality, the highly-praised principle of the smallest mean, is incessantly converting the last units of the economy: firms and men alike. The most advanced form at any given time dominates. At one time, department stores took over the old specialized shops. After growing beyond mercantile control, this specialization took over initiative, disposition and organization, and became free enterprise just as the old mills and forges grew into small factories. The risks of competition led to the more productive centralized form of retail trade represented by department stores. The individual—the psychological corner-shop —suffers the same fate. He arose as a dynamic cell of economic activity. Emancipated from tutelage at earlier stages of economic development, he was interested only in himself: as a proletarian, by hiring his services through the labor market, and through continual adaptation to new technical conditions; and, as an entrepreneur, through tireless attempts to approximate to the ideal type *homo economicus*. Psychoanalysis represented the internal "small business" which grew up in this way as a complex dynamic system of the conscious and unconscious, the id, ego, and super-ego. In conflict with the super-ego, the social check-mechanism of the individual, the ego holds the psychological drives within the limits of self-preservation. The friction surfaces are large, and neuroses—the *faux frais* of this instinctive economy—are inescapable. However, the complex mental apparatus made possible to some extent that free interplay of subjects on which the marked economy was based. But in the era of great business enterprises and world wars the mediation of the social process through innumerable monads proves retrograde. The subjects of the economy are psychologically expropriated, and the economy is more rationally operated by society itself. The individual no longer has to decide what he himself is to do in a painful inner dialectic of conscience, self-preservation and drives. Decisions for men as active workers are taken by the hierarchy ranging from the trade associations to the national administration, and in the private sphere by the system of mass culture which takes over the last inward impulses of individuals, who are forced to consume what is offered to them. The committees and stars serve as the ego and super-ego, and the masses, who have lost the last semblance of personality, shape themselves more easily according to the models presented to them than the instincts ever could by the mechanism of inner censorship. In the system of liberalism, individuation of a sector of the population belonged to the process of adaptation of society as a whole to technological development, but today the operation of the economic apparatus demands that the masses be directed without any intervention from individuation. The economically determined direction of society as a whole, which has always dominated in the mental and physical constitution of men, allows those organs of the individual which helped to arrange his independent existence to atrophy. Since thought has become a mere sector of the system of division of labor, the plans of the competent experts and leaders have made it superfluous for individuals to plan their own happiness. The irrationality of the unresisting and busy adaptation to reality becomes more reasonable than reason for the individual. In an earlier age, the citizens introjected compulsion as a duty of conscience for themselves and the workers, but today the whole man has become the subject-object of repression. As industrial society progresses and is supposed to have overcome its own law of impoverishment, the notion which justified the whole system, that of man as a person, a bearer of reason, is destroyed. The dialectic of Enlightenment is transformed objectively into delusion.

Delusion is also an insanity of political reality. As a dense network of modern means of communication, the world has become so unified that differences in the breakfast eaten by diplomatists in Dumbarton Oaks and Persia have come to be seen as national features, like the hunger for rice of the millions who have fallen through the tight meshes. While the profusion of goods which could be produced everywhere simultaneously, makes the struggle for raw materials and markets seem increasingly anachronistic, mankind has been divided up into a few armed power blocs. They compete more pitilessly than the companies producing consumer goods ever could, and strive to liquidate each other. The more ridiculous the antagonisms are, the more rigid the blocs become. Only if the inhabitants of these power blocs become totally identified with them and accept their dictates as second nature while all the pores of the consciousness are blocked, can the masses be kept in the state of total apathy which makes them capable of fantastic exploits. Any decision-taking functions which still appear to be left to individuals are in fact taken care of in advance. The irreconcilable nature of ideologies as thundered out from the political platforms is simply itself an ideology of the blind constellation of power. The ticket thinking which is a product of industrialization and its advertising machine, extends to international relations. The choice by an individual citizen of the Communist or Fascist ticket is determined by the influence which the Red Army or the laboratories of the West have on him. The objectification by which the power structure (which is made possible only by the passivity of the masses) appears as an iron reality, has become so dense that any spontaneity or even a mere intimation of the true state of affairs becomes an unacceptable utopia, or deviant sectarianism. The illusion has become so concentrated that a mere attempt to penetrate it objectively itself appears as an illusion. On the other hand, support for a political ticket means support for the illusion-reality, which is thus prolonged indefinitely. The person who has doubts is already outlawed as a deserter. Since Hamlet, hesitation has been a sign of thinking and humanity for modern thinkers. The time which was wasted represented and mediated the distance between the individual and the general, just as circulation represented and mediated the distance between consumption and production in the economy. Today individuals receive their tickets direct from the powers that be in the same way as consumers receive their automobiles from the manufacturers' sales agencies. Accordance with reality and adaptation to power are no longer the results of a dialectical process between the subject and reality, but are produced directly by the cogwheel mechanism of industry. The process is one of liquidation instead of sublation of formal instead of specific negation. The unleashed colossi of the manufacturing industries did not overcome the individual by granting him full satisfaction but by eliminating his character as a subject. This is the source of their complete rationality, which coincides with their madness. The heightened maladaptation between the collective system and the individual destroys tension, but the faultless harmony between omnipotence and importance

205

is itself direct contradiction, the absolute opposite of reconciliation.

The psychological determinants of the individual have not
disappeared with him; they have always been the human agencies
of the false society. But the character types now find their exact
position in the system of power. Their coefficients of action and
friction are allowed for. The ticket itself is a cogwheel. Everything which was compulsive, unfree and irrational in the psychological mechanism is precisely incorporated and adapted.
The reactionary ticket which contains anti-Semitism suits the
conventional destructive syndrome. The reaction against the
Jews is heightened into a true object for persecution—an object
of instinctual release—by the political ticket. The "elements of
anti-Semitism," which are based on experience but are defused
by the loss of subjective experience shown in ticket-thinking,
are remobilized by the ticket. Already proved to be inadequate,
these elements give the neo-anti-Semite a bad conscience, and
thereby lead to insatiable evil. Because the psychology of the
individual and its contents can be built up only through synthetic patterns of social behavior, contemporary anti-Semitism
acquires its impenetrable, meaningless character. The Jewish
go-between is turned into a devilish character after he ceases to
exist in the economy. This makes the triumph easy, and the
anti-Semitic family man becomes a spectator—with no responsibility—of the irresistible historical trend, who only acts to the
extent that his role as a party employee or a worker in the factories manufacturing gas crystals for the extermination camps
so requires. The administration of totalitarian states, which
seeks to eliminate sections of the nation that have lost their
contemporary relevance, merely implements economic verdicts
issued long ago. The members of other sectors of the labor system can watch with the same indifference which the reader of a
newspaper shows when confronted with a report on the work
needed to clear up after a catastrophe. The special character by
reason of which the victims are killed, itself ceased to exist
long ago. The human beings who are outlawed as Jews must
first be located on the basis of complex questionnaires, because
—under the leveling pressure of late industrial society—the

hostile religions which once constituted the difference have been already converted into mere culture articles by successful assimilation. The Jewish masses themselves are as prone to ticket-thinking as the hostile youth organizations. The Fascist variety of anti-Semitism must first invent its own object. Paranoia no longer pursues its aim simply on the basis of the individual case history of the persecutor; having become a social existential, it must define a position in the context of wars and economic performance before the *Volksgenossen* with the right psychological predisposition can, as "patients," relate to, and support themselves inwardly and outwardly on, the resulting system.

The fact that anti-Semitism tends to occur only as part of an interchangeable program is sure hope that it will die out one day. Jews are being murdered at a time when the Fascist leaders could just as easily replace the anti-Semitic plank in their platform by some other just as workers can be moved from one wholly rationalized production center to another. The basis of the development which leads to the acceptance of programs and tickets is the universal reduction of all specific energy to the one, some abstract form of labor, from the battlefield to the studio. But the transition from these conditions to a more human state cannot occur because the good suffer the same fate as the evil. Freedom on the progressive ticket is just as removed from the structures of political power on which progressive decisions are necessarily based, as anti-Semitism is external to a chemical cartel. It is true that the more humane individuals are attracted by the progressive policy, but the growing loss of experience ultimately changes even the supporters of the progressive ticket into foes of difference. The ticket mentality as such is as anti-Semitic as the anti-Semitic ticket. The anger against all that is different is teleologically inherent in the mentality, and, as the dominated subjects' resentment of natural domination, is ready to attack the natural minority—even when the social minority is threatened first. The socially responsible elite is in any case much more difficult to define than other minorities. In the fog of relationships between property, possessions, ordinance, and management it successfully escapes theoretical determination. Only the abstract difference from the

207

majority appears in racial ideology and class reality. But if the progressive ticket strives for something which is worse than its own content, the content of the Fascist program is so meaningless that, as a substitute for something better, it can only be upheld by the desperate efforts of the deluded. Its horror lies in the fact that the lie is obvious but persists. Though this deception allows of no truth against which it could be measured, the truth appears negatively in very extent of the contradiction; and the undiscerning can be permanently kept from that truth only if they are wholly deprived of the faculty of thought. Enlightenment which is in possession of itself and coming to power can break the bounds of enlightenment.

NOTES
AND DRAFTS

WHY IT IS BETTER NOT TO
KNOW ALL THE ANSWERS

ONE of the lessons which Hitler has taught us is that it is better not to be too clever. The Jews put forward all kinds of well-founded arguments to show that he could not come to power when his rise was clear for all to see. I remember a conversation during which a political economist demonstrated—on the basis of the interests of the Bavarian brewers—that the Germans could not be brought into line. Other experts proved that Fascism was impossible in the West. The educated made it easy for the barbarians everywhere by being so stupid. The farsighted judgments, the forecasts based on statistics and experience, the comments beginning "this is a subject I know very well," and the well-rounded, solid statements, are all untrue.

Hitler was opposed to mind and to men. But there is also a spirit which is opposed to the interests of men: its characteristic is clever superiority.

Note

There is a historical tendency for cleverness to prove stupid. Reasonableness in the sense which Chamberlain called Hitler's demands at Bad Godesberg "unreasonable" is all very well if the balance of give and take is respected. Reason is based on an exchange. Specific objectives should only be achieved, as it were on the open market, through the small benefits which power can obtain by playing off one concession against another and following the rules of the game. But cleverness becomes meaningless as soon as power ceases to obey the rules and chooses direct appropriation instead. The medium of the traditional bourgeois intelligence—that is, discussion—then breaks down. Individuals can no longer talk to each other and know it: they therefore make the game into a serious and responsible institution which requires the application of all available strength to ensure that there is no proper conversation and at the same time no silence. On a wider scale, the same is true: it is not possible to have a conversation with a Fascist. If anyone else speaks, the Fascist considers his intervention a brazen interruption. He is not accessible to reason, because for him reason lies in the other person's agreement with his own ideas.

The contradiction between stupidity and cleverness is necessary. The bourgeois form of reasoning must lay claim to universality and at the same time seek to set limits. Just as in the process of exchange each person is given his due while social injustice still occurs, so the form of reflection in an economy founded on exchange is just, general, and at the same time biased—an instrument of privilege in equality. The Fascists reveal this form of reasoning in its true colors. They openly defend particular interests and therefore show the limits of the rationale based on generality. The fact that the clever suddenly become stupid proves the unreasonableness of reason.

But the Fascists also labor under contradiction. Bourgeois reason is in fact not only particular but general, and its generality speeds the progress of Fascism by denying it. Those who came to power in Germany were cleverer and yet more stupid than the liberals. The progress towards the new order was supported to a large extent by those whose consciousness was not involved in progress: by bankrupt individuals, sectarian interests, and fools. They are protected against error as long as their power prevents any kind of competition. But, in the competition between states, the Fascists are not only equally capable of making mistakes but through such characteristics as short-sightedness, obstinacy, and lack of knowledge of economic forces, and above all through their inability to see the negative side of things and include this factor in their estimate of the overall position, they contribute subjectively to the catastrophe which they have always expected in their heart of hearts.

TWO WORLDS

Here in America there is no difference between a man and his economic fate. A man is made by his assets, income, position, and prospects. The economic mask coincides completely with a man's inner character. Everyone is worth what he earns and earns what he is worth. He learns what he is through the vicissitudes of his economic existence. He knows nothing else. The materialistic critique of society once objected against idealism that existence determined consciousness and not vice versa, and that the truth about society did not lie in its idealistic conception of itself but in its economy; contemporary men have rejected such idealism. They judge themselves by their own market value and learn what they are from what happens to them in the capitalistic economy. Their fate, however sad it may be, is not something outside them; they recognize its validity. A dying man in China might say, in a lowered voice:

> Fortune did not smile on me in this world.
> Where am I going now? Up into the mountains
> to seek peace for my lonely heart.

I am a failure, the American says—and that is that.

THE TRANSFORMATION OF IDEAS
INTO DOMINATION

The ancient history of Eastern countries sometimes reveals trends which have been repeated much more recently in times more familiar to us. The distance makes these similarities particularly clear.

211

In his notes on the Isa-Upanishad, Deussen[1] points out that the progress made by Indian thought in this work beyond earlier thinking is similar to that made by Jesus beyond John the Baptist in the Gospel according to St. Matthew,[2] and by the Stoics beyond the cynics. This observation is historically biased because the uncompromising ideas of John the Baptist and the cynics—like the ideas beyond which the first verses of the Isa-Upanishad were thought to represent progress[3]—pointed towards left-wing ideas split off from the powerful cliques and parties, rather than toward the main lines of the historical movements from which European philosophy, Christianity, and the living religion of Veda branched off. As Deussen himself states, the Isa-Upanishad was generally placed at the beginning of the Indian collections, long before the other works which it is supposed to have replaced. However, this first work shows traces of the betrayal of youthful radicalism and revolutionary opposition to the dominant reality.

The step forward to the Vedic religion, stoicism or Christianity, which are capable of assuming an organized form, consists in the participation in social activity, in the development of a unified theoretical system. This is reflected in the doctrine that an active role in life is not incompatible with the salvation of the soul, provided that the correct mental attitudes are adopted. Christianity only reached this stage with St. Paul. The idea which alienates from existing circumstances is transformed into religion. The uncompromising individuals are criticized. They "rejected the desire to bear children, to own property, to be involved in the world and walked the highways as beggars. Because the desire for children is the desire for possession and the desire for possession is the desire to participate in the world and all such desire is vain."[4] The critic who talks thus may speak the truth in the eyes of the civilizing philosophers, but he is not in step with the course of social life. And so he be-

1. Paul Deussen, *Sechzig Upanishad's des Veda* (Leipzig, 1905), p. 524.
2. 2nd chapter, verses 17–19.
3. Especially *Brihadaranyaka-Upanishad*, 3.5.1 and 4.4.22. Deussen, *op. cit.*, pp. 436f. and 479f.
4. *Op. cit.*, p. 436.

comes mad in an attempt to resemble John the Baptist. He "was clothed with camel's hair, and with a girdle of a skin about his loins; and he did eat locusts and wild honey."[5] "The cynics," Hegel tells us, "have little philosophical training and have not developed a system or a science; the stoics were the first to develop a philosophical discipline."[6] Their successors called them "hogs and brazen beggars."[7]

The uncompromising people who are recorded in history did not lack all forms of organized society, otherwise not even their names would have been handed down to us. They set up at least a certain systematic doctrine and rules of conduct. Even the more radical Upanishads which came in for bitter criticism were verses and sacrificial sayings developed by gilds of priests.[8] John the Baptist did not found a religion but he did found an order.[9] The cynics formed a school of philosophy; their founder Antisthenes even outlined a theory of the state.[10] The theoretical and practical systems of these outsiders of history are, however, not very rigid and centralized; they differ from the successful systems by an element of anarchy. They set greater store by the idea and the individual than by administration and the collective. They therefore arouse anger. Plato was thinking of the cynics when he attacked the tendency to equate the office of the king with that of a common shepherd, and the loose organization of mankind without national frontier with a state of pigs.[11] The uncompromising individuals may have been in favor of unity and cooperation but they were not able to build a strong hierarchy. Neither in their theory (which was lacking in unity and logic), nor in their practical behavior (which was not adequately coordinated) did their being reflect the world as it really was.

5. Gospel according to St. Mark, 1.6.
6. *Vorlesungen über die Geschichte der Philosophie*, Vol. II; *Werke*, Vol. IV. pp. 159f.
7. *Op. cit.*, p. 168.
8. Cf. Deussen, *op. cit.*, p. 373.
9. Eduard Meyer, *Ursprung und Anfänge des Christentums* (Stuttgart and Berlin, 1921), Vol. I, p. 90.
10. Diogenes Laertius, IV, 15.
11. Cf. *Politeia*, 372. *Politikos*, 267ff.; and Eduard Zeller, *Die Philosophie der Griechen* (Leipzig, 1922), pt. 2.1, pp. 325f.

This was the formal difference between the radical and con-
formist movements in religion and philosophy; the difference
did not lie in terms of isolated content. The sects of the ascetic
Gautama conquered the Asiatic world. In his own lifetime he
showed a real talent for organization. Unlike the reformer Kan-
kara, he did not yet exclude the lower strata of society from the
message,[12] but he specifically recognized the ownership of men
by others, and boasted of the "sons of noble family" who joined
his order in which "Pariahs appear to have been rare excep-
tions."[13] At the outset the disciples were classified on the system
of the Brahmans.[14] Cripples, the sick, criminals, and many
others could not join.[15] Various questions were put to would-be
adherents: "Are you suffering from leprosy, consumption, or
vertigo? Are you a human being? Are you a man? Are you
your own master? Do you have no debts? Are you not in royal
service?" and so on. In conformity with the brutal patriarchism
of India, women were only accepted reluctantly as disciples in
the original Buddhist order. They were subordinate to the men
and remained dependent.[16] The whole order enjoyed the favor
of the rulers and fitted in perfectly with Indian life.

Asceticism and materialism, these opposites, are both ambiguous. Asceticism as the refusal to participate in a bad existing order coincides, from the standpoint of domination, with
the material claims of the masses, just as asceticism as a means
of discipline imposed by cliques aims to promote adaptation to
the state of injustice. Materialistic acceptance of the status quo
and private egotism have always been associated with renunciation, while the gaze of the non-bourgeois fanatic travels beyond
the existing order materialistically to the land of milk and
honey. True materialism abolishes asceticism, and true asceticism abolishes materialism. The history of the old religions and

12. Cf. Deussen, *Das System des Vedanta* (Leipzig, 1906), 2nd ed.,
pp. 63ff.
13. Hermann Oldenberg, *Buddha* (Stuttgart and Berlin, 1914), pp.
174f.
14. Cf. *op. cit.*, p. 386.
15. *Op. cit.*, pp. 393f.
16. Cf. *op. cit.*, pp. 184ff. and 424ff.

schools like that of the modern parties and revolutions teaches us that the price for survival is practical involvement, the transformation of ideas into domination.

ON THE THEORY OF GHOSTS

Freud's theory that belief in ghosts stems from the evil thoughts of living people about the dead, and from the memory of old death wishes, is too limited. Hatred of the dead is made up of envy no less than of a feeling of guilt. The living individual feels deserted and attributes his pain to the dead person who caused this state of affairs. At the stages of humanity in which death appeared as the direct continuation of existence, the desertion in death necessarily seems to be a betrayal, and even the enlightened individual has not completely overcome the old belief. It is not possible for the consciousness to conceive of death as absolute nothingness, since absolute nothingness is inconceivable. If the burden of life weighs on the living, the position of the dead may easily seem preferable. The manner in which many people reorganize their lives after the death of someone close to them as an active cult of the dead, or as rationalized oblivion, is the modern counterpart of the belief in ghosts which lives on in unsublimated form as spiritualism. Only the conscious horror of destruction creates the correct relationship with the dead: unity with them because we, like them, are the victims of the same condition and the same disappointed hope.

Note

The disturbed relationship with the dead—forgotten and embalmed—is one of the symptoms of the sickness of experience today. One might almost say that the notion of human life as the unity in the history of an individual has been abolished: the life of the individual is defined only by its opposite, destruction,

215

but all harmony and all continuity of conscious and involuntary memory have lost their meaning.

Individuals are reduced to a mere sequence of instantaneous experiences which leave no trace, or rather whose trace is hated as irrational, superfluous, and "overtaken" in the literal sense of the word. Just as every book which has not been published recently is suspect, and the idea of history outside the specific sphere of historical science makes modern men nervous, so the past becomes a source of anger. What a man was and experienced in the past is as nothing when set against what he now is and has and what he can be used for. The well-meaning if threatening advice frequently given to emigrants to forget all their past because it cannot be transferred, and to begin a completely new life, simply represents a forcible reminder to the newcomer of something which he has long since learned for himself. History is eliminated in oneself and others out of a fear that it may remind the individual of the degeneration of his own existence—which itself continues. The respect for something which has no market value and runs contrary to all feelings is experienced most sharply by the person in mourning, in whose case not even the psychological restoration of labor power is possible. It becomes a wound in civilization, asocial sentimentality, showing that it has still not been possible to compel men to indulge solely in purposeful behavior. That is why mourning is watered down more than anything else and consciously turned into social formality; indeed, the beautified corpse has always been a mere formality for the hardened survivors. In the funeral home and crematorium, where the corpse is processed into portable ashes—an unpleasant item of property—it is not considered proper to show emotion, and the girl who proudly described the first-class burial of her grandmother, adding "a pity that Daddy lost control" (because he shed a few tears), accurately reflects the situation. In reality, the dead suffer a fate which the Jews in olden days considered the worst possible curse: they are expunged from the memory of those who live on. Men have ceased to consider their own purpose and fate; they work their despair out on the dead.

216

QUAND MÊME

The pressure of circumstances around them has forced men to overcome their own problems and produce material and intellectual works. The thinkers from Democritus to Freud who have stressed this fact are not wrong. The resistance of external nature to which the pressure can ultimately be reduced continues through the classes in society, and acts on every individual from childhood on as the obduracy of his fellows. Men are soft to the extent that they want to get something out of those who are stronger, and they are hard when weaker individuals want something from them. This has been the key to the essential nature of the individual in society up to now.

The conclusion that terror and civilization are inseparable, as drawn by the conservatives, is well-founded. What could bring men to develop in such a way that they are able to master more complex stimuli in a positive manner, but their own development tied up with a hard effort to overcome outside resistance? The resistance is first embodied in the father, and later on assumes a thousand different forms: the schoolmaster, the superior, the customer, the competitor, the representatives of social and governmental forces. Their brutality stimulates individual spontaneity.

It seems illusory to suppose that in the future the degree of severity could be accurately adjusted, and that the bloody penalties which have been inflicted on tame men over the centuries could be replaced by sanatoria. Simulated force is powerless. Culture has developed with the protection of the executioner. Here the book of Genesis, which tells of the fall from Paradise, coincides with the *Soirées de Petersbourg*. All work and pleasure are protected by the hangman. To contradict this fact is to deny all science and logic. It is impossible to abolish the terror and retain civilization. Even a lessening of terror implies a beginning of the process of dissolution. Various conclusions can be drawn from this—from the groveling respect for Fascist barbarity to refuge in the circles of Hell. But there is another con-

217

clusion: to laugh at logic if it runs counter to the interests of men.

ANIMAL PSYCHOLOGY

A big dog stands on the highway. He walks on confidently and is run over by a car. His peaceful expression shows that he is usually better looked after—a domestic animal to whom no harm is done. But do the sons of the rich bourgeois families who also suffer no harm have the same peaceful expression? They were cared for just as lovingly as the dog which is now run over.

IN PRAISE OF VOLTAIRE

Your reason is one-sided, one-sided reason whispers, and you have done wrong to those in power. You have cried out— pathetically, tearfully, sarcastically, noisily—against the shameful nature of tyranny. But you have forgotten the good achievements of power. Without the security provided by power alone, this goodness could never have existed. Life and love have played under the protective wings of power and won a little happiness from hostile nature. This apology has true and false elements. Only power is capable of injustice, because only the execution which follows a judgment is unjust, and not the speech of a lawyer which is not implemented. Only if the speech itself aims to suppress, and defends power instead of the weak, does it share in the general injustice. But power (so the voice of one-sided reason continues) is represented by men. By exposing power, you make men the target. And their place will perhaps be taken by others who are still more evil. The lie has some truth in it. If the Fascist murderers are already waiting, the people must not be egged on to attack a weak régime. But even the alliance with less brutal power does not necessarily lead to the concealment of infamy. The likelihood that the good cause will suffer if the injustice which protects the individual against the devil is denounced, was still even less than the advantage which the devil gained by allowing him to denounce injustice. How far must a society have come when only evil men speak the truth and Goebbels keeps alive the memory of cheerfully continued lynchings. Evil rather than good is the object of theory. It presupposes reproduction of life in its specifically determined forms. Its element is freedom and its theme suppression. When language becomes apologetic it is already corrupted, and it can neither be neutral nor practical in its essence. Can you not show the good side of things and announce the principle of love instead of endless bitterness? There is only one expression for the truth: the thought which denies injustice. If insistence on the good aspects is not abolished in the negative system it highlights its own contrast: violence. I can intrigue, propagate and suggest with words; this is the feature by which all action is caught up in reality, and also the feature which understands lies. It insinuates that the contradiction of existing circumstances is effected in the service of incipient forms of violence, competing bureaucracies, and powerful rulers. In its nameless fear it can and will only see itself. The components which are used in its medium, language, as mere instruments, become identical with lies just as things become identical in darkness. But however true it may be that there are no words which cannot be used in the service of lies, goodness does not appear through these words but only in the obduracy of thought against the ruling power. Uncompromising hatred for the terror wrought on the least being provides the basis for the legitimate gratitude felt by those who are spared. The appeal to the sun is idolatry. The sight of the burning tree inspires a vision of the majesty of the day which lights the world without setting fire to it at the same time.

CLASSIFICATION

General concepts determined axiomatically or by the individual sciences on the basis of abstraction, form the material for representation in the same way as names for individual things. It is futile to reject general concepts. But this does not exhaust the dignity of universals. That which is common to many individuals or returns constantly in the individual does not have to be more stable, eternal, or deeper than the particular. The scale of types is not identical to the scale of significance. This was the mistake of the Eleatics and of all who followed them, especially Plato and Aristotle.

The world is unique. The simple repetition of the aspects which constantly recur in the same way is more like a vain and compulsory litany than the redeeming word. Classification is a condition for cognition and not cognition itself; cognition in turn dispels classification.

AVALANCHES

In modern times there are no more changes. A turn in events is always for the better. But if in times like the present the need is greatest, the heavens open and cast their fire on those who are already lost.

Social and political affairs give this impression first. The front pages of newspapers which once appeared strange and vulgar to happy women and children—newspapers recalled the inn and swaggering pretense—have now come to be a real threat. The armaments race, events overseas, tension in the Mediterranean, and all kinds of complicated notions induced a genuine fear among men until World War I broke out. And then inflation came with figures which were giddily high. When the inflation was brought under control this was not a turning point but an even greater misfortune: rationalization and a tightening of belts. When Hitler's electoral success began to increase, modestly at first but steadily all the same, it was already clear that this was an avalanche. Electoral figures always characterize this phenomenon. When the results are received from a few constituencies on the evening of the Fascist polling day, one-eighth or one-sixteenth of the votes already foreshadow the general results. If ten or twenty districts have chosen *en masse* one particular direction, the other hundred will chose otherwise. There

220

is a general spirit of uniformity. The essence of the world coincides with the statistical law according to which its surface is classified.

In Germany, Fascism won the day with a crassly xenophobic, collectivist ideology which was hostile to culture. Now that it is laying the whole world waste, the nations must fight against it; there is no other way out. But when all is over there is nothing to prove that a spirit of freedom will spread across Europe; its nations may become just as xenophobic, pseudocollectivistic, and hostile to culture as Fascism once was when they had to fight against it. The downfall of Fascism will not necessarily lead to a movement of the avalanche.

The principle of liberal philosophy was that of "both/and." Today the principle of "either/or" seems to apply, but as though a decision had already been taken for the worse.

ISOLATION BY COMMUNICATION

Modern communications media have an isolating effect; this is not a mere intellectual paradox. The lying words of the radio announcer become firmly imprinted on the brain and prevent men from speaking to each other; the advertising slogans for Pepsi-Cola sound out above the collapse of continents; the example of movie stars encourages young children to experiment with sex and later leads to broken marriages. Progress literally keeps men apart. The little counters in railroad stations or banks enabled clerks to talk and joke with their colleagues. The glass windows of modern offices and the great halls in which innumerable employees sit down together and can easily be supervised by the public and managers prevent private conversations and moments out of time. In administrative offices the taxpayer is now protected against time wasting by employees. They are isolated in the collective system. But means of communication also isolate men physically. Railroads have given way to private automobiles, which reduce acquaintanceships made during journeys to contacts with hitchhikers—which may even be dangerous. Men travel on rubber tires in

221

complete isolation from each other. The conversations in their vehicles are always identical and regulated by practical interests. The families in specific income brackets spend the same percentage on housing, movies, and cigarettes as the statistics prescribe; the themes of conversation vary with the category of vehicle. When visitors meet on Sundays or holidays in restaurants whose menus and rooms are identical at the different price levels, they find that they have become increasingly similar with their increasing isolation. Communication establishes uniformity among men by isolating them.

ON THE CRITIQUE OF THE PHILOSOPHY OF HISTORY

The human race is not, as has sometimes been asserted, a chance phenomenon of natural history, a freak due to hypertrophy of the brain. This is only true of reason in certain individuals and perhaps for short periods of history—even for certain countries in which the economy allowed these individuals freedom of action. The brain or human intelligence is strong enough to form a regular epoch in the history of the world. The human race with its machines, chemicals, and organizations—which belong to it just as teeth belong to a bear, since they serve the same purpose and merely function more effectively—is the *dernier cri* of adaptation in this epoch. Men have not only overtaken their immediate predecessors, but thoroughly exterminated them in a manner which is not reflected in any other modern species, including the flesh-eating saurians.

On the other hand, there is a tendency to interpret the history of the world as Hegel did, in categories such as freedom and justice. These originate in the isolated individuals, who are insignificant by comparison with the system as a whole, except to the extent that they help to bring about a temporary social condition in which a particularly large number of machines and chemicals are created to strengthen the race and subjugate others. In the sense of this serious history, all ideas, prohibitions, religions, and political faiths are only interesting in so far as they increase or reduce the natural prospects of the human race on earth or in the universe. The liberation of citizens from the injustice of the feudalistic and absolutist past served to unleash modern machinery through liberalism, just as the emancipation of women led to their development into a military force. The spirit and all that is good in its origins and existence are inextricably caught up in this network of horror. The serum which a doctor gives a sick child is obtained by attacking defenseless animals. The endearing words of lovers and the holiest symbols of Christianity contain traces of the pleasure felt in devouring the flesh of a kid, just as this pleasure itself reflects an ambiguous respect for the totem animal. The differentiated understanding of cooking, the Church, and the theater is a consequence of the refined division of labor which works at the expense of nature inside and outside human society. The historical function of culture lies in the retrospective heightening of this organization. True thought which detaches itself from such considerations therefore assumes that trace of delusion which the establishment has also observed. If such thought were to win a decisive victory in mankind it would endanger the powerful position of the race. The theory of the sideward movement would ultimately still be true. But this theory which cynically wished to serve the critique of the anthropocentric philosophy of history is itself too anthropocentric to be maintained. Reason plays the part of an instrument of adaptation, and not of the tranquilizer which it may seem to be because of the use which the individual sometimes made of it. Its cunning consists in turning men into animals with more and more far-reaching powers, and not in establishing the identity between subject and object.

A philosophical interpretation of world history would have to show how the rational domination of nature comes increasingly to win the day, in spite of all deviations and resistance, and integrates all human characteristics. Forms of economy, rule, and culture would also be derived from this position. The notion of the superman only becomes applicable in the sense of the transition from quantity to quality. Just as the aviator who can rid the last continents of the last free animals in a few flights by dropping a toxic substance may be called a superman in contrast to the troglodyte, a human super-amphibian may ultimately appear in relation to whom the aviator of today will seem to be a harmless swallow. It is doubtful whether a genuine "next-higher" race can arise after men. Anthropomorphism contains a measure of truth in that natural history did not reckon with the play of chance which led to the development of men. Their destructive capacity risks becoming so great that a clean sweep will be made if the race is ever exhausted. Either men will tear each other to pieces or they will take all the flora and fauna of the earth with them; and if the earth is then still young enough, the whole thing will have to be started again at a much lower stage.

When the philosophy of history shifted the position of humane ideas as an active force into history itself, and caused the latter to end with the triumph of these forces, humane ideas were robbed of the innocence which is an integral part of their content. The scorn which they showed when the economy—the center of power—was not with them, is the scorn for all weakness; in it the authors identified themselves against their own will with the suppression which they wanted to abolish. The philosophy of history repeats a process which occurred in Christianity: the goodness which in reality remains at the mercy of suffering is concealed as the force which determines the course of history and ultimately triumphs. It is idolized as the spirit of the world or as an immanent law. In this way, however, history is transformed directly into its opposite, and the idea itself (which wanted to arrest the logical course of events) is distorted. The risk of the lateral movement is averted. The impotence which appears as power is once again denied by this heightening effect and removed from the memory. Christianity, idealism, and materialism, which in themselves contain truth, are therefore also responsible for the barbaric acts perpetrated in their name. As representatives of power—even if of power for good—they themselves became historical forces which could be organized, and as such played a bloody role in the true history of the human race: that of the instruments of organization. Because history as the correlation of unified theory and as something which can be built is not good but horror, so thought is in fact a negative element. Hope for better circumstances—if it is not a mere illusion—is not so much based on the assurance that these circumstances would be guaranteed, durable, and final, but on the lack of respect for all that is so firmly rooted in the general suffering. The infinite patience, the permanent and tender urge of the being for expression and light which seems to calm and satisfy the violence of creative development, does not define, as the rational philosophies of history do, a specific practice as beneficial—not even that of non-resistance. The first appearance of reason which comes to light in this driving force and is reflected in the memories of men, also meets its inevitable contradiction on Judgment Day: the fate which reason alone cannot avert.

MONUMENTS OF HUMANITY

Humanity has always been more at home in France than elsewhere. But the French themselves were not aware of this. Their books simply contained the ideology which everyone already recognized. The better things in life still led a separate existence: the special tone of voice, the feats of gastronomy, the brothels and the cast-iron urinals. But the Blum government already opened an offensive against this respect for the individual, and even the conservatives did little to protect its monuments.

A THEORY OF CRIME

. . . The criminal has always been bourgeois—like the retribution which consists in robbing him of his freedom. In the Middle Ages the children of princes were imprisoned when they represented a disagreeable claim to an inheritance. Criminals, on the other hand, were tortured to death in order to imbue the mass of the population with a respect for law and order, because the example of severity and cruelty is supposed to have an educa-

225

tive effect. The regular punishment of imprisonment presupposes a growing need for manpower. It reflects the bourgeois way of life as suffering. The rows of cells in a modern prison are monads in the true sense of the word defined by Leibniz: "Monads have no windows through which it is possible to see in or out. The accidents cannot be detached or move about outside the substances as the perceptible forms of the Scholastics once did. Neither substance nor accidence is introduced into a monad from without."[1] The monads have no direct influence on each other; their life is regulated and coordinated by God, or direction.[2] Absolute solitude, the violent turning inward on the self, whose whole being consists in the mastery of material and in the monotonous rhythm of work, is the specter which outlines the existence of man in the modern world. Radical isolation and radical reduction to the same hopeless nothingness are identical. Man in prison is the virtual image of the bourgeois type which he still has to become in reality. Those who cannot manage outside are forcibly held in a terrible state of purity in prison. The rationalization of the existence of prisons by the need to separate the criminal from society or to "improve" him does not strike at the heart of the problem. The prison is an image of the bourgeois world of labor taken to its logical conclusion; hatred felt by men for everything that they would themselves wish to become but is beyond their reach, is placed as a symbol in the world. The weak or retarded individual must suffer the order of life in which he finds himself without love while introverted violence is wreaked on him. The criminal who simply sets absolute store by self-preservation in reality has the weaker personality; the habitual criminal is an inadequate individual.

Prisoners are sick persons. Their weakness has put them in a situation which has already attacked—and continues to attack—body and soul. Most of them were already sick when they committed the act which led to their imprisonment; sick in their constitution or circumstances. Others acted as any healthy person faced with the same set of stimuli and motives would have

1. Leibniz, *La Monadologie*, Ed. Erdmann (Berlin, 1840), Sec. 7, p. 605.
2. Cf. *op. cit.*, Sec. 51, p. 709.

acted—they were simply unlucky. And a few remaining individuals were more evil and cruel than most free persons, as evil and cruel as the Fascist masters of the world are in their attitudes. The act of the common criminal is narrow-minded, personal, and directly destructive. The probability is that the living substance which is the same in everyone exerts identical pressure on all individuals, so that when we consider the circumstances under which extreme acts of violence are committed we would ourselves have acted in the same way as the assassin, had we not possessed the insight granted to us by a fortunate chain of events. But the prisoner merely suffers a blind penalty, something alienated from him, a misfortune like cancer or the collapse of a house. The prison is a disease. This is confirmed by the expression, cautious movements, and circumstantial thinking of prisoners. Like the sick, they can only talk of their sickness.

Today the boundary line between respectable and illegal rackets has become objectively blurred and in psychological terms the different forms merge. As long as criminals were still diseased individuals (as was the case in the nineteenth century), imprisonment reversed their weakness. The ability to stand apart from the environment as an individual, and at the same time to enter into contact with that environment—and gain a foothold in it—through the approved forms of communication, was eroded in the criminal. He represented a trend which is deep-rooted in living beings, and whose elimination is a sign of all development: the trend to lose oneself in the environment instead of playing an active role in it; the tendency to let oneself go and sink back into nature. Freud called it the death instinct, Caillois *"le mimétisme."*[3] This urge underlies everything which run counter to bold progress, from the crime which is a shortcut avoiding the normal forms of activity, to the sublime work of art. A yielding attitude to things, without which art cannot exist, is not so very remote from the violence of the criminal. The inability to say No which leads a teenage girl to lapse into prostitution also conditions the criminal's career.

3. Cf. Caillois, *Le Mythe et l'Homme* (Paris, 1938), pp. 125ff.

There is negation in the criminal which does not contain resistance. Weakness which, with no specific conscience, timidly imitates and at the same time destroys pitiless civilization is opposed by the solid walls of the prisons and labor camps, its own stone ideal. Since de Tocqueville, the bourgeois republics have attacked man's soul, whereas the monarchies attacked his body; similarly the penalties inflicted in these republics also attack man's soul. The new martyrs do not die a slow death in the torture chamber but instead waste away spiritually as invisible victims in the great prison buildings which differ in little but name from madhouses.

Fascism includes both forms. The concentration of control over all production brings society back to the stage of direct rule. When the market system is abolished in a nation, intervening intellectual operations, including law, also disappear.

Thought which developed in the transaction as a result of an egotism which had to negotiate, is diverted for plans of violent appropriation. The mass-murdering Fascist appeared as the pure essence of the German manufacturer, different from the criminal only in that he enjoyed power. The diversion ceased to be necessary. Civil law which continued to function to settle differences between the entrepreneurs living in the shadow of heavy industry, became a kind of court of arbitration judging those who were subject to it without considering their real interests—in short, the rule of terror. The legal protection which now disappears did, however, define property. Monopoly as the ultimate form of private ownership destroys the notion of property. Fascism replaces the state and social contract by secret agreements, and retains only the rule of the supposedly general power, which is enforced by its servants on the rest of mankind. In the totalitarian state, crime and punishment are liquidated as superstitious relics; and the naked extermination of resisting individuals aware of their political aim, spreads across Europe under the criminal regime. By comparison with the concentration camp, an ordinary prison reminds us of the good old days, just as the intelligent newspaper which once existed to reveal the truth contrasts with the glossy magazines whose literary content—even if the subject is Michelangelo—simply serves to promote the interests of the ruling power. In former times prisoners were placed in enforced isolation. Today that isolation has entered into men's body and soul. The well-trained soul and happiness of the individual are as bleak as the prison cell now that the Fascist rulers have seized the whole labor force of the nation. The punishment of imprisonment is as nothing when set against the social reality in which we live.

LE PRIX DU PROGRÈS

A recently discovered letter by the French physiologist, Pierre Flourens, who once enjoyed the bittersweet fame of having been elected to the French Academy in competition with Victor Hugo, contains the following striking passage:

"I still cannot decide to agree to the use of chloroform in general surgical practice. As you probably know, I have devoted extensive study to this substance and was one of the first to describe its specific properties on the basis of experiments with animals. My scruples are founded on the simple fact that operations with chloroform, and presumably also with the other known forms of narcosis, have an illusory success. These substances act solely on certain motor and coordination centers and on the residual capability of the nervous substances. Under the influence of chloroform, the nervous substance loses a considerable part of its ability to absorb traces of impressions, but it does not lose the power of sensation as such. On the contrary, my observations suggest that in conjunction with the general innervation paralysis, pain is experienced even more strongly than in the normal condition. The public is misled by the fact that after an operation the patient is unable to remember what he has undergone. If we told our patients the truth, it is probable that not one of them would wish to have an operation performed under chloroform, whereas they all insist on its use now because we shroud the truth in silence.

"But quite apart from the fact that the only questionable gain is a loss of memory lasting for the duration of surgery, I consider that the extended use of this substance entails another serious risk. With the increasing superficiality of the general academic training of our doctors, the unlimited use of chloroform may encourage surgeons to carry out increasingly complex and difficult operations. Instead of using these methods on animals in the interests of research, our own patients will then become the unsuspecting guinea pigs. It is possible that the painful stimuli which because of their specific nature may well exceed all known sensations of this kind, may lead to permanent mental damage in the patient or even to an undescribably painful death under narcosis; and the exact features of this death will be hidden for ever from the relatives of the patient and the world at large. Would this not be too high a price to pay for progress?"

If Flourens had been right here, the dark paths of the divine world order would have been justified for once. The animal would have been avenged through the suffering of his executioners: every operation would have been a vivisection. The suspicion would then arise that our relationship with men and creation in general was like our relationship with ourself after an operation—oblivion for suffering. For cognition the gap between us and others was the same as the time between our own present and past suffering; an insurmountable barrier. But perennial domination over nature, medical and non-medical techniques, are made possible only by the process of oblivion. The loss of memory is a transcendental condition for science. All objectification is a forgetting.

IDLE HORROR

The observation of evil is a fascinating occupation. But this observation implies a measure of secret agreement. The bad social conscience of everyone who participates in an evil deed, and hatred for fulfillment in life, are so strong that under critical circumstances they turn against their own interests as a form of immanent revenge. One fatal example of this is provided by the French bourgeois who observed ironically the heroic ideal of the Fascists: they were delighted by the triumph of their

230

fellows expressed in Hitler's rise to power, even if it threatened their own destruction; indeed they took their own destruction as evidence of the justice of the order they represented. This behavior pattern is prefigured in the attitude of many rich people toward impoverishment, which they use to rationalize a thrifty attitude: their latent inclination—while fighting for every penny—to abandon all their possessions or gamble them away irresponsibly. In Fascism they are presented with a synthesis of the desire to rule and self-hatred; idle horror is always accompanied by the words "I told you so!"

THE IMPORTANCE OF THE BODY

Europe has two histories: a well-known, written history and an underground history. The latter consists in the fate of the human instincts and passions which are displaced and distorted by civilization. The Fascist present in which the hidden side of things comes to light also shows the relationship between written history and the dark side which is overlooked in the official legend of the nationalist states, as well as in the critique of the latter.

The relationship with the human body is maimed from the outset. The division of labor which made a distinction between utilization on the one hand and work on the other, outlawed crude force. The more dependent the ruling classes become on the work of others the more they despise that work. A stigma attaches to work as it does to slavery. Christianity extolled the virtues of work but declared the flesh to be the root of all evil. It ushered in the modern bourgeois order, joining forces here with the pagan Machiavelli, by praising work which was still accursed in the Old Testament. For the desert patriarchs, Dorotheus, Moses the Robber, Paul the Simple, and others of the poor in spirit, work was a key to the kingdom of heaven. For Luther and Calvin the link between work and salvation was so complex that the Protestant insistence on work appeared almost like scorn, like the jackboot stamping on a worm.

The princes and patriarchs were able to step across the

231

religious gap which had opened between their days on earth and their eternal destiny by thinking of the income which they derived from the working hours of others. The irrational way in which men were chosen for salvation left the possibility of redemption open to them. But the workers were merely exposed to greater pressure. They realized vaguely that the humiliation of the flesh by the ruling power was simply the ideological reflection of the suppression to which they were themselves subject. All sacrificial victims, right up to the modern colonial peoples, have experienced the same fate as the slaves of ancient times: they were treated as lesser people.

There were two races by nature: the greater and the lesser. The liberation of the European individual took place in the context of a general, cultural transformation which increased the gap among the "free" people all the more on the internal plane as the physical compulsion from outside declined. The exploited body was defined as "evil," and the spiritual occupations in which the higher people were free to indulge were asserted to be the greatest good. This process made possible the supreme cultural achievements of Europe, but the suspicion of the trickery which was apparent from the outset heightened the love-hate relationship with the body which permeated the thinking of the masses over the centuries, and found its authentic expression in the language of Luther. The relationship between the individual and the body—his own and that of others—shows the irrationality and injustice of rule as cruelty which is as far removed from the relationship of insight and happy reflection as the practice of cruelty is from freedom. Nietzsche's theory of cruelty, and certainly that of Sade, recognized the importance of this factor, while Freud's doctrines of narcissism and the death instinct provided a psychological interpretation.

The love-hate relationship with the body colors all more recent culture. The body is scorned and rejected as something inferior, and at the same time desired as something forbidden, objectified, and alienated. Culture defines the body as a thing which can be possessed; in culture a distinction is made between the body and the spirit, the concept of power and command, as the object, the dead thing, the *"corpus."* In man's denigration of his own body, nature takes its revenge for the fact that man has reduced nature to an object for domination, a raw material. The compulsive urge to cruelty and destruction springs from the organic displacement of the relationship between the mind and body; Freud expressed the facts of the matter with genius when he said that loathing first arose when men began to walk upright and were at a distance from the ground, so that the sense of smell which drew the male animal to the female in heat was relegated to a secondary position among the senses. In Western civilization, and probably in all other forms of civilization, the physical aspect of existence is taboo—an object of attraction and repulsion. For the Greek rulers and in the feudal system, the relationship with the body was still conditioned by personal strength as a requisite of rule.

In naïve terms, the concern for the body had its social objectives. The *kalos kagathos* was only partly a semblance; in part, too, the gymnasium was a necessary aid to maintaining the individual's own power, or at least as training for the posture of a ruler. The complete transition of rule into the bourgeois form determined by commerce and communication, led to a formal change. Men are no longer enslaved by the sword, but by the gigantic apparatus which ultimately again forges the sword. The rationale for improving the functional properties of the male body disappeared; the romantic attempts to bring about a renaissance of the body in the nineteenth and twentieth centuries simply idealize a dead and maimed condition. Nietzsche, Gauguin, Stefan George, and Klages recognized the nameless stupidity which is the result of progress. But they drew a false conclusion. They did not denounce injustice as it is, but glorified injustice as it was. The revulsion against mechanization became an ornament of mass culture which cannot do without noble gestures. The artists prepared the lost image of the unity of body and soul against their own will for publicity purposes. The idolizing of the vital phenomena from the "blond beast" to the South Sea islanders inevitably leads to the "sarong film" and the advertising posters for vitamin pills and skin creams which simply stand for the immanent aim of publicity: the new, great, beautiful and noble type of man—the Führer and his

233

storm troopers. The Fascist leaders take the weapons of murder into their own hands again; they execute their prisoners with pistol and riding crop, not because of their superior force, but because the gigantic apparatus and its true centers of power deliver the victims of the state into the cellars of their headquarters.

The body cannot be remade into a noble object: it remains the corpse however vigorously it is trained and kept fit. The metamorphosis into death was simply a part of that perennial process which turned nature into substance and matter. The feats of civilization are the product of sublimation, that acquired love-cum-hatred for the body and earth from which the rulers have separated all men. Medicine uses the mental reaction to the physical incarnation of man for productive purposes, while technology uses the reaction to the reification of nature as a whole.

The murderer, the bestial colossus who is used by the rulers —legal or illegal, great or small—to execute their dark purposes, the violent men who are always there when somebody has to be done away with, the lynchers and KKK members, the strong-armed man who stands up when someone fears him, the terrible vultures to whom everyone is delivered up immediately he loses his money and position, and all the werewolves who exist in the darkness of history and keep alive that fear without which there can be no rule—all these men stand for the love-hate relationship with the body in its crudest and most direct form; they pervert all they touch, they destroy what they see in the light and this destruction is their rancor for reification; they repeat in their blind anger against the living object all that they cannot unmake: the division of life into spirit and its object. They are irresistibly attracted by man: they want to reduce him to a physical substance; nothing must be allowed to live. This hostility—which was once carefully fostered by the worldly and spiritual rulers—felt by the lowly against the life which held out nothing for them and with which they could establish a homosexual and paranoiac relationship by murdering, was always an essential instrument of the art of government. The hostility of the enslaved against life is an undying force on the dark side of history. Puritanical excess takes its desperate revenge against life.

The love of nature and destiny expressed in totalitarian propaganda is simply a veiled reaction to failed civilization. Men cannot escape from their body and sing its praises when they cannot destroy it. The "tragic" philosophy of the Fascist is the ideological party which precedes the real blood wedding. Those who extolled the body above all else, the gymnasts and scouts, always had the closest affinity with killing, just as the lovers of nature are close to the hunter. They see the body as a moving mechanism, with joints as its components and flesh to cushion the skeleton. They use the body and its parts as though they were already separated from it. Jewish tradition contains a disinclination to measure men with a foot-rule because the corpse is measured in this way for the coffin. This is what the manipulators of the body enjoy. They measure others, without realizing it, with the gaze of a coffin maker. They betray themselves when they speak the result: they call men tall, short, fat or heavy. They are interested in illness and at mealtimes already watch for the death of those who eat with them, and their interest is only thinly rationalized by concern for their health. Language keeps pace with them. It has transformed a walk into motion and a meal into calories just as the English and French languages make no distinction between living and dead wood (whereas in German it is possible to speak of *Wald* or *Holz*). Society with its death statistics reduces life to a chemical process.

The diabolical humiliation of the prisoner in a concentration camp which the modern executioner adds—with no rational purpose—to a martyred death, expresses the unsublimated but repressed rebellion of tabooed nature. The full horror is reserved for the martyr of love, the supposed sexual criminal and libertine, because sex represents the body in its pure state—for which the murderers despairingly long in secret. In free sexuality the murderer fears lost directness, the original unity in which he can no longer exist. It is death which stands up and lives. The murderer makes everything one by seeking to destroy all around him because he has to stifle unity within himself.

235

For him, the victim represents life which has overcome the separation; it must be broken and the universe must be mere dust and abstract power.

MASS SOCIETY

The cult of celebrities (film stars) has a built-in social mechanism to level down everyone who stands out in any way. The stars are simply a pattern round which the world-embracing garment is cut—a pattern to be followed by the shears of legal and economic justice with which the last projecting ends of thread are cut away.

Note

The opinion that the leveling-down and standardization of men is accompanied on the other hand by a heightened individuality in the "leader" personalities that corresponds to the power they enjoy, is false and an ideological pretense. The modern Fascist bosses are not so much supermen as functions of their own propaganda machine, the focal points at which identical reactions of countless citizens intersect. In the psychology of the modern masses, the Führer is not so much a father-figure as a collective and overexaggerated projection of the powerless ego of each individual—to which the so-called "leaders" in fact correspond.

They look like hairdressers, provincial actors, and hack journalists. Part of their moral influence consists precisely in the fact that they are powerless in themselves but deputize for all the other powerless individuals, and embody the fullness of power for them, without themselves being anything other than the vacant spaces taken up accidentally by power. They are not excepted from the break-up of individuality; all that has happened is that the disintegrated form triumphs in them and to some extent is compensated for its decomposition. The "leaders" have become what they already were in a less developed form throughout the bourgeois era: actors playing the part of leaders. The distance between the individuality of Bismarck and Hitler is scarcely less than that between the prose of *Thoughts and Memories* and the mumbo-jumbo of *Mein Kampf*. One important component of the fight against Fascism is to cut the inflated "Führer" images down to size. Chaplin's *Great Dictator* touched on the core of the problem by showing the similarity between the ghetto barber and the dictator.

CONTRADICTIONS

Philosophers are asked to provide a moral system containing principles and conclusions, with watertight logic and reliable applicability to every moral dilemma. In general they have fulfilled this expectation. Even if they did not establish a practical system and a well-developed casuistics, they derived the need for obedience to authority from their theoretical considerations. Generally, they provided logical reasons and evidence in support of the whole scale of values already approved by public practice. "Honor the gods through your traditional native religion," wrote Epicurus, and Hegel echoed these words. Anyone who is slow in confessing his faith is asked even more energetically to put forward his belief in a general principle. If thought is to do more than merely confirm dominant regulations, it must appear more universal and authoritative than when it simply justifies something which already holds. You consider the existing power to be unjust—Do you want power to be replaced by chaos? You criticize the monotonous uniformity of life and progress— Shall we then light wax candles in the evening and allow our cities to be full of stinking refuse as they were in the Middle Ages? You do not like slaughter-houses—Is society to live on raw vegetables from now on? However absurd it may seem, the affirmative answer to questions such as these still falls on friendly ears. Political anarchy, a reaction against existing forms of culture, radical vegetarianism, and deviant sects and parties have a certain publicity appeal. The doctrine need only be general, sure of itself, universal, and imperative. What seems intolerable is the attempt to break away from the "Either-Or," to overcome mistrust for the abstract principle and infallibility without doctrine.

A discussion between two young people:

A. You don't want to be a doctor then?

B. Doctors have so much professional contact with dying people that they become hardened. As institutionalization advances, the doctor also comes to represent the establishment and its hierarchy for the patient. Often he is tempted to appear as the controller of life and death. He becomes an agent of the establishment against the consumer. This does not matter when it is a question of selling automobiles, but when the goods dealt in are life, and the consumers are suffering individuals, this is a situation which I would not like to be placed in. The profession of the family doctor may have been less harmful but it is declining today.

A. Do you then maintain that there should be no doctors or that the old quacks should return?

B. I did not say that. I am simply horrified at the prospect of becoming a doctor myself, especially a consultant with responsibility over a large hospital. Nevertheless, I consider it better for doctors and hospitals to exist than for sick people to be left to die. I also don't want to be a public prosecutor, yet I consider the existence of robbers and murderers to be a much greater evil than that of a system which sends them to prison. Justice is reasonable. I am not opposed to reason—I simply wish to define clearly the form it has taken.

A. I do not agree with you at all. You yourself make use of the benefits created by doctors and judges. You share their guilt. But you do not want to take part in the work which others do for you. Your own existence presupposed the principle you would like to escape.

B. I do not deny that, but the contradiction is necessary. It is the answer to the objective component of society. With the complex division of labor which we have today, horror may arise at one point and involve the guilt of everyone. If it develops and if only a small proportion of mankind become aware of it, mental homes and prisons could perhaps be humanized and courts of law might become unnecessary in the long run. But that is not the reason why I want to become a writer. I simply wish to explain more clearly for myself the terrible state in which everyone lives today.

A. But if everyone thought as you do and nobody wanted to dirty his hands, there would be no more judges or doctors, and the world would be even more terrible than it is today.

B. I am not so sure; if everybody thought as I do, I hope that evil itself as well as the means to combat it would diminish. Mankind has other possibilities. I am not the whole of mankind and my thoughts cannot stand for those of everybody else. The moral principle that each of my actions should be able to stand as a general maxim is very dubious. It overlooks the lesson of history. Why should my own disinclination to become a doctor be equated with the assumption that there should be no doctors? In reality there are very many individuals who are capable and have a real chance of becoming good doctors. If they remain within the moral limits placed on the profession today, I admire them greatly. Perhaps they even help to reduce the burden of evil which I have described to you, or perhaps at the other extreme they increase it despite all their professional skill and morality. My own existence as I imagine it to be, my fear and will to understand my condition seem as justified to me as the profession of the doctor, even though I cannot directly help anyone.

A. But if you knew that you could save the life of a person who is dear to you by studying medicine would you not then take up this study, especially if you knew that the person concerned would die unless you did so?

B. Probably, but you will agree that you have had to take an absurd example with your preference for taking an argument to its ultimate conclusion, whereas I—with my impractical stubbornness and contradictions—have still remained within the bounds of common sense.

This discussion is always repeated when individuals are unwilling to give up their right to think rather than become directly involved in practical affairs. Logic and rationality always seem to be on the other side. If you are opposed to vivisection, you should not breathe another breath which is likely to cost the life of one bacillus. Logic serves progress and reaction—or at all events reality. But in an age of education which centers squarely on reality, discussions like this have become less frequent, and the neurotic partner B needs superhuman power if he is not to become healthy too.

A PERSONAL OBSERVATION

When men reach the age of forty or fifty they tend to observe a curious change. They discover that most of the individuals with whom they grew up and maintained contact now behave in a disturbed manner. One may stop working so that his business fails; another may break his marriage, though the fault does not lie with his wife; and yet another may embezzle money. Even those individuals who show no such striking behavioral changes still show signs of degeneration. Conversation with them becomes shallow, threadbare, and boastful. Previously the aging individual found mental stimulus in others but now he feels that he is almost the only one to present objective interest.

At first, he is inclined to consider the development of his fellows as an unpleasant quirk of fate. They have changed for the worse. Perhaps this change has something to do with his particular generation and its external fate. Finally, he discovers that he had already had the same experience but from a different angle: that of the conflict between young people and adults. He always used to be convinced that there was something wrong with a teacher, his uncles and aunts, friends of his parents, and, later, his university professors or the training supervisor in a business concern. They either showed a laughable side to their character, or else he felt their presence to be particularly burdensome, disappointing, and meaningless.

At the time he gave the matter no more thought and simply accepted the inferiority of adults as a fact of nature. Now the facts are confirmed to him: under the given conditions, the mere continuation of an existence maintaining individual skills of a technical or intellectual nature leads to cretinism even in the prime of life. Men of the world are not excluded from this general rule. It is as though people who betray the hopes of their youth and come to terms with the world, suffer the penalty of premature decay.

Note

The breakdown of individuality today not only helps us to understand its category as a historical feature but also evokes doubt about its positive nature. The injustice experienced by the individual was the essential principle of his existence in the phase of competition. This does not apply only to the function of the individual and his particular interest in society, but to the internal composition of individuality as such. The trend toward the emancipation of men resulted from this, but it is also a consequence of the mechanisms from which mankind must be emancipated. The independence and incomparability of the individual crystallize resistance to the blind, repressive force of the irrational whole. But, historically, this resistance was only made possible by the blindness and irrationality of each independent and incomparable individual. Conversely, all that is opposed to the whole because of its individuality remains a permanent feature of existence. The radically individual features of a person are both components in one, the facor which has been able to escape the ruling system and fortunately lives on, and the symptom of the injury by which the system maims its members. The basic principles of the system are repeated in an exaggerated manner in these features: the desire for property is reflected in avarice and the urge to self-preservation in imaginary illness. Because the individual uses such features in a firm attempt to assert himself against the compulsion of nature and society, illness and bankruptcy, they necessarily themselves assume a compulsive character. In his innermost essence, the individual comes up against the same force which he is trying to escape. Escape therefore becomes a hopeless illusion. Molière's comedies highlight the curse of individuality just as Daumier's caricatures do; but the National Socialists who abolish the individual, comfortably thrive on this curse and appoint Spitzweg as their classical painter.

The hardened individual represents that which is better only in relation to a hardened society, and not in absolute terms. He reflects the shame felt at everything the collective system inflicts on the individual and what happens when there are no more individuals. The disembodied yes-men of today are the direct descendants of the irritable apothecaries, the passionate rose-growers and the political cripples of yesteryear.

PHILOSOPHY AND THE DIVISION OF LABOR

It is not difficult to see where science fits into the social division of labor. Its task is to accumulate facts and their functional relationships in the greatest possible quantities. The storage system used must be clearly designed, so that any industry can instantly pick out the particular assortment of intellectual goods it is seeking. To a large extent, these are in fact already assembled with an eye on the demands of specific branches of industry.

Historical works, too, furnish material. Ways of applying it are to be sought not directly in industry but indirectly in the administrative sphere. Just as Machiavelli once wrote for princes and republics, so today work is undertaken on behalf of economic and political committees. The historical form has of course now become a hindrance, and it is far better to order historical material right away in the light of a given administrative task, such as the manipulation of commodity prices or of mass emotions. The interested parties include not only the authorities and industrial consortia but also trade unions and political parties.

The official philosophy ministers to science operating on these lines. It is expected, as a sort of Taylorism of the mind, to help improve its production methods, to rationalize the storage of knowledge, and to prevent any wastage of intellectual energy. It is allotted a place in the division of labor in the same way as chemistry or bacteriology. If the few remnants of philosophy that recall the medieval worship of God and the contemplation of eternal essences are still tolerated at secular universities, it is precisely because these establishments are so reactionary. Furthermore, a few historians of philosophy are still at work tirelessly expounding Plato and Descartes while remarking that these are already outdated. Here and there they are joined by some veteran exponent of sensualism or an accomplished personalist. They are employed in rooting out the dialectical weeds that might overrun the field of science.

But, unlike those who administer it, philosophy is concerned with thought, in so far as this does not succumb to the prevailing division of labor or allow it to dictate its tasks. The status quo compels men not merely by virtue of physical force and material interests but also through its overpowering suggestion. Philosophy is not synthesis; and it is not the fundamental or master science. It is the attempt to resist this suggestion, the determination to hang on to intellectual and real freedom.

The division of labor, as it has developed under domination, is by no means overlooked in the process. Philosophy sees in it only the lie that there is no escaping it. Resisting the fascination of superior strength, it follows it in every nook and cranny of the social apparatus, which *a priori* should be neither stormed nor redirected, but grasped for what it is, divested of the spell exerted by it. If the officials whom industry sponsors in its intellectual centers—the universities, the Churches, and the press—require philosophy to declare its principles as a condition for continuing its searching, it is in a mortal dilemma. Philosophy knows of no workable abstract rules or goals to replace those at present in force. It is immune to the suggestion of the status quo for the very reason that it accepts bourgeois ideals without further consideration. These ideals may be those still proclaimed, though in distorted form, by the representatives of the status quo; or those which, however much they may have been tinkered about with, are still recognizable as the objective meaning of existing institutions, whether technical or cultural. Philosophy believes that the division of labor exists to serve mankind, and that progress leads to freedom. This is why it is so apt to come into conflict with both of them. It gives utterance to the contradiction between faith and reality while keeping close to the time-conditioned phenomenon. Unlike the press, it does not attach greater weight to mass slaughter than to the murder of a few mental defectives. It does not pay more attention to the intrigues of a statesman flirting with Fascism than to a lynching spree of modest proportions. For philosophy, the frenzied publicity of the film industry rates no higher than an intimate funeral announcement. Philosophy has little taste for sheer size. Therefore it is simultaneously alien and sympathetic to the status quo. Its voice belongs to the object, though without its will. It is the voice of contradiction, which would otherwise not be heard but triumph mutely.

THOUGHT

The belief that the truth of a theory is the same as its productiveness is clearly unfounded. There are some, however, who appear to maintain the opposite: that theory has so little need of application in thinking that it should dispense with it entirely. They falsely interpret every utterance as an ultimate avowal, command, or taboo. They would bow down to the idea as to a god, or attack it as if it were an idol. Where ideas are concerned they are completely lacking in freedom. But it is an essential aspect of truth that one should play a part in it as an active subject. One may encounter propositions that are inherently true, but their truth can only be discovered after a great deal of thought during and after their postulation.

Nowadays this sort of fetishism takes the most drastic forms. Thoughts have to be answered for as though they were deeds. Not just the word as authority's target but the tentative, experimenting word, testing the possibility of error, is for this very reason regarded as intolerable. Nevertheless, to be incomplete and at the same time conscious of the fact remains a feature of such thought, and particularly of the kind of thought worth dying with. The proposition that truth is the whole turns out to be identical with its contrary, namely, that in each case it exists only as a part. Of all the excuses that intellectuals have found for executioners—and during the past ten years they have not been idle in the matter—the most pitiable of all is that the victim's thought—for which he was murdered—was fallacious.

MAN AND ANIMAL

The idea of man in European history is expressed in the way in which he is distinguished from the animal. Animal irrationality is adduced as proof of human dignity. This contrast has been reiterated with such persistence and unanimity by all the predecessors of bourgeois thought—by the ancient Jews, Stoics, Fathers of the Church, and then throughout the Middle Ages down to modern times—that few ideas have taken such a hold on Western anthropology. The antithesis is still accepted today. The behaviorists only appear to have forgotten it. The fact that they apply to humans the same formulas and findings that, without restraint, they force from defenseless animals in their nauseating physiological laboratories stresses the contrast quite adroitly. The conclusion they draw from mutilated bodies applies not to animals in the free state but to man as he is today. It shows that because he does injury to animals, he and he alone in all creation voluntarily functions as mechanically, as blindly and automatically as the twitching limbs of the victim which the specialist knows how to turn to account. The professor at the dissecting-table defines these spasms scientifically as reflexes, just as the soothsayers at the altar once proclaimed them to be signs vouchsafed by his gods. Reason, mercilessly advancing, belongs to man. The animal, from which he draws his bloody conclusion, knows only irrational terror and the urge to make an escape from which he is cut off.

The want of reason has no words. Its possession, which dominates manifest history, is full of eloquence. The whole earth bears witness to the glory of man. Unreasoning creatures have encountered reason throughout the ages—in war and peace, in arena and slaughterhouse, from the lingering death-throes of the mammoth overpowered by a primitive tribe in the first

245

planned assault down to the unrelenting exploitation of the animal kindom in our own days. This visible process conceals the invisible from the executioners—existence denied the light of reason, animal existence itself. That should be the true theme of psychology since only the animal's life is governed by mental impulses. Where psychology has to be called in to explain human beings they are already disordered, and where its aid is enlisted on their behalf the already exiguous sphere of their immediate relationships is narrowed down still further, reducing them even there to things. To resort to psychology in order to understand one's fellow man is an effrontery; to use it to account for one's own motives is pure sentimentality. Animal psychology, however, has lost sight of its true purpose and, in its games with traps and mazes, has forgotten that it is to the animal alone that it can turn to discuss and conceive the soul. Even Aristotle, who allowed them a soul (though of an inferior kind), preferred to concern himself with animals' bodies and parts, with their movements and manner of reproduction, than with their actual existence.

The animal's world is devoid of concept. It lacks any word to seize the identical in the flux of phenomena, to isolate the same species in the alternation of specimens, or the same thing in altered situations. Even though the possibility of recognition is not lacking, identification is limited to what has been already vitally established. There is nothing in the flux of things that could be labeled as permanent. Yet everything remains one and the same for the lack of any certain knowledge of the past and of any clear expectation of the future. An animal answers to its name and has no self; it is shut up in itself and yet at the same time utterly exposed. Every moment brings a new constraint beyond which no idea can reach. Deprivation of comfort does not secure an animal alleviation of fear; or unconsciousness of happiness any respite from pain and sorrow. If happiness is to materialize, bestowing death on existence, there must be an identifying memory, a mitigating cognition, the religious or philosophical idea—in short, a concept. Happy animals there are, but then how short-lived is their happiness! The life of an animal, unrelieved by the liberating influence of thought, is dreary and harsh. Escape from the dismal emptiness of existence calls for resistance, and for this speech is essential. Even the strongest of animals is infinitely weak. Schopenhauer's definition of life as an endless oscillation between pain and boredom, between split seconds of stifled urges and unbounded passion, applies to animals, which cannot apply the brake of cognition to their destiny. The diverse emotions and needs of men, the very rudiments of the spirit, are planted in the animal soul, but without that curb which only the organizing faculty of reason can supply. The best days rush past in a flurry of change as in a dream, which the animal in any case can scarcely distinguish from waking life. The animal knows nothing of the clear-cut transition from play to serious activity, or of the joy of waking from a nightmare to the world of reality.

The metamorphosis of men into animals is a recurring theme of national folklore. To be condemned to inhabit an animal body was to be damned. Such metamorphoses were immediately understandable and familiar to whole peoples as they remain so to children. Believers in the transmigration of souls in the earliest cultures also regarded reincarnation in animal form as a dire punishment. The mute savagery in an animal's features reflects the same dread men felt about such a transformation.

Every animal suggests some crushing misfortune that took place in primeval times. The fairy tale betrays man's misgivings. But its prince preserves his reason, so that he can explain his predicament when the time comes and be set free by the fairy. An animal, however, is doomed by its lack of reason to inhabit its form for ever—that is, unless man, who is one with it through the past, discovers the redeeming formula and succeeds in softening the stony heart of eternity at the end of time.

For rational beings, however, to feel concern about an irrational creature is a futile occupation. Western civilization has left this to women. Women have no personal part in the efficiency on which this civilization is based. It is man who has to go out into an unfriendly world, who has to struggle and produce. Woman is not a being in her own right, a subject. She produces nothing but looks after those who do; she is a living monument to a long-vanished era when the domestic economy was self-contained. The division of labor imposed upon her by man brought her little that was worthwhile. She became the embodiment of the biological function, the image of nature, the subjugation of which constituted that civilization's title to fame. For millennia men dreamed of acquiring absolute mastery over nature, of converting the cosmos into one immense hunting-ground. It was to this that the idea of man was geared in a male-dominated society. This was the significance of reason, his proudest boast. Woman was weaker and smaller. Between her and man there was a difference she could not bridge—a difference imposed by nature, the most humiliating that can exist in a male-dominated society. Where the mastery of nature is the true goal, biological inferiority remains a glaring stigma, the weakness imprinted by nature as a key stimulus to aggression. The Church, which throughout the ages has missed scarcely an opportunity of exerting its telling influence on popular institutions—whether in slavery, crusades, or plain pogroms—has sided, despite the Ave Maria, with Plato's assessment of woman. The image of the Mother of God stricken with sorrow was merely a sop to the last traces of the matriarchate. The Church set the seal of its authority on that very doctrine of female inferiority which that same image was intended to redeem. De Maistre, a true son of the Church if ever there was one, gave a warning: "We have only to weaken in some degree the influence of divine Law in a Christian country by countenancing the freedom of women that stemmed from it, to see freedom, noble and moving though it be, degenerating soon enough into utter shamelessness. Women would become the baneful instruments of a general decline which would not be long in infecting the vital organs of the State. This would fall into decay and, in its gangrenous decomposition, spread abroad ignominy and terror."[1] The witchcraft trials which the associated feudal racketeers used to terrorize the masses when they felt themselves threatened, served at once to celebrate and to confirm the triumph of male society over prehistoric matriarchal and mimetic stages of development. The auto-da-fé was the Church's heathen

1. *Eclaircissement sur les Sacrifices, Oeuvres* (Lyon, 1892), Vol. V, pp. 322ff.

bonfire, a triumph of nature in the form of self-preserving reason, to celebrate the glory of the mastery of nature.

The bourgeoisie profited from female chastity and propriety —the defense mechanisms left by matriarchal revolt. Woman herself, on behalf of all exploited nature, gained admission to a male-dominated world, but only in a broken form. In her spontaneous submission she reflects for her vanquisher the glory of his victory, substituting devotion for defeat, nobility of soul for despair, and a loving breast for a ravished heart. At the price of radical disengagement from action and of withdrawal into the charmed circle, nature receives homage from the lord of creation. Art, custom, and sublime love are masks in which nature reappears transformed into her own antithesis. Through these masks she acquires the gift of speech; out of her distortion emerges her essence. Beauty is the serpent that exhibits a wound in which a thorn was once embedded. Behind male admiration of beauty, however, lurks always the ribald laughter, the withering scorn, the barbaric obscenity with which strength greets weakness in an attempt to deaden the fear that it has itself fallen prey to impotence, death, and nature. Ever since the stunted jester, to whose gambolling and cap-and-bells the melancholy lot of broken nature once clung, made his escape from the service of kings, woman has been made the caretaker of all things beautiful. The modern female puritan eagerly took up the office. She identified herself fully with the status quo, with nature domesticated, not red in tooth and claw. What remained of the fans, songs, and dances of Roman slave girls was finally whittled down in Birmingham to the pianoforte, needlework, and similar attainments, until the last vestiges of female wantonness had been clarified down to an emblem of patriarchal civilization. Under the pressure of all-pervasive advertising, lipstick and powder were severed from their origins among courtesans and used to signify skin care; bathing dress became a matter of hygiene. The process is inescapable. Its mere occurrence in the tightly organized system of a male-dominated society imprints a trademark even on love. In Germany those involved in it still betray by their promiscuity, as once by their modesty, their obedience to the powers that be; and by their indiscriminate indulgence in the sexual act their rigid subordination to the rule of reason.

The shrew, a fossilized survival of the bourgeois esteem of woman, is invading society today. With her endless nagging she takes revenge in her own home for the misery inflicted upon her sex from time immemorial. If sufficient deference is not shown to her, a cross old woman will continue her scolding outside the house, knocking off the hat of any absentminded individual who neglects to rise in her presence. That whatever happens, his head should roll, she has always demanded in her politics— whether in recollection of the maenadic era or outdoing man and his organization in her helpless fury. The blood-lust a woman displays in a pogrom outdoes that of a man. Subjected woman in the guise of a Fury has survived and still wears the grimace of mutilated nature at a time when our rulers are already busy modeling trained bodies of both sexes, in whose uniformity the grimace disappears. Against the background of this kind of mass production the scoldings of the Fury, who at least re- tained her own distinctive features, will become a sign of hu- manity, and her ugliness a mark of the spirit. If a girl in past ages bore her subjection in the form of melancholy mien and loving devotion—an alienated image of nature, an aesthetic chattel—the Fury has eventually hit upon a new female pursuit. She bustles about after cultural goals like a social hyena. Her ambition runs to honors and the limelight, but her feeling for masculine culture is not yet so well developed that, weighed down as she is by additional sorrow, she can prevent herself from stumbling, and betraying that she is still not at home in a man's world. The lonely woman seeks refuge in a hotchpotch of science and magic, in monstrosities bred in the fancy of the civil servant and the Nordic clairvoyante. She feels drawn to disaster. The last vestiges of female opposition to the spirit of a male-dominated society are engulfed in a morass of paltry rackets, religious sects, and hobbies. They find some outlets in the perverse aggressiveness of social work and theosophical chitchat, in the petty malice of charity and Christian Science. In this wasteland, fellow-feeling for other living creatures ex- presses itself not so much in societies for the prevention of cruelty to animals as in an interest in neo-Buddhism and in Pekingese dogs whose distorted faces, today just as in the old paintings, remind one of those of the jesters who were overtaken by the march of progress. The tiny dog's features, like the hunchback's clownish leaps, still display the mutilated lineaments of nature. Mass industry and mass culture, on the other hand, have already learned how to apply scientific methods to manipulate bodies—both of pedigree animals and of humans. The masses, having been forced to toe the same line, are becoming so oblivious of the transformation they are undergoing —a transformation to which they themselves are contributing— that they no longer need to have it symbolically displayed. Now and again, if we scan the trivial news-items on the second and third pages of a newspaper—the front page is crammed with men's frightful deeds of glory—we may come across a few lines about a circus fire or poisoned elephants. Animals are only remembered when the few remaining specimens, the counterparts of the medieval jester, perish in excruciating pain, as a capital loss for their owner who neglected to afford them adequate fire protection in an age of concrete and steel. The tall giraffe and the white elephant are oddities of which now even the shrewdest schoolboy would now hardly feel the loss. In Africa, the last part of the earth where a futile attempt is made to preserve their dwindling herds, they are an obstacle to the landing of bombers in the latest war. They will be completely eradicated. The earth, now rational, no longer feels the need of an aesthetic reflection. The demonic element is wiped out by directly applying the desired imprint on mankind. Domination no longer needs numinous images; it produces them itself on an industrial scale and uses them as a more reliable means of winning over the masses.

Distortion, an essential aspect of a work of art just as mutilation is an added luster to female beauty (that display of the wound in which subjugated nature recognizes herself) has been taken up by Fascism, and not merely in a symbolic form. It is directly practiced on the condemned. In this society there is no sphere in which authority as contradiction expresses itself as in art. Expressive media, formerly implied not beauty alone but

251

thought, spirit, and language itself. Today language calculates, describes, betrays, incites to murder; but it expresses nothing. The culture industry, like science, seeks a standard to work to outside itself . . . in facts. Film stars are experts; their performances are protocols of natural behavior, a guide to approved responses. Producers and scriptwriters produce models for proficiently adjusted conduct. The precision work of the culture industry rules out distortion as mere error, chance, the unwholesomeness of the subjective and natural. Deviation is permitted only on practical grounds that bring it within the realm of reason. Then, and only then, is it excused. Now that nature reflects domination, tragedy and comedy have vanished. The masters summon up just so much gravity as there is opposition to overcome, and just so much humor as is needed to deal with the despair they see before them. Intellectual pleasure was associated with representative suffering, but authority now sports with naked terror itself. Sublime love attached itself to the phenomenon of strength through weakness, to womanly beauty; but the masters cling directly to strength. The current ideal of society is a masculine face that is a blend of smartness and nobility. Woman exists to work and to bring forth children, or to enhance with her attractions the prestige of her mate. She does not overwhelm man with her charms; once again adoration slumps into self-esteem. The world and its purposes need the whole man. No one can any longer step out of it to serve another ideal. Nature, on the other hand, is seen as something outside practical life and at a lower level, like the soldier's moll in the popular mind. Now emotion is reserved to power conscious of itself as power. Man surrenders to man, cold, bleak, and unyielding, as woman did before him. Man turns into woman gazing up at her master. In the Fascist collective with its teams and labor camps, everyone spends his days from the tenderest years in solitary confinement. The seed of homosexuality is sown. It is the animal still that has to carry the nobler features. An over-accentuated human face, an embarrassing reminder of its origin in and degeneration from nature, now arouses only an irresistible urge to indulge in efficient manslaughter. Anti-Semitic cartoonists have always known this, and

Goethe's aversion to apes also indicated the limits of his humanitarianism. When industrial magnates and Fascist leaders want to have pets around them, their choice falls not on terriers but on Great Danes and lion cubs. These are intended to add spice to power through the terror they inspire. The murderous Fascist colossus stands so blindly before nature that he sees animals only as a means of humiliating men. It is he who deserves the criticism unjustly leveled by Nietzsche at Schopenhauer and Voltaire that they "knew how to mask their hate of certain men and things as compassion for animals."[2] The Fascist's passionate interest in animals, nature, and children is rooted in the lust to persecute. The significance of the hand negligently stroking a child's head, or an animal's back, is that it could just as easily destroy them. One victim is fondly stroked shortly before the other is struck down, and the choice made has nothing to do with the victim's guilt. The petting demonstrates that all are equal in the presence of power, that none is a being in its own right. A creature is merely material for the master's bloody purposes. Thus the Führer takes the innocent into his service, picking them out regardless of merit just as, for no apparent reason, they may be slaughtered. Nature is so much filth. Only the cunning power that knows how to survive has any right on its side. This power itself is once again only nature; just as the whole sophisticated machinery of modern industrial society is nature bent on tearing itself apart. There is no longer any medium in which to express this contradiction. It rounds itself off with the dogged earnestness of a world from which art, thought and the negation have completely vanished. Men have become so utterly estranged from one another and from nature that all they know is what they need each other for and the harm they do to each other. Each of them has become a factor, the subject or object of some practice or other, something with which one need no longer reckon.

In this world divested of illusion in which men, following the loss of reflection, have again become the cleverest of animals and are busy enslaving the rest of the universe (assuming

2 Nietzsche, *Die fröhliche Wissenschaft*, *Werke*, Vol. V, p. 135.

always that they do not tear themselves to pieces), respect for animals is regarded no longer as sentimental but as a betrayal of progress. Goering, in the good old reactionary tradition, has bracketed the protection of animals with race hatred, the German-Lutheran relish for joyous killing with the sporting attitude of the aristocrat. The opposing fronts are clearly demarcated: anyone who is against Hearst and Goering sides with Pavlov and the vivisectionists. Anyone who sits on the fence is fair game for both camps. He ought to listen to reason. The choice is already ordained and inevitable. Anyone who wants to change the world must on no account finish up in the swamp of petty rackets where fortune tellers languish with political sectarians, utopians, and anarchists. The intellectual whose thinking does not attach itself to some effective historical force, who gravitates to neither of the poles toward which industrial society is sweeping, will apparently be reduced to a shadow and his thought have no solid basis. The world of hard facts alone is to be regarded as reasonable. The progressives also maintain that if anyone stands on the sidelines, no one will lift a finger to help him. Everything, it appears, depends on society, and even the most precise thinking must throw in its lot with the dominant social trends if it is not to degenerate into a mere fad. This realization binds together all the champions of reality; it accepts human society as a wholesale racket in nature. The voice that does not pursue the aims of one of the branches of that society throws its members into an ungovernable rage. It is a reminder that only that which exists to be broken still has a voice— namely, nature, from which the lies of nationalists and folklorists issue in streams. Whenever the voice is heard, even momentarily, above the clamor of their chorus of yells, it is accompanied by the fearful reverberations which, as in every animal, sound even in one's own rationalized and broken heart. The tendencies revealed by such a voice are blind, yet ubiquitous. Nature herself is neither good, as the ancients believed, nor noble, as the latterday Romantics would have it. As a model and goal it implies the spirit of opposition, deceit, and bestiality.

Only when seen for what it is, does nature become existence's craving for peace, that consciousness which from the very beginning has inspired an unshakable resistance to Führer and collective alike. Dominant practice and its inescapable alternatives are not threatened by nature, which tends rather to coincide with them, but by the fact that nature is remembered.

PROPAGANDA

How absurd it is to try to change the world by propaganda. Propaganda makes language an instrument, a lever, a machine. It fixes the condition of men, as they have come to be in under social injustice, by setting them in motion. It counts on being able to count on them. Deep down all men know that through this tool they too will be reduced to a tool as in a factory. The anger they feel mounting inside them as they succumb to propaganda is the age-old resentment against the yoke, heightened by the suspicion that the remedy it prescribes is the wrong one. Propaganda manipulates people; when it cries freedom it contradicts itself. Deceit and propaganda are inseparable. A community in which the leader and his followers come to terms through propaganda—whatever the merits of its content—is a community of lies. Truth itself becomes merely a means of enlisting support and is falsified in the very utterance. This is why genuine resistance knows no propaganda. Propaganda is misanthropic. It assumes that to say that policy ought to spring from mutual understanding is not a basic principle but conveniently empty phraseology.

In a society that prudently sets limits to the threat of superfluity, suspicion attaches to whatever one person recommends to another. The warning against commercial advertising—namely, that no business ever gives anything away—applies everywhere, and particularly to the modern fusion of industrial and political interests. The louder the boasts, the poorer the quality. The publicity on which the Volkswagen depends is different to that for the Rolls Royce. Producer and consumer interests are not brought into line, even where the former has something serious to offer. Propaganda for freedom itself can be a source of confusion in that it must bridge the gap between

255

theory and the special interests of its audience. The workers' leaders defeated in Germany were robbed even of the truth of their own action by Fascism, which undermined solidarity through its choice of a method of retaliation. If intellectuals are tortured to death in prison camps, the workers outside do not have to be worse off. Fascism did not mean the same thing to Ossietzky as to the proletariat. But both were betrayed by it.

It is not the portrayal of reality as hell on earth but the slick challenge to break out of it that is suspect. If there is anyone today to whom we can pass the responsibility for the message, we bequeath it not to the "masses," and not to the individual (who is powerless), but to an imaginary witness—lest it perish with us.

THE GENESIS OF STUPIDITY

The true symbol of intelligence is the snail's horn with which it feels and (if Mephistopheles is to be believed)[1] smells its way. The horn recoils instantly before an obstacle, seeking asylum in the protective shell and again becoming one with the whole. Only tentatively does it re-emerge to assert its independence. If the danger is still present it vanishes once more, now hesitating longer before renewing the attempt. In its early stages the life of the mind is infinitely fragile. The snail's senses depend on its muscles, and muscles become feebler with every hindrance to their play. Physical injury cripples the body, fear the mind. At the start the two are inseparable.

The higher animals have earned their greater freedom; their mere presence proves that once feelers groped out in new directions and were not then withdrawn. Each of their species is a monument to countless others whose attempts to develop were doomed from the start, whom terror struck low the moment a feeler reached out in the direction of their development. The suppression of this potential by the direct resistance of the

1. Goethe, *Faust* I (*Walpurgisnacht*): ". . . with its delicately groping face, it has scented me already."

natural environment is carried a stage further as internal organs begin to atrophy with fear. In every questioning glance of an animal there flickers a new form of life that could emerge from the distinctive species to which the individual belongs. It is not merely this distinctive character that keeps it within the shelter of familiar being. The might that glance encounters dates back millions of years. From time immemorial it has kept the creature at its appointed stage, and has constantly inhibited its initial attempts to progress beyond it. A preliminary groping of this kind is always easily thwarted; it is always backed by good will and faint hope but not by unflagging energy. When facing in the direction from which it is finally scared into retreat, the animal grows timid and stupid.

Stupidity is a scar. It can stem from one of many activities—physical or mental—or from all. Every partial stupidity of a man denotes a spot where the play of stirring muscles was thwarted instead of encouraged. In the presence of the obstacle the futile repetition of disorganized, groping attempts is set in motion. A child's ceaseless queries are always symptoms of a hidden pain, of a first question to which it found no answer and which it did not know how to frame appropriately.[2] Its reiteration suggests the playful determination of a dog leaping repeatedly at the door it does not yet know how to open, and finally giving up if the catch is out of his reach. It also has something in it of the desperation of the lion pacing up and down in its cage, or of the neurotic who renews a defensive reaction that has already proved futile in the past. If the child's repeated attempts are balked, or too brutally frustrated, it may turn its attention in a different direction. It is then richer in experience, as the saying goes, but an imperceptible scar, a tiny calloused area of insensitivity, is apt to form at the spot where the urge was stifled. Such scars lead to deformities. They can build hard and able characters; they can breed stupidity—as a symptom of pathological deficiency, of blindness and impotency, if they are quiescent; in the form of malice, spite, and fanati-

2. Cf. Karl Landauer. "Intelligenz und Dummheit," in: *Das Psycho-analytische Volksbuch* (Berne, 1939), p. 172.

cism, if they produce a cancer within. The coercion suffered turns good will into bad. And not only tabooed questioning but forbidden mimicry, forbidden tears, and forbidden rashness in play can leave such scars. Like the species of the animal order, the mental stages within the human species, and the blind-spots in the individual, are stages at which hope petered out and whose petrifaction demonstrates that all things that live are subject to constraint.